John Mandeville, John Ashton

The voiage and travayle of Sir John Maundeville knight

John Mandeville, John Ashton

The voiage and travayle of Sir John Maundeville knight

ISBN/EAN: 9783337204600

Printed in Europe, USA, Canada, Australia, Japan

Cover: Foto ©Andreas Hilbeck / pixelio.de

More available books at **www.hansebooks.com**

THE VOIAGE AND TRAVAYLE OF SIR JOHN MAUNDEVILLE, KNIGHT.

THE VOIAGE AND TRAVAYLE

OF

SIR JOHN MAUNDEVILLE KNIGHT

WHICH TREATETH OF THE WAY TOWARD HIERUSALEM

AND OF MARVAYLES OF INDE WITH OTHER

ILANDS AND COUNTREYS

Edited, Annotated, and Illustrated in Facsimile

BY

JOHN ASHTON

Author of "Chap Books of the 18th Century," "Social Life in the Reign of Queen Anne," "English Caricature and Satire on Napoleon I.," &c.

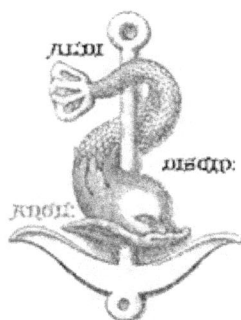

LONDON
PICKERING & CHATTO
66, HAYMARKET
1887

CHISWICK PRESS :—C. WHITTINGHAM AND CO., TOOKS COURT,
CHANCERY LANE.

PREFACE.

HAVE edited, and illustrated "The Voiage and Travayle of Syr John Maundeville, Knight," for two reasons. First, that a popular edition has not been published for many years—so much so, that many otherwise well educated people hardly know his name ; or, if they do, have never read his book of Marvels. Secondly, a good edition has not yet been published. Putting aside the chap-books of the eighteenth century, which could only cram a small portion of his book into their little duodecimos, the only English versions of this century are the reprint by Halliwell, in 1839, of the *reprint* in 1725-1727, of the early fifteenth century MS. (Cotton, Tit. c. 16), which he again reprinted in 1866,[1] the edition in " Bohn's Classical Library" (" Early Travels in Palestine "), 1848 ; and "The English Explorers," which forms part of Nimmo's "National Library," 1875. There was also a small edition published in Cassell's " National Library " in 1886 in modern English.

[1] This has again been reprinted in 1884.

Halliwell's reprint of the Cotton MS. is open to objection, because the language of the MS. is specially rude, and can only be understood by professed antiquaries, no footnotes explanatory of the text being given, only a glossary at the end of the book. Also, Mr. Halliwell has taken his illustrations from various sources, not confining himself to English woodcuts—the Cotton MS. having no illustrations. If, however, the language in Halliwell's edition is too archaic, Bohn and Nimmo err in the opposite direction. Without illustrations, and clothed in modern English, they are bald in the extreme ; whilst the editors of both have not been over careful to closely copy the text.

Seeing these difficulties, and dearly loving Sir John, in spite of his romancing, I cast about for a book which should fulfil the conditions of an edition I should like for my own reading ; which should have the spice of the old language, without being unreadable, like the Cotton MS., and which contained the original quaint illustrations. This I have found in a reprint of Pynson's unique edition (now in the Grenville Library, British Museum), from which it varies very slightly, except in the modernizing of the language, which is rather an advantage ; and which, by means of the copious footnotes I have made, will, I hope, be easily read by anybody.

This edition, too, was particularly rich in woodcuts, which I have faithfully facsimiled ; and, in the Appendix, I have reproduced a few from other editions, showing the different treatment of some subjects. In the Appendix, also, I have given a list of all the editions of Sir John Mandeville's Travels now in the British Museum. A glance at this will show how popular his book was, in all civilized countries, and in all ages, since its first publication.[1] I have thought that an edition should be produced which could be read by all, and therefore have given explanations of words and facts, perfectly familiar to advanced students, by means of which they will not be inconvenienced, and the general reader much benefited.

Perhaps the Illustrations in one or two of the early foreign editions are quainter, but I wanted, and have got, a thoroughly representative *English* Edition, which gives Sir John's adventures, with their concomitant "Travellers' Tales," without the apocryphal stories which were introduced into some of the MSS. and foreign editions.

Of East, the printer of the exemplar I have chosen, very little is known ; and, curiously, he is ignored in Herbert and Dibdin's edition of *Ames' Typographical Antiquities*. According to Ames, he was made free of the Stationers' Company 3rd December, 1565, and he gives his first known printed book as 1569, or a year later than the book I have copied. East, according to the same authority, was granted a patent for ruled paper for music, and worked both for Bird and Tallis. The

---

[1] Colonel Yule, in "The Book of Ser Marco Polo," &c. (1871), says :—" And from the great frequency with which one encounters in catalogues both MSS. and early printed editions of Sir John Maundeville, I should suppose that the lying wonders of our English knight had a far greater popularity and more extensive diffusion than the veracious and more sober marvels of Polo. In Quaritch's last catalogue (November, 1870) there is only one *old* edition of Polo ; there are nine of Maundeville. In 1839 there were nineteen MSS. of the latter *catalogued* in the British Museum Library. There are *now* only five of Marco Polo. At least twenty-five editions of Maundeville, and only five of Polo were printed in the fifteenth century."

date of his death does not seem to be known, but his widow, or daughter, printed a book of Bird's music in 1610.

JNO. ASHTON.

INTRODUCTION.

I KNOW of nothing more likely to be pro-
vocative of a literary war than the question
of Sir John Mandeville's personal entity.
Were I to express an opinion either way—
that he was a real being, or that he never existed—
fierce would be the criticism on my views, and much
good ink be spilt, which might well be devoted to a
better purpose, so that I prefer letting the reader form
his own opinion thereon,—a course which will save every-
body any trouble or vexation of spirit.

We labour under this difficulty—all that is known
about him is what he tells us himself, and no one who
reads the book can altogether trust his absolute verity.
If his book is a mere compilation from other sources, so
then is that of Odorico (who died January, 1331), which
I place in an Appendix, and which agrees with Mandeville in so many particulars, that one might reasonably
suppose him to be the " fellawe," or companion, whom
he frequently mentions, and connect him with that
Minorite friar from Lombardy (for Odorico was born
at Udine or Friuli) who shrove them before their

entrance into "ye Valey of Divels."[1]   According to
his own account, he was a knight, that he was born at
St. Albans, and that he left England on his wonderful
voyage on 29th September, 1322.   He informs us that
he travelled through Asia Minor, Armenia, Tartary,
Persia, Syria, Arabia, Upper and Lower Egypt, Libya,
Chaldæa, a large portion of Ethiopia, Amazonia, Lower
India, and the greater part of Upper India, together
with the neighbouring islands.   If his narrative can be
trusted, he lived in most friendly relations with the ruler
of Egypt, whom he served in his war against the
Bedouins, and was on such familiar terms that they
would privately argue on religious topics, and he was
even offered a richly dowered princess as a wife, if he
would but change his creed, and become a Mahometan.
If he can be believed, he wandered all over the then
known world, and gratified his military instincts by
helping the Emperor of China in his war against the
sovereign of Manzi.   He tells us that after thirty-four
years of wandering and exile he returned to England,
taking Rome in his way home, in order to get the Pope's
Imprimatur to his book, for which he naïvely gives as
reason : "and, for as much as many men beleve not that
they see with theyr eyen, or y^t they may conceiue &
know in their mynde, therefore I made my way to Rome
in my coming homewarde, to shew my boke to the holy
father the pope, and tell him of the mervayles y^t I had
sene in diverse countreys ; so that he with his wise

---

[1] "And there were in our company two friers minours of Lombardy, & sayd, if any of us wold go in, they wold also, as they had
sayd so, and upon trust of them we sayd that we wold go, & we
dyd sing a masse, and were shriven & houseled, and we went in
xiiii men, and whē we came out we were but x."

counsel wold **examine it,** with diverse folke y' are at
Rome, for there dwell men of all nations of the world,
and a lytle time after whan he & his coûsel had examined
it all through, he sayde to me for a certayne that it was
true, for he sayd he had a boke of latin contayning all
that, and much more, of y' which *Mappa Mundi* is
made, the which boke I saw, & therefore the **pope hath**
ratyfied & confirmed my boke in all poyntes." If any
portion of this is true, it is probable that the " boke of
latin" may have been Pliny, Solinus, or some other
equally veracious writer.

As to the "Mappa Mundi" constructed from such
sources, that at Hereford may be taken as a type of
ideal geography of the time. This was almost contemporary with Mandeville, and is ascribed to the very **early**
part of the fourteenth century. Indeed, it can be proved
to be of **this date,** for, among other inscriptions on the
map, is the following :—

> "Tuz Ki cest estoire ont.
> Ou oyront ou lirront ou veront.
> Prieut a ihesu su deyte.
> De Richard de Haldingdam e de Lafford eyt pite.
> Ki lat fet e compasse.
> Ki ioie eu cel li seit donc."

Which may be thus translated :—

> "All who **have, or shall have, or shall** read, or shall see this his-
> tory—pray **to** Jesu in deity (or **as God) that** he may have pity on
> Richard of Haldingham and of Lafford, who **has** made and **con-
> trived it, that joy** in heaven may be given **unto him."**

Richard of Haldingham, or Holdingham, whose real
name was Richard de la Battayle, or de Bello,[1] held the

---

[1] Havergal's *Fasti Herefordenses,* p. 161.

prebend of Lafford (now Sleaford), in Lincoln Cathedral up to the year 1283, and afterwards held the prebend of Norton, in Hereford Cathedral. Hardy, in his edition of Le Neve's *Fasti Ecclesiæ Anglicanæ*, says he was appointed to this stall in 1305. He was afterwards preferred to the Archidiaconate of Berkshire. Perhaps the best description of this map is in a paper read before the Geographical Society of Paris, 30th November, 1861, by M. D'Avezac, President of the Society, a translation of which may be found in the *Gentleman's Magazine* of May, 1863. He considers it to have been executed early in the year 1314, because Lyons was not annexed to France till the 30th of April, 1313, and gives other reasons, equally strong, in support of his argument.

Thus, then, we have a contemporary map as a guide, and on this Hereford map are portrayed all the monsters described by Mandeville—the one-eyed men, those with their heads in their breasts, even the big-footed one-legged man—all those things which are regarded as fable in Mandeville—are here drawn, and evidently must have been currently believed in. So that when Mandeville, or some subsequent editor, challenged the *Mappa Mundi* as confirmatory evidence, he clearly knew what he was about.

A strong presumption of his personal being is drawn from the fact that Liège is said to be the place of his burial, *see Appendix Harl.*, 3589. 2, "qui obiit Leodii A.D. 1382." That he was believed to have lived at Liège is also shown in *Appendix Grenville*, 6728/3, where he is said to have written his book in the year 1355 ; and if Weever [1] is to believed, he died there, but at an earlier

---

[1] "Ancient Funerall Monuments, &c. Composed by the Travels

date, namely, 1371. Speaking of St. Albans, he says : " This Towne vaunts her selfe very much of the birth and buriall of *Sir Iohn Mandeuill* Knight, the famous Trauailer, who writ in Latine, French, and in the English tongue, his Itinerary of three and thirty yeares. And that you may beleeue the report of the Inhabitants to bee true, they haue lately pensild a rare piece of Poetry, or an Epitaph for him, vpon a piller ; neere to which, they suppose his body to haue beene buried, which I think not much amisse to set downe ; for although it will not bee worth the reading, yet do but set it to some lofty tune, as to the *Hunting of Antichrist*, or the leke, I know it will be well worth the singing : marke how it runs.

and Studie of John Weever." Lond. 1631. It is exceedingly singular that a book published at Antwerp in 1584, " The Itinerarium per nonnullas Galliæ Belgicæ partes Abrahami Ortelii et Joannis Viviani," confirms Weever, in such almost identical words, that it is not worth while to append a translation. Ortelius, or Ortell, writes (p. 16):—" *Est in hac quoq. regione Gulielmitarū Cænobium in quo epitaphiū hoc Joannis à Mandeuille excepimus :* HIC IACET VIR NOBILIS DÑS JOËS DE MANDEVILLE AL' DCVS AD BARBAM, MILES DÑS DE CÃPDI, NATUS DE ANGLIA, MEDICIË PFESSOR DEVOTISSIMVS ORATOR ET BONORUM LARGISSIMVS PAU-PERIBUS EROGATA QUI TOTO QUASI ORBE LUSTRATO LEODII DIEM VITE SUE CLAVSIT EXTREMUM AÑO DÑI Mº CCCº LXXI MENSIS NOVÊBRE' DIE XVII.

" *Hæc in lapide, in quo cælata viri armati imago, leonem calcantis, barba bifurcata, ad caput manus benedicens, & vernacula hæc verba :* VOS KI PASEIS SOR MI POVR LAMOVR DEIX PROIES POR ME. *Clypeus erat vacuus, in quo olim laminam fuisse dicebant æream, & eius in ea itidem cælata insignia, leonem videlicet argenteum, cui ad pectus lunula rubea, in campo cæruleo, quem limbus ambiret denti-culatus ex oro. Eius nobis ostendebãt & cultros, ephippioque, & calcaria, quibus usum fuisse afferebãt in perigrando toto fere ter-rarum orbe, vt clarius eius testatur Itinerarium, quod typis etiam excusum passim habetur.*"

"'All yee that passe, on this pillar cast eye,
 This Epitaph read if you can ;
'Twill tell you a Tombe onc't stood in this roome,
 Of a braue spirited man.
Iohn Mandeuill by name, a knight of great fame,
 Borne in this honoured Towne.
Before him was none that euer was knowne,
 For trauaile of so **high** renowne.
As the Knights in the Temple, **crosse-legged** in marble,
 In armour, with sword and with sheeld,
So was this Knight grac't, which time hath defac't,
 That nothing but ruines doth yeeld.
His Trauailes being donne, he shines like the Sun,
 In heauenly Canaan.
To which blessed place, O Lord of his grace
 Bring vs all man after man.'

"That he was borne heere in this Towne I cannot much deny ; but I am sure that within these few yeares, I saw his Tombe in the Citie of Leege, within the Church of the religious house of the *Guilliammits*, with this Inscription vpon it, and the verses following hanging by on a table.

"*Hic iacet vir nobilis D. Ioannes de Mandevile, Al ;*[1] *D. ad Barbam miles ; Dominus de Campdi : natus de Anglia, Medicine professor, deuotissimus* **orator** *: et bonorum largissimus pauperibus erogator* **qui toto** *quasi orbe lustrato. Leodij diem vite sue clausit extremum. Ann. Dom. M.C.C.C.lxxi. Mens. Nouemb. die xvi.*

ALIUD.

"'*Hoc iacet in tumulo, cui totus patria* **vino** *Orbis erat ; totum quem peragrasse ferunt. Anglus Equesque fuit, nunc ille Britannus Vlysses Dicatur, Graio* **clarus** *Vlysse magis.*

---

[1] "Otherwise called the Bearded Knight."

Moribus, ingenio, candore, & sanguine clarus
Et vere cultor Relligionis erat.
Nomen si queras, est Mandevil, Indus, Arabsque
Sat notum dicet finibus esse suis.'

"The Churchmen will shew you here his kniues, the furniture of his horse, and his spurres, which he vsed in his trauells."

Thus speaks Weever, and nobody doubts but that there was a tomb of a Jehan de Maundeville in the Abbey of the Guilelmites,[1] which is mentioned by Bollandus in his *Acta Sanctorum* (Februarius, Tom. 2, p. 481, edit. 1658) as " Domus de Motta extra Leodium, inchoata, anno CIƆCCLXXXI." The abbey, or hospital, is now destroyed ; but, as side proofs, let me give two extracts from different works of the eighteenth century. One, " Abrégé curieux et nouveau de l'histoire de Liege," &c. (no date), 24mo., p. 117. " L'Hôpital & la Chapelle de S. Guilleaume aux Faux-bourgs de S. Walburge furent fondez l'an 1330," and in " Abrégé Chronologique de l'histoire de Liege, jusqu'a l'année 1784, &c." Liege, 1784, 12mo., p. 66. It says, " L'hôpital & la chapelle de Saint Guillaume au fauxbourg de Sainte Walburge furent fondés l'an 1330."

As I said before, regarding Mandeville it must be a question of faith. If Weever is to be relied on, he was a physician, and from the fact of his wearing a beard, probably acquired in his eastern travels, he received the sobriquet of " ad Barbam." This title, however, is claimed for a certain " Jehan de Bourgoigne dit à la

---

[1] An order founded by Sir William of Maleval—a hermit—who died 10th Feb., 1157. The order was somewhat austere, as the members went barefoot, and their fasts were almost continual. They have nearly all been absorbed into the Augustines.

Barbe," but the bare fact of anyone wearing a beard in France, in the clean-shaven fourteenth century, was sufficient to make him remarkable.

If, again, Weever and others are to be relied on, he died in 1371, and it is a curious fact that the earliest French, or Romance, manuscript known in this country is one of that date, and, moreover, it is circumstantially dated, as will be shown hereafter. This MS. is in the Earl of Ashburnham's collection (catalogued Barrois 24), which every lover of literature will regret was not secured for the nation in its entirety. Its text is most beautiful, and the few illuminations are fine examples of fourteenth century French art. But what I want particularly to point out, is the curious coincidence of dates—absolutely contemporaneous. Whether there were any MSS. published before then I cannot tell, but here is a book published the year of his death, when inquiry would have proved easily whether such a man had ever lived, but the whole style of the MS. shows that he was well known as a traveller, and it is evidently copied from an earlier edition, as at the end it says, " Ce livre cy fist escrire honorables homes sages et discret maistre Gervaise crestien, maistre en medicine, et premier phisicien de tres puissant noble et excellent prince Charles, par la Grace de Dieu, roy de France, Escript par Raoulet dorliens lan de grace mil ccclxxj le xviij jour de Septembre."

Here we have an authentic date, which there could be no earthly reason to falsify, and this MS. was written— unless Weever and others are liars—during the man's lifetime. For, according to their authority, he did not die until *November* of that year, and we must not fail to remember that Liege was not a very far cry from Paris, and that his fame must have been great, or his book would never have been written as a present for the king, as it probably was.

This manuscript, being the earliest known, is also useful in another way. By some singular chance, all the English versions make out that Mandeville wrote his book first in Latin, then in French, and afterwards in English. But this manuscript settles the point, as it says, " Et sachies q̄ je eusse cest livret mis en latin pour plus briefment deviser. Mais pour ce que pluseurs entendent mieulx rom̄ant que latin je lay mis en rom̄ant par quoy q̄ chacun lentende." Which I translate : "And know that I should (or might) have written this book in Latin, for the sake of brevity. But, because more people know the Romance (or French) tongue, than Latin, I have written it in Romance, so that anyone may understand it." And this translation is endorsed by E. M. Thompson, Esq., the head of the MS. department in the British Museum. It all depends on the words "je eusse." They do not mean *I had ;* and, even in modern French, might be used for *I should have*, although of course *j'aurais* would be better.

For many years he has been called the "father of English Prose," but this title, after the above, is doubtful, even if his existence is granted, and belongs of right to Wyclif.

Another book, and a very rare and curious one it is, is attributed to Mandeville. There is a copy of this book in the British Museum (C. 27, f. 2), which, although in Gothic letter, gives no clue as to its date, or place of birth, nor do any of the bibliographical authorities which I have consulted (and they are all that can be found in the British Museum) throw any light upon it. The museum authorities catalogue it

b

as *Lyons ? 1530 ?* Its title is "LE LAPIDAIRE *en fran-
coys compose par messire Jehan de mandeuille chevalier.*"
Its contents are of little worth, except that they contain a
store of legendary lore relating to precious stones, such
as are met with in most medieval treatises on jewels and
it winds up with a prayer. The authorship of this book,
too, must be a matter of faith, since it has nothing to
guarantee it but its title-page.

It is somewhat singular too, that the Latin letter sup-
posed to be written by Mandeville to King Edward the
Third, and which is *apropos* of nothing, only exists in the
French edition.

In the appended Travels of Oderico, the Minorite
Friar, I have italicized many of the passages which are
identical with Mandeville's description in order that the
reader may have easier reference.

THE TABLE.

APPENDIX.

THE journall of Frier Odoricus.—Of the maners of the Chal-
deans, and of India.—How peper is had : and where it
groweth.—Of a strange and uncouth idole : & of certaine
customes and ceremonies.—Of certaine trees yeelding
meale, honey, and poyson.—Of the abundance of fishes
which cast themselues upon the shore.—Of the Island of
Sylan : and of the mountaine where Adam mourned for his
sonne Abel.—Of the upper India : and of the province of
Mancy.—Of the citie of Fuco.—Of a Monastery where
many strange beastes of divers kindes doe live upon an hill.
—Of the citie of Cambaleth.—Of the glory and magnificence of the great Can.—Of certain Innes or hospitals
appointed for traveilers throughout the whole empire.—Of
the foure feasts which the great Can solemnizeth euery yeere
in his court.—Of divers provinces and cities.—Of a certaine
riche man, who is fed and nourished by 50 virgins.—Of the
death of Senex de monte.—Of the honour and reverence
done unto the great Can.—Of the death of frier Odoricus. 221

The Voiage and Travayle of Syr John Maundeville, Knight.

Here beginneth a lyttle treatise or boke, named John Maundevile Knight, borne in England in the towne of Sainct Albone, & speaketh of the wayes to Hierusalem, to Inde, and to the greate Cane,[1] and also to Prester Johns land, & to many other countreys, & also of many marvailes that are in the holy Lande.

FOR AS MUCH as the lande over the sea, that is to say, the holy land, that men cal the land of Behest,[2] among all other lands is most worthy & Soveraine, for it is blessed, halowed, and sacred of the precious bloud of our Lord JESU CHRIST, in the which land, it liked him to take flesh and bloud of the Virgin Mary, & to environ that lande with his owne feete, and there he wold do many myracles, preach and teach the fayth and the law of Christen men, as unto his children, & there he would suffer many reprouves and scornes for us, and he that was King of heaven and hell, of ayre, of sea, of lande, and of all things that are contained in them, wold alonely[3] be called King of that land, when he sayde, *Rex sum Judeorum*, I am King of Jewes : For that tyme was that lande of Jewes, and that lande he chose before

---

[1] Khan. [2] Promise. [3] *Pynson*, all oonly.

all other landes, as the best & most worthy of vertues
of all the world.   And as the Philosopher sayth, *Virtus
rerum in medio consistit.* That is to say, the vertue of
things is in the midst : and in that lande he would leade
his lyfe, and suffer passion and death of the Jewes for
us, to save and deliver us from the paines of hell, and
from deathe without ende, the which was ordeyned to us
for the sinne of our father Adam, and our owne synnes
also, for as for himself he had none evil done ne[1] deserved,
for he never thought ne dyd any evyll, for he that was
King of Glory and of joy might best in that place suffer
death.   For he that will do any thinge that he will haue
knowen openly, he wyll proclayme it openly in the
myddle place of a towne or of a citie, so that it may bee
knowne to all parties of the citie, so he that was King of
glory and of all the worlde would suffer death for us at
Hierusalem, which is in the mydst of the worlde, so that
it might be knowen to all nations of the worlde how
deare he bought man, that he made with his handes in
his owne likenesse, for the great loue that he had to us.
Ah dere God, what love he had to his subjects, when he
that had done no trespasse, would for us trespassours
suffer death : for a more worthy catell[2] he might not
have sette for us, then his owne blessed bodie and his
owne precious bloud the which he suffered for us : right
wel ought men to love, worship dreade, and serve such
a Lord, and prayse such an holy lande that brought
forth a lord of such fruite, through the which eche man
is saved but if it be his own defaute.   This is that
lande prepared for an heritage to us, and in that lande
would he dye as seased,[3] to leaue it to his children.   For

[1] Nor.   [2] Treasure, money, goods, property, possessions.
[3] Possessing (seized).

the which eche good Chrysten man that may & hath
wherewith, should strengthen him for to conquere our
righte heritage, and purchace[1] out of the evill peoples
handes : for we are cleped[2] christen men of Christ our
father, and if we be the ryght children of Christ, we
oughte to challenge the heritage that our father lefte us
& take it out of straunge mens handes.   But now
Pryde, Covetyse and Envy hath so inflamed the hearts
of the lordes of the worlde, that they are more busy for
to disheryte theyr neighbours than to challenge or conquere their right heritage aforesayde.   And the common
people that would put their bodies and theyr catell for
to conquere our heritage, they may not do so without
lordes : for assembling of the people without a chiefe
lorde, is as a flocke of sheepe without a sheepherd, the
which depart asunder, and wot not whether they shall go.
But would[3] God, the worldly Lordes were at a good
accorde, and with other of their common people would
take this holy voyage over the sea.   I trust well that
within a little tyme our right heritage before sayd should
be reconsiled and put into the hands of the right heires
of Jesu Christ.   And for as much as it is long time that
there was any general passage over the sea, and that
many men desire to here speaking of the holy lande,
and have therefore great solace and comfort, therefore
ye shall here by me John Maundevile Knight which
was borne in England in the towne of Saint Albones,
and passed the sea in the yeare of our Lord JESU
CHRIST A. MIII.C.[4] on the day of Sainct Michael, and
there remained long tyme, and went through many landes,

---

[1] *Pynson*, "and *chase* out the ylle troward."
[2] Called.   [3] (to) omitted.
[4] *Pynson* and other authorities say MCCCXXXII.

and many provinces, kingdomes and yles, & have
passed through Turkey, and through Armony[1] the lyttle
and the great, through Tartary, Percy,[2] Surre,[3] Araby,
Egypt the high and the low, through Libie, Caldee and
a great part of Ethiope, through Amazonie through
Inde the lesse & the more a great part, and through
many other yles which are about Inde, where many
people dwelleth of divers lawes and shapes. Of the men
of which landes and yles I shall speake more plainly and
I shall devise[4] a parte of the things what they are when
time shall be, after it may best come to my mynde &
specially for them that will, and are in purpose, for to
visite the holy citie of Hierusalem and the holy places
that are there aboute & I shall tell the way that they
shall holde[5] thither, for I have many times passed and
ridden it with good company and with many lordes.

CAP : I.

*He that will go toward Hierusalem on horse, on foote, or
by sea.*

IN the name of God Almightie. He that will passe
over the sea, he may go many wayes both by sea
and by lande, after the countreys that he cometh from,
and many of them cometh to one ende, but think not
that I will tell all the townes, cities & castelles that men
shall goe by, for then I should make to long a tale, but
only some countries and most principall cities and townes
that men shall go by and through to go the right way.

---

[1] Armenia.   [2] Persia.   [3] Syria.   [4] Relate.
[5] Travel or journey.

First, if a man come from the west side of the worlde
as England, Ireland, Wales, Scotland and Norway, he
may if he wyl, go through Almayne[1] and throughout the
Kingdome of Hungary, which Kinge is a great lord and
a mightie, and holdeth many landes & great, for he
holdeth the land of Hungarie, Savoy,[2] Camonie,[3] a great
part of Bulgary, that men call the land of Bugres, and a
great part of the Kingdome of Rossie,[4] and that lasteth
to the land of Mifland,[5] and marcheth on Siprus,[6] and
men passe thus through the land of Hungary and through
the Citie that men call Cipanum,[6] and through the castell
of Nuburgh,[7] and by the yll Torwe,[8] towarde the ende of
Hungarie and so by the river of Danubie, that is a full
great ryver and goeth into Almayne, under the hilles of
Lumbardy, and it taketh into him 40 other ryvers and it
runneth throughout Hungary and through Cresses[9] and
Crochie,[9] and goeth into the sea so strongely and

[1] Germany.   [2] Sclavonia.

[3] Comania may now be placed as being on the north-west side of
the Caspian Sea.

[4] Or Rosia, was Russia proper, by the Baltic ; the huge Empire
now so termed being then called Muscovy.

[5] *Pynson* says Nyflond, and in some MSS. it is written indiffe-
rently Nyfland, Nyflond, Nislan, and Neflond; but I have no doubt
but that by it is meant Livonia, as is explained Apian's *Cosmo-
graphie:* " qui est la derniere Province d'Alemaigne, et de la Chres-
tiété, vulgairement appelee Liefland ; " and this is the more likely
as Siprus is spelt in *Pynson* and other editions Pruysse, *i.e.*,
Prussia.

[6] *Pynson* says Chypron, other authorities Schyppronne, Cypron,
and Chippronne.

[7] Neuburgh ; sometimes written Neaseburghe, Newbow, or New-
borewe.

[8] In other editions " evyll."

[9] Cresses is rendered in other editions as Grece or Greece,
but this is impossible, as also is Crochie, which *Pynson* calls
Tracy, and others call Thracie or Thrace. It probably means

with so great might that the water is freshe xxx[1] myle within the sea and afterwards go men to Belgrave[2] and entereth the lande of Bugres and there pass men a bridge of stone that is over the river Marrock,[3] and so men passe through the lande of Pinseras[4] and come to Grece to the citie of Stermis,[5] and to the citie of Affinpane,[6] that was sometime called Bradre[7] the noble and so to the citie of Constantinople that was sometime called Bessameron[8] and there dwelleth commonly the Emperor of Grece.

Croatia, and he has muddled up the Save or Sau, a tributary to the Danube, which rises not far from Lombardy, joining the Danube at Belgrade.

[1] *Pynson* and others say 20 miles.
[2] Belgrade.   [3] Now called the Morava.
[4] *Pynson* says Pynteras, others Pyncemartz, and Pyncoras.
[5] *Pynson* says Sternys, others Sternes, or Scernys.
[6] Written elsewhere Affynpayn, Assynpayn, and ad fines Epapie.
[7] This will best explain the difficulty of placing the localities, for this means Adrianople.
[8] Byzantium, the ancient name for Constantinople, the seat of the Western Empire.

At Constantinople is the best and the fairest church of the worlde, and it is of sainct Steven.[1] And before this church is a gylte image of Justinian the Emperour, and it is sitting upon an horse and crowned, and it was wont to holde a round appell[2] in his hand, & men say there that it is a token that the Emperour hath lost a part of his landes, for the appell is fallen out of the images hand : and also he hath lost a great parte of his lordshippe. For he was wont to be Emperour of Rome, of Grece, and of all Asia the lesse, of Surry, and of the land of Jude,[3] in the which is Jerusalem, & of the land of Egipt, of Percie & Arabia, but he hath lost all but Grece, and that lande he holdeth all onely. Men would put the appell in the images hande, but it will not holde it. This appell betokeneth the lordship that he had over all the world, and the other hand he lifteth up against the East,[4] in token to manasse[5] misdoers. This image standeth upon a pyller of marble.

[1] *Pynson* has Sophy, now the Mosque of St. Sophia.
[2] Probably an orb.   [3] Judæa.
[4] *Pynson* says West, but others give East.   [5] Menace.

At Constantinople is the crosse of our Lord and his cote
without seame, the sponge and the rede with which the
Jewes gave our Lord gall to drinke on the Crosse, and
there is one of the nayles that our Lorde Jesu Christ
was nayled with to the Crosse. Some men think that
halfe the Crosse of Christ be in Cipres in an Abbey of
Monkes, that men call the hill of the holy crosse, but it
is not so, for the crosse that is in Cipres is the crosse on
which Dysmas¹ the good theefe was hanged, but all men

---

¹ The names of the penitent and impenitent thieves vary slightly
in different accounts.   In the Apocryphal book of Nicodemus, cap.
7, vv. 10, 11, they are thus given : "But one of the two thieves
who were crucified with Jesus, whose name was Gestas, said to
Jesus, If thou art the Christ, deliver thyself and us. But the thief
who was crucified on his right hand, whose name was Dimas,
answering, rebuked him, and said, Dost thou not fear God, who art
condemned to this punishment? We indeed receive rightly and
justly the demerit of our actions : but this Jesus, what evil hath he
done?"

But in the Apocryphal book, I. Infancy, cap. 8, vv. 1-7 (a
Nestorian and Gnostic book), the names are given differently: "In
their journey from hence they came into a desert country, and were
told it was infested with robbers ; so Joseph and St. Mary prepared
to pass through it in the night.

And, as they were going along, behold they saw two robbers
asleep in the road, and with them a great number of robbers, who
were their confederates, also asleep.

The names of those two were Titus and Dumachus ; and Titus
said to Dumachus, I beseech thee let those persons go along
quietly, that our company may not perceive any thing of them ;

But Dumachus refusing, Titus again said, I will give thee forty
groats, and as a pledge, take my girdle, which he gave him before
he had done speaking, that he might not open his mouth, or make
a noise.

When the Lady St. Mary saw the kindness which this robber did
show them, she said to him, The Lord God will receive thee to his
right hand, and grant thee pardon of thy sins.

Then the Lord Jesus answered and said to his mother, When

wot[1] not that, & that is evil done but for the getting of
the offering they say that it is the crosse of our Lorde,
and ye shall understande that the crosse of our Lorde
Jesus Christ was made of foure maner of trees, as it is
conteyned in this verse following.

In cruce fit Palma, Cedrus, et Cypressus, Oliva.

For the piece that went ryght up from the earth unto
the head was of Cipres, and the piece that went overthwart, to the which his handes were nayled, was of ·
Palme, and the stock that stood within the earth in the
which they had made a morteys, was of Cedre, and the
table aboue his head was a foote and a half long, on
which ye tytle was written, y^t was of Olyve. Y^e Jewes

thirty years are expired, O Mother, the Jews will crucify me at
Jerusalem.

And these two thieves shall be with me at the same time upon
the cross, Titus on my right hand, and Dumachus on my left, and
from that time Titus shall go before me into Paradise."

[1] Know.

made this crosse of these foure maner of trees for they
thought y^t our Lord shold have hanged as long as y^e
crosse might last, therefore they made the foote of
Cedre, for Ceder may not in the erth ne^1 in water rot ;
they thought that the body of Christ shold have stonken,
they made the piece y^t went from the yearth upwarde of
Cipres so that the smell of his body shold greve no man
that came by, and that overthwart was made of Palme
in signification of Victory. And the table of the tytle
was made of Olive, for it betokeneth peace, as the story
of Noe witnesseth, when ye dove brought ye braunch of
Olive that betokened peace made between God and man.
And you also shal understande, that the Christen men
that dwell over the sea, say that the pece of the Crosse
that we call Cipres was of the tree that Adam eate the
appell of, and so finde they written, and they say also
that their scripture saith, that when Adam was sicke he
sayd to his son Seth that he shold go to Paradise and
pray that the Aungel that kepeth Paradise, y^t he wold
send him oyle of the tree of mercy for to anoynte him
that he might have health, & Seth went, but the
Aungel would not let him com in at the gate, but said
unto him that he might not have ye oyle of mercy, but
he took him three carnels^2 of the same tree that his
father eate the appell of, and bad him as sone as his
father was dead, that he should put these carnels under
his tongue and bury him, and he did so, and of these
three carnels sprang a tree, as the Angel sayd and when
the tree bare fruite, then shold Adam be made whole.
And when Seth came againe and founde his father dead,
he did with the carnels as the Aungell commaunded him,
of the which came three trees, whereof a crosse was

^{1} Nor. ^{2} Kernels—another edition says Greynes.

made that bare good fruite, that is to say, our saviour
Jesu Christ, through whom Adam and all that came of
him should be saved and delivered from everlasting
death, but[1] if it be their owne defaute.[2] This holy
crosse had the Jewes hid under the earth in yᵉ rock of
the mount of Calvery, & it laye there two hundreth
yeares and more, as they say, unto the tyme that Saint
Elene found it, the which Saint Elene was daughter of
Coel King of Englande, that then was called Britaine,
and after maried to Constantius, fyrst Consul and after
Emperour of Rome, who had by hir issue Constantine
the great, born in England and afterward Emperour of
Rome, which Constantine turned the name of Bezansium
into Constantinople, he reedified that citie, and made it
monarcall seate of all Europa and Asia Minor. Also
ye shall understande that the crosse of our Lord was in
length viii cubites and that the piece that went overthwart was three cubites[3] and a halfe.

[1] Except. [2] Fault.
[3] This measure varied. It was generally accepted as being the

A part of the crowne of our Lord Jesu wherewith he was crowned & one of the nayles, and the speare head and many other reliques are in France at Paris in the chapell of the King, and the crowne lyeth in a vessell of cristall wel dight and richly, for y⁰ French King bought these reliques sometime of the Jewes, to whome the Emperour had laid them to pledge for a great sume of golde. And although men say that this Crowne was of thornes—ye shall understand that it was of Jonkes[1] of the sea, which be white and pricketh as sharp as thornes, for I have seene and beheld many times that at Paris, and that at Constantinople, for they were both of one, and made of Jonkis of the sea. But men have departed him in two partes, of the which one parte is at Paris, and the other part at Constantinople, and I haue a point thereof that seemeth a white thorne, and that was given me for a great friendeship—for there are many of them broken and fallen into the vessell, when they shew the Crowne to great men or lordes that come theither. And ye shall understande that our Lord in that night that he was taken, he was led into a garden, and there he was examined sharply, & there the Jewes crowned him with a crown of abbespine[2] braunches that grew in the same garden & set it on his head so fast, that the blood came downe by many places of his visage, necke, and shoulders, and therefore hath the abbespine many vertues, for he that beareth a braunche of it about him, no thunder, nor any maner of tempest may hurt him, nor the house that it is

length of a man's arm from the elbow to the extremity of the little finger. The Roman cubit is usually reckoned as $17\frac{4}{10}$ in., the Scriptural cubit at 22 in., and the English cubit at 18 in.

[1] Rushes. *Juncus Maritimus.*

[2] Albespine—probably meant for *White thorn.*

in may no evill ghost come, nor in no place where it is.
And in that same garden Sainct Peter denied our Lord
thrise. And afterward was our Lord led before the Bishop
and ministers of the lawe into another gardein of Anne[1]
and there was he examined, scorned & crowned efte[2] with
a swete thorn that men called barbareus[3] that grew in
the same gardein and that hath many vertues.   And
afterward he was led to a gardein of Caiphas, and there
he was crowned again with eglentine,[4] and after that he
was led to a chamber of Pilate & there he was crowned,
and the Jewes set him in a chaire and clad him in a mantell
of purpure[5] and then made they a crowne of Jonkes of
the sea and there they kneled to him & scorned him
saying *Ave rex Judeorum*   That is to say, haile King of
Jewes.   And of this crowne, halfe is in Paris and the
other halfe at Constantinople, the which our Saviour
Jesu Christ hadde on his head, when he was nayled on
the crosse, and therefore shall men honour and worship
it, and holde it more worthy then any of the other.   And
the speare shaft hath the Emperour of Almaine, but the
head which was put in his side is at Paris they say, in
the holy chappell, and oft tymes sayth the Emperour of
Constantinople, that he hath the speare head & I have
often seen it, but it is greater than that at Paris.   Also
at Constantinople lyeth Sainct Anne our ladie's mother,
whom Saint Elene caused to be brought from Hierusalem, and there lieth also the body of Saint John
Chrisostome that was bishop of Constantinople.   There
lyeth also sainct Luke the Evangelist, for his bones were
brought from Bethany where he was buried: and many
other relyques are there, and there is of the vessell of

---

[1] Annas.   [2] Again.   [3] ? *berberis.*
[4] Honeysuckle.   [5] Purple.

stone as it were marble, which men call Idryus, that evermore droppeth water & fylleth himselfe every yeare once.
And ye shall wete that Constantinople is a fayre citie
and well walled & it is three cornered, and there is an
arme of the sea that men call Hellespon, and some men
call it the bunch[1] of Constantinople and some call it the
brace[2] of sainct George, and this water encloseth two
partes of the citie, and upward to the sea upon that
water was wont to be the great citie of Troy in a fayre
plaine, but that citie was destroyed by the Grekes.

CAP: II.

Of the Ilandes of Grece.

ABOUT Grece be many yles that men cal Calastre,[3]
Calcas Settygo, Thoysoria, Mynona, Faxton, Molo,

[1] *Bouche*, the mouth.
[2] Arm. *Lat. brachium*, as we should say, an arm of the sea.
[3] Calliste, which Ferrarius, in his *Lexicon Geographicum* (edit.

Carparte and Lempne, and in this yle is mount Athos
that passeth the clowdes & there are divers speaches
and many countries that are obedient to the Emperour
of Constantinople, that is to say Turcoply, Pyncy, Narde,
Comage and many other, Tracy & Macedony, of which
Alexander was king.   In this countrey was Aristotle
borne, in a citie that men call Strages, a little from the
citie of Tragie, .& at Strages is Aristotle buried, and
there is an aulter on his tombe, and there they make a
greate feast every yeare as he were a saint, & upon his
aulter the lordes holde their great counsayles and as-
semblies and they think, that through the inspiration of
God & him, they should have the better councill.   In
this countrey are right highe hilles, there is an hill that
men call Olimphus that departeth Macedonie and Tracy,
and is as high as the cloudes, and the other hill that
men call Athos is so highe, that the shadow of him
stretcheth unto Olimphus and it is neare lxxvii myle
between, and above that hill is the aire so cleere, that
men may fele no wynde there, and therefore may no
beast live there the ayre is so drye, and men say in the

1670), says is an island in the Ægean Sea. The other islands have
different names in different MSS., but are not worth the trouble of
identifying, except Lampne as Lemnos—where Mandeville places
Mount Athos. *Plutarch* and *Pliny* said that, in the summer
solstice this mountain projected its shadow on the market-place of
Myrina, the capital city of Lemnos, and that a brazen cow was
there erected to mark the termination of the shadow ; but this is
as probable as the distance given, namely, seventy-seven miles,
which is manifestly erroneous. The spelling of the geographical
names is very bad, and renders it a difficult task to identify them :
for instance, if it were not a well-known fact that Aristoteles was
born and buried at Stagira, it would be very difficult to identify
Strages as being the same place. Again, Olimphus is used instead
of Lemnos, in connection with the shadow of Mount Athos.

countrey that Philosophers somtyme went up to these
same hilles and helde to their noses a sponge wet with
water for to have ayre, for the ayre was so drye there
& above in the pouder[1] of the hill they wrote letters
with their fingers, and at the yeares ende they came
againe and found those letters which they had written
the yeare before without any defaute,[2] and therefore it
seemeth well that these hilles passe the cloudes to y^e
pure aire.

At Constantinople is the Emperours palaice which is
fayre and well dight,[3] and therein is a palaice for justing,[4]
and it is made about with stages that eche man may
well see and none greve,[5] other & under these stages are
stables vauted for the Emperours horses and all the
pillers of these stables are of marble. And within the
church of Saint Sophy, an Emperour wold haue layd
the body of his father when he was dead, and as they
made the grave they found a body in the earth & upon
that body lay a great plate of fine gold & there upon
was written in Ebrew, Greke & Latin letters that sayde
thus : *Jesus Christus nascetur de virgine Marie, et ego
credo in eum.* That is to say, Jesu Christ shal be borne
of the Virgin Mary & I believe in him. And the date
was that it lay in the earthe 200[6] yeare before our Lord
Jesu Christ was borne, and yet is that plate in the
treasory of the Church, and men say that it was Hermogenes[7] the wise man. And neverthelesse if it be so
that men of Grece be Christen, yet they vary from our

---

[1] Powder, dust.   [2] Uninjured.   [3] Furnished.
[4] Jousting or tilting.   [5] Inconvenience.
[6] *Pynson* and other editions say Two thousand.
[7] Here the chronology is somewhat involved, as Hermogenes
lived in the time of Marcus Aurelius Antoninus, *who was born*
A.D. 121.

fayth, for they say that the holy ghoste commeth not
out of the sonne, but all onely of the father, and as they
are not obedient to the Church of Rome, nor to the
Pope, and they saye that theyr Patryarkes haue as much
power over the sea, as the Pope hath on this syde the
sea. And therefore Pope John the XXII. sente letters
to them, how Christen fayth should be all one, and that
they shoulde be obedient to a pope that is Christes
Vykar in earthe, to whome God gave plaine¹ power to
binde and to assoyle,² and therefore they should be
obedient to him. And they sent him divers aunsweres,
and among other they said thus. *Potentiam tuam sum-
mam circa subjectos tuos firmiter credimus. Superbitatem
tuam sustinere non possumus. Avaritiam tuam satiare
non intendimus. Dominus tecum fit, quia Dominus
nobiscum est. Vale.* That is to say, we beleve wel that
thy power is great upon thy subjectes. We may not
suffer thy pryde. We are not in purpose to fulfille thy
covetyse.³ Our Lorde be with thee, for our Lorde is
with us. Farewell. And other aunswere might not be
haue of them. And also they make theyr sacrament of
the aulter of therf bread,⁴ for our Lord made it of therf
bread when he made his maunde.⁵ And on sherthursday⁶
make they theyre bread in tokening of the maunde, and
they dry it at the sonne,⁷ and kepe it all the yeare &
give it to sick men instede of gods body. And they
make but one unction when they Christen Children, and
they anoynt no sick men, and they say there is no pur-
gatory, and soules shall haue neither joy ne payne untill
the day of dome.⁸ And they say that fornication is no

---

¹ Plenary.   ² Absolve.   ³ Covetousness.
⁴ Unleavened bread.   ⁵ Last Supper.   ⁶ Shrove Thursday.
⁷ In the sun.   ⁸ Doom, or the day of judgment.

C

18

THE VOIAGE AND TRAVAYLE OF

deadly sinne, but a kindly thing, and that men & women
shoulde wed but once, and who so weddeth more than
once theyr children are bastards and gotten in sinne,
and theyr priestes also are wedded, and they say that
usury or simony is no deadly sinne and they sell benefices of holy churche, and so did men of other places
and is great sclaunder,[1] for now is Simony King crowned
in holy churche, God amende it when his will is. And
they say that in Lent men should not singe masse but
on the Saterday and on the Sonday, and they fast not
the Saterday no tyme in the yeare, but if it be Christmas
or Easter even. And they suffer no man that is on this
side the Grece sea to sing at theyr aulters, and if it fall
that they do through any hap,[2] they wash theyr aulters
as sone without tarieng with holy water, and they say
that there should be but one masse sayde at one aulter
in a day. And they say that our Lorde did neuer eate
meate but that he made a token[3] of eating. And also
they say that we sinne deadly in shaving of our berdes,
for the berde is a token of a man, and a gift of our Lord
and they saye that we sinne in eating of beastes that
were defended[4] in the olde lawe, as swyne, hares and
other beastes.

And thus they saye that we sinne in eating of fleshe
on the dayes before Ashwednesday, and in eating of
fleshe on the Wednesdaye, and when we eate chese or
egges on the Fryday and they curse all those that eate
no fleshe on the Saterday. Also the Emperour of Constantinople maketh the Patriarkes, Archebishoppes and
Bishoppes, and he giveth all the dignities of the churches,
and depryveth them that are unworthy, although it be so

[1] Scandal.   [2] If by chance they should do so.
[3] Only seemed to eat.   [4] Forbidden.

that these touch not the way, nevertheless they touch
that which I haue behight[1] to shew a parte of the custome, maners, and diversitie of countries, and for this is
the first countrey that is discordaunt from our faithe and
letteth[2] our faithe on this side the sea, therefore haue I
sette it here that ye may see the diversitie between our
faith & theirs, for many men haue great liking to here
speake of straunge things.

CAP: III.

*To come againe to Constantinople for to go toward the
holy land.*

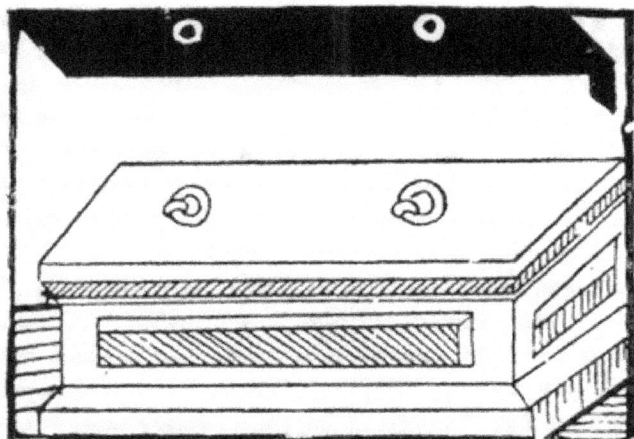

NOW come we againe for to know the way from
Constantinople. He that will go through Turkey,
he goeth through the citie of Nyke,[3] and passeth through

---

[1] Promised.   [2] Hinders.   [3] ? Salonika.

the gate of Chivitot that is right highe, and it is a myle
and a halfe from Nyke, and who so wyll go by the
brache [1] of Sainct George, and by the Greeke sea there
as Sainct Nicolas lyeth, and other places.   First men
come to the yle of Silo, and in that ile groweth mastike
upon small trees as plomtrees, or chery trees.   And
then after men go through the ile of Pathmos, where
Saint John the Evangelist wrote the Apocalips and I do
you to wete,[2] when our Lorde Jesu Christ died, Saint
John the Evangelist was of the age of xxxii yeare and
he lived after the passion of Christ lxiii [3] year and then
died.   Fro Pathmos men go to Ephesim which is a faire
citie and neare to the sea, and there died sainct John
& he was buried behind the high aulter in a tombe, and
there is a fayre church, for Christen men were wont to
holde that place, but in the tombe of sainct John is
nothing but Manna, for his body was translated [4] into
paradise, & the Turkes hold now that citie and the
church, and all Asia the lesse, & therefore is Asia the
lesse called Turkey.   And ye shall understand that
sainct John did make his grave ther in his lyfe and laied
himselfe therein all quick [5] & therefore some say he
dyed not, but that he resteth there unto the day of
judgement, and therefore truely there is a great marvaile,
for men may see there apertly [6] ye earth of the tombe
many times stirre and move, as there were a quick thing
under.   And from Ephesim, men go through many iles
in the sea unto the citie of Pateran [7] where sainct Nicolas
was borne and so to Marca [8] where he by the grace of
God was chosen Bishop, and there groweth right good

---

[1] See foot note, *ante*, p. 19.   [2] Know.   [3] *Pynson* says 67.
[4] Taken up to heaven.   [5] Living, alive.   [6] Openly.
[7] Patera, a city of Lycia.   [8] Myra, also in Lycia.

wyne and strong, that men call the wyne of Marca.
From thence men go to the yle of Crete, which the
Emperor gave sometime to Jonais.[1]   And then men
passe through the yles of Cophos and Lango[2] of the
which yles Ipocras[3] was lord, and some say that in the
yle of Lango is Ipocras daughter in maner of a Dragon,
which is a hundred foote long as men saye, for I have
not seene it, and they of the yles call hir the lady of
the countrey, and she lyeth in an olde castell and
sheweth hir thrise in the yeare, and she doth no man
harme and she is thus changed from a damosell to a
dragon through a goddesse that men call Diana, and
men say that she shall dwell so unto the tyme that a
knighte come that is so hardy as to go to hir and kisse
hir mouthe, and then shall she tourne againe to hir owne
kinde, and be a woman, and after that she shall not live
long   And it is not long sith[4] a knight of the Rodes[5]
that was hardy and valiant said that he would kisse hir,
and whan the Dragon began to lifte up hir head againste
him, and he saw it was so hideous, he fled awaye, and
the Dragon in hir anger bare the knight on a roche, and
of[6] that cast him into the sea and so he was lost.

[1] The Genoese.   [2] The island of Cos.
[3] Hippocrates, the famous physician, who was born at Cos.
[4] Since.   [5] The island of Rhodes.   [6] Off.

CAP: IIII.

Yet of the same Dragon.

ALSO a young man that wist not of the Dragon, went out of a shippe and went through the yle till he came to a Castell, and came into the cave and went so long till he founde a chamber, and there he saw a damosell that kemde[1] hir heade & loked in a mirrour, and she had much treasure aboute hir, and he trowed[2] she had been a common woman that dwelled ther to kepe men, and he abode[3] the damosel, and the damosel saw the shadowe of him in the mirrour, & she tourned toward

---

[1] Kemped or combed.   [2] Thought.

[3] *Pynson* says " obeyed unto the damsell"—that is, made obeisance, or bowed to her.

him and asked what he would, and he said he would be
hir paramoure or lemman,[1] and she asked him if he were
a knight, and he sayd nay, and she sayd then might he
not be hir lemman, but she bad him go againe to his
fellowes and make him knighte and come againe on the
morow and she woulde come oute of the cave and then
hee shoulde kisse hir on the mouth, and she badde him
haue no dread, for she would do him no harme, although
she semed hidious to him, she sayd it was done by in-
chauntment, for she sayd that she was such as he saw
hir then, and she sayd that if he kissed hir, he should
haue all the treasure, and be hir lord, and lord of all
those yles.   Then he departed from hir and went to his
fellowes in the ship, and made him knight, and came
againe on the morow to kisse the damosel, and when he
saw hir come out of the cave in forme of a dragon, he
had so great dread, that he fled to the ship, and she
folowed him, and when she saw that he tourned not
againe, she began to crye as a thing that had much
sorow, and tourned again, and sone after the knight
dyed, and sithen[2] hetherto might no knight see hir but
he died anon.   But when a knight commeth that is so
hardy to kisse hir, he shall not dye, but he shall tourne
that damosel into hir right shape and shal be lord of the
countrey aforsayde.   And from thence men go to the
yle of Rodes, the which the hospitallers held and governed, and that they took sometime from the Emperour,
and it was wont to be called Colles[3] and so yet the
Turkes call it Colles.   And sainct Paule in his Epistels
writeth to them of the yle Collocenses.[4]   This yle is

[1] Sweetheart.   [2] Since then.
[3] From the Colossus there, a statue of Jupiter 70 cubits high,
and which was accounted as one of the wonders of the world.
[4] This is not so. The Epistle to the Colossians was addressed

nere CLxxx[1] myle from Constantinople. And from this yle of Rodes, men go into Cipres where are many vines, the first is red and after a yeare they war all white, and those vines that are most white, are most cleare and best smelling, And as men passe by the way by a place where was wont to be a great citie that men call Sathalay, and all that countrey was lost through the folly of a young man, for he had a faire damosell that he loved well, and she dyed sodenly & was buried in a grave of Marble & for the great love he hadde to hir, he went in a nighte to hir tombe and opened it, & went and lay by hir and when he had done he went away, & when it came to the ende of ix monthes a voice came to him & sayd in this maner as in the next chapter foloweth.

to the inhabitants of Colossæ, a city in Phrygia—which is clearly shown by his referring in cap. 4, v. 13, to two neighbouring cities. " For I bear him record, that he hath a great zeal for you, and them that are in *Laodicea*, and them in *Hierapolis*."
  [1] *Pynson* and others say 800.

CAP: V.

Of a young man and his lemman.

G O unto the tombe of the same woman that you
hast lien by & opē it, behold well that which thou
hast begotten on hir and if thou let for to go, thou shalt
haue a great harme, and he went and opened the tombe
and there flew out an head[1] right hideous for to see, the
which head flew all about the citie and countrey, and
sone after the citie and the countrey sanke downe, &
ther are many perilous passages.   Fro Rodes to Cipres

---

[1] An edder, or adder—really meaning a winged serpent.

is five hundred mile and more, but men may go to
Cipres and come not at Rodes.   Cipres is a good yle &
a great, and there are many good cities, and there is an
Archbishoppe at Nichosy,[1] and foure other Bishops in
the lande.   And at Famagost is one of the best havens
on the sea that is in the worlde, and there are christen
men and Sarasins and men of all nations.   In Cipres is
the hill of the holy crosse, and there is the crosse of the
good thefe Dismas, as I sayd before, and some wene[2]
that there is halfe of the crosse of our lord, but it is not
so, and they do wrong that make men to believe so.   In
Cipres lieth S. Simeon, of whome the men of the countrey
make a great solempnitie, and in the Castell of Amours
lyeth the body of Saint Hillarion, and men kepe it
worshipfully, and beside Famagost was sainct Barnarde[3]
borne.

[1] Nicosia.   [2] Imagine.   [3] Barnabas.

CAP: VI.

Of the maner of hunting in Cipres.

IN Cipres men hunte with Pampeons[1] that be lyke
to Leopards, and they take wylde beastes right well
and they are somewhat more than lions, and they take
more sharply wilde beastes then houndes. In Cipres is
a maner that lordes and other men eate upon the earthe,
for they make diches within the earth all about the hall
depe to the knee, and they pave them, and when they

---

[1] Large wild dogs; they are described by *Jacobus de Vitriaco*
(the Cardinal), in his *Historiæ Orientalis*, thus: "*Papiones* quos
appellant, canes silvestres, acriores quam lupi."

will eate, they goe therein & sit there, this they do to be
more freshe, for that lande is hotter then it is here. And
at great feastes and for strange men, they set formes and
bordes as they do in this countrey, but they had lever [1]
sit in the earth.   From Cipres men go by lande to
Hierusalem, and by sea, and in a day and a night he
that hath good wind may come to that haven of Tyre
that now is called Sur, and it is also at the entre of
Surry.[2]   There was sometime a fayre citie of christen
men, but the Sarasins haue destroyed the most parte
thereof, and they kepe ye hauen righte well, for dread that
they haue of Christen men.   Men might go right to that
haven and come not in Cipres, but they go gladly to
Cipres to rest them on the lande, or else to by[3] thinges
that they haue nede of to their living.   Upon the sea
side men may find many rubies, and there is a well that
holy write speaketh of

Fons ortorum et puteus aquarum viventum.   That is to
say, The well of gardeines and diches of waters living.
In the citie of Tyre sayde the woman to our Lorde,
Beatus venter qui te portavit et ubera que succisti.   That
is as much to say, Blessed be the body that bare thee,
and the pappe of the which thou suckest.   And there
our Lorde forgave the woman of Canee hir sinnes, and
there was also in that place wont to be the stone on
which our Lord sat and preached & on the same stone
was founded the Church of Sainct Saviour.   And upon
that See is the citie of Saphon, Sarep, or Sodome and
there was wont to dwell Elias the prophet & there was
raised Jonas the prophete the widowes sonne, and fiue
myle from Saphen is the citie of Sydon, of which citie
Dido that was Eneas wife after the destruction of Troy

---

[1] Liefer, rather.   [2] Syria.   [3] Buy.

was queene, and that founded the Citie of Carthage in
Affryke and now is called Didonsart. And in the citie of
Tyre raigned Achilles, the father of Dido and a myle[1]
from Sidon is Beruth, & from Beruth to Sardena is
three days journey and from Sardena is five myle to
Damas.

CAP. VII.

Of the haven of Jaffe also named.

WHO so will go lenger upon the sea and come
nerer to Hierusalem—you shall go from Cipres
by sea to porte Jaffe, for that is the next haven to
Hierusalem, for from that haven it is but a days journey
& a halfe to Hierusalem And that haven is called
Jaffe, and the towne Affe after one of Noyes[2] sonnes
that men call Japheth that founded it, and now it is
called Jops. And ye shall understand that it is the
eldest town of the world, for it was made before Noes
floud and there be the bones of a giaunts side that be
XL fote long.

CAP : VIII.

Of the haven of Tyre.

AND who arriveth at the first haven of Tyre, or of
Surrey beforesayde, may go by land if he will to
Hierusalem, and he goeth to the citie of Acon in a day,

---

[1] Other editions say 16 miles.   [2] Noah's.

it was called Tholomayda, and it was a citie of christen
men sometime, but it is now destroyed and it is on the sea.
And it is from Venice to Acon by the sea two thousand
and Lxxx myle of Lombardy & from Calabre or fro
Cicill it is to Acon a thousand three hundred miles of
Lombardy.

CAP. IX.

Of the hill Carme.

A ND the yle of Grece[1] is right in the mid way,
and beside this citie of Acon towarde the sea at

[1] Crete.

viii[1] hundred furlonges on the righte hande towarde the
southe is the hil Carme[2] where Elias the prophet dwelled,
and there was the ordre of Carme[3] fyrst founded.   This
hyl is not ryghte greate, ne hygh, and at the foote of
this hill was sometime a good citie of chrysten men,
that was called Cayphas, for Cayphas founded it, but it
is nowe all wasted.   And at the lyfte syde of the hyll is
a Town that men call Saffre, and that is sette upon
another hil, there was Sainct James and saynt John
borne, and in the worshippe of them is there a faire
church made.   And from Tholomayda that men now
call Acon, to a great hill that men call Ekale[4] de Tyrreys
is an hundred furlongs, and beside that citie of Acon
runneth a lyttle ryver that men call Belyon, and there
nere is the fosse of Minon[5] all round that is a hundred
cubytes or shaftments[6] broade, and it is all full of
gravell, cleare shyninge, whereof men make white glasse
cleare, and men come from far countreys by shippe, and
by lande with cartes to take of the gravell & if there be
never so much taken thereof in a daye, on the morow it
is full againe as ever it was, and that is great marvaile,
and there is alwaye winde in that fosse that styreth
alway the gravell and maketh it troubled.   And if a man
put or do therein any mettal, as sone as it is therein it
waxeth glasse, and the glasse that is made of this
gravell if it be done[7] into the gravell tourneth againe

[1] *Pynson* and others say 120 furlongs.
[2] Carmel.   [3] Carmelite friars.
[4] The scale, or ladder, of Tyre.
[5] Meaning the sepulchre of Memnon.
[6] A shaftment was a measure taken from the top of the extended
thumb to the outmost part of the palm—usually taken as six
inches.
[7] Buried.

into the gravell as it was before & some say that it is a
swallow[1] of the sea gravell.[2]

CAP. X.

How Sampson slew the King and his enimies.

ALSO from Acon beforesaid, men go three[3] journeys
to the citie of Philisten, that now is called Gaza,
that is to say the rich citie & it is right fayre and full

[1] Whirlpool.

[2] This story is said to come from Solinus, and is mentioned in
Münster's Cosmographia, and in other books.

[3] *Pynson* and others say four.

of folke and it is a little uppon the sea, and from that
citie broughte the strong Sampson the gates of the Citie
uppon a highe hill, where he was taken in the Citie,
and there he slewe the King in his palace, and many
thousande more with him, for he made an house to fall
on them.   And from thence shal men go to the citie of
Cesaryen,[1] and so to the castell of Pylleryns[2] and then
to Askalon, and so forth to Japhat[3] and so unto the holy
citie of Hierusalem.

CAP. XI.

The waye to Babylon whereas the Soudan dwelleth.

AND whoso wyll go through the lande of Babylon
where the Soudan[4] dwelleth, to have leave to go

---

[1] Cæsarea.   [2] Pilgrims.   [3] Jaffa.   [4] Sultan.

more sykerly [1] throughe the Churches & countreys,
and to go to mount Sinay before he come to Hierusalem, and then turne agayne by Hierusalem ; he shall goe
from Gaza to the castell Dayre.   And after a man commeth out of Surry, and goeth in the wildernesse, where
the waye is full sandy, and the wyldernesse lasteth eyght
Journeys,[2] where men findeth all that them nedeth of
vytayles and men call that wyldernesse Archelleke,[3] and
whan a man commeth out of this deserte, hee entreth
into Egypte, and they call Egypte, Canopat,[4] and in
another language men call it Mersyne,[5] and the fyrste
goode towne that men fynde is called Beleth, and it is
at the ende of the Kingdome of Alape,[6] and from thence
men come to Babylon and to Kayre,[7] and in Babylon is
a fayre churche of our lady, where she dwelled vii yeare
when she was oute of the lande of Jewes, for dreade of
Kynge Herode.   And there lyeth the bodye of Saynte
Barbara vyrgyn, and there dwelled Joseph whan he was
solde of his brethrene, and there made Nabugodonosor
put the children in (the) fire, for they were of right[8]
trouth, the which chyldren men call Anania, Azaria, and
Misael (as y⁰ psalme of Benedicite saith) but Nabugodonosor called them thus, Sydrac, Mysac, Abdenago, that
is to say, God glorious, God victorious, God over all
Kingedomes, and that was for myracle that he made
Goddes sonne, as he sayd, go wyth those chyldren
throughe the fyre.   There dwelleth the Soudan, for there

---

[1] Certainly, surely.   [2] Day's march.
[3] Athylec, Abylech, Alhylet, Alhelet, Abylet.
[4] Query Canopus, a city 12 miles from Alexandria, named after
the pilot of Menelaus' vessel, who was buried here.
[5] Mersur, Morsyn.   [6] Aleppo.   [7] Cairo.
[8] True faith.

is a faire citie and a stronge castell and it standeth upon
a rocke.   In that Castell is always dwellyng to kepe the
castell and to serve the soudan, above viii[1] thousand
persons or folk that take all theyr necessaries at the
Soudans courte.   I should well knowe it, for I dwelled
with him soudiour[2] in his warres a great while agayne
the Bedions,[3] and he wold haue wedded me to a great
princes daughter ryght richly, if I would haue forsaken
my faith.

CAP. XII.

*Yet here followeth of the Soudan and of his Kingdomes
that he hath conquered, which he holdeth strongly with
force.*

AND ye shall understand that the Soudan is lorde of
v Kingdomes : the which he hath conquered and
gotten to him by strength, and these be they—the Kingdome of Canopate (*that is*) the Kingdome of Egipte, the
Kingdome of Hierusalem : whereof David and Salomon
were Kings, the Kingdome of Surry, of the which the
citie of Damas[4] was the chiefe, the Kingdome of Alape
in the lande of Dameth, and the Kingdome of Arabya :
which was one of the three Kinges that made offeryng
to our Lorde when he was borne, and many other landes
he holdeth in his hande, and also he holdeth Calaphes[5]
that is a great thing to the Soudan, that is to say, among
them Roys[6] yle and this vale is colde.

---

[1] Other editions say 6,000.   [2] Soldier.   [3] Bedouins.
[4] Damascus.   [5] Khalifs.
[6] Who are accounted there as kings.

And then men go uppon the mount of Sainct Katherina
and that is much higher than the mount Moyses.   And

there as saint Katheryn was graven[1] is no church ne
castell, ne other dwelling place, but there is an hyll of

[1] Buried.

stones gathered togither, about the place there she was graven of Aungels, there was wont to be a chapell, but it is all cast downe & yet lyeth there a great parte of the stones.

But under the foote of mount Sinay is a monasterie of Monkes, and there is the church of Sainct Katherine wherein be many lamps brenning, and they have oyle onlye enough to eate and to brenne, and that they haue by myracle of God, there come certaine of all maner of byrdes euery yeare once, lyke pylgrymes and eche of them bringeth a braunch of olyve in token of offering, whereof they make much oyle.

CAP. XIII.

For to returne fro Sinay to Hierusalem.

NOW sythen a man hath visited this holy place of Sainct Katheryn and he will torne to Hierusalem, he shall fyrst take leave of the Monkes, and recommend him specially to their prayers, then those Monks will freely giue to Pilgrims victuals to pass through the Wildernesse to Surry & that lasteth well xiii Journeys. And in that wyldernesse dwell many Arabyns that men call Bedoins and Ascoperdes,[1] these are folk that are full of all maner of yll condycyons, and they have no houses, but tentes, the wyche they make of beastes skinnes, as of camelles and other beastes the whyche

---

[1] Or Giants from the Arabic *askhaf*, a tall, big-boned man. It will be remembered that Sir Bevis of Southampton brought home a Giant Ascapart—who probably was one of them.

they eate, and thereunder they lye, and they dwell in
places where they maye fynde water, as on the rede sea,

for in that wildernesse is greate defaute of water, and it
faileth ofte where a man findeth water one time, he
fyndeth it not another tyme, and therefore make they no
houses in those countreys.   These men that I speake of
tyll not the land, for they eate no breade, but[1] yf it be
anye that dwelleth neare a goode towne. And they rost
al theyre fishes and flesh upon the hote stones agaynst
the sonne, and they are stronge men and well fyghtynge,
and they do nothinge but chace wyld beastes for theyr
sustenaunce, and they sette[2] not by theyr lyves, therfore
they dreade not the Soudan nor no prince of all the
worlde.   And they haue greate warre wythe the Soudan,
and the same tyme that I was dwelling with him they
bare but a shelde and a speare for to defende them with,
and they holde[3] none other armour, but they wynde

---

[1] Unless.   [2] They value not.   [3] Have.

theyr heades and neckes in a great lynnen clothe,[1] and
they are men of full yll kynde.

. CAP. XIIII.

As men are passed this wyldernesse againe comming to
Hierusalem.

AND when men are passed this wyldernesse towarde
Hierusalem they come to Barsabe[2] that was sometime a fayre and a lykyng towne of Christen men, and
yet is some of their churches, and in that towne dwelled
Abraham the Patryarke. This towne of Barsabe founded
Uryas wife, of whom David engendred Salomon the
wyse that was Kyng of Hierusalem, and of the xii kindes[3]
of Israell, and he raigned xl yeare. And from thence

---

[1] A turban.　　　[2] Beersheba.　　　[3] Tribes.

go men to the vale of Ebron, that is from thence nere
xii myle and some call it the vale of Mambre,[1] and also
it is called the vale of Teeres, for as much as Adam in
that vale he wept a hundred yeare the death of his sonne
Abel that Cayne slew.   And Ebron was sometime[2] the
principall Citie of the Philistines & there dwelled giaunts
& there it was so free, that all that had done evill in
other places were there saved.   In Ebron Josue and[3]
Calope and theyr felowship came fyrst to espy how they
might wynne the lande of promyssion.   In Ebron David
raigned fyrst vii yeare and a halfe & in Hierusalem he
raigned xxxii[4] yeare and a halfe, and there be the graves
of the Patryarkes—Adam, Abraham, Jacob and theyr
wyves, Eve, Sare, Rebecca[5] and they are in the hanging[6]
in the hyll.   And under them is a right fayre Churche
Kirnelde[7] after the facion and maner as it were a Castell,
the which the Sarasins keepe right well, and they haue
that place in greate worship for the holy Patryarkes that
lieth there, and they suffer no Christen men ne Jewes to
come therein but they have speciall grace of the Soudan,
for they holde Christen men and Jewes but as houndes
that should come in no holy place, and they call the
place Spelunke[8] or double cave or double grave ; for one
lyeth on another, and the Sarasins call it in theyr language Caryatharba, that is to say the place of Patryarkes,
and the Jewes call it Arboth.   And in that same place

---

[1] Mamre.   [2] Formerly.

[3] Jehoshua and Caleb (see Numbers, cap. 13).

[4] *Pynson* and others say 33 years and a half.

[5] All other editions have " and of Lya," or Leah, who is evidently
here forgotten.

[6] Caves cut in the side of the rock.

[7] Crenelated or battlemented.

[8] Lat. *Spelunca*, a cave.

was Abrahams house, and that was the same Abraham which sat in his dore, and saw three persons and wor- shipped but one, as holy wryt witnesseth saying, *Tres videt et unum adoravit.* That is to saye, he saw three and worshipped but one, and him took Abraham into his house.

CAP. XV.

Here foloweth a lyttle of Adam & Eve and other things.

A ND right nere to that place is a cave in a Roche where Adam and Eve dwelled whan they were dryven out of Paradyse, and there got they theyr chyldren. And in that place was Adam made as some men saye, for men called sometime that place the felde

of Damasse,[1] for it was in the worshippe[2] of Damasse;
and fro thence he was translated into Paradyse as they
saye, and afterwarde he was driven out of Paradyse, and
put there agayne, for the same daye that he was put into
Paradyse, the same day he was driven out, for so soone
he synned.   And there begynneth the yle[3] of Ebron that
lasteth nere to Hierusalem, and the Aungell bad Adam
that he should dwell wyth his wyfe, and there they engendred Seth, of the which kyndred[4] Jesu Christ was
borne.   And in that vale is the felde where men draw
out of the earth a thinge the which men in that countrey
call Chambell and they eate that thinge in the stede
of spyce & they beare it to sell, and men may not
grave[5] there so deepe ne so wyde, but it is at the yeares
ende full againe up to the sydes through the grace of
God.   And two myle from Ebron is the grave of Loth[6]
that was Araham's brother.

[1] Damascus.   [2] *Pynson* and others say lordship.
[3] Vale.   [4] Kindred or tribe.   [5] Dig.   [6] Lot.

CAP. XVI.

Of the dry tree.

WHEN a lyttle from Ebron is the mounte of
Mambre, of the which mount the vale toke his
name, and there is the tree of oke that the Sarasins call
dypre,[1] that is of Abraham's time, that men call the dry
tree. And they say that it hath ben from the beginning
of the worlde, and was sometime grene and bare leaves,
unto the tyme that our Lorde dyed, and so did all the
trees in the worlde, or else they fayled in their heartes,
or else they faded, and yet is there many of those in the
worlde. And some prophesies say, that a lorde or prince
of the weste syde of the worlde shall winne the lande of

[1] *Pynson* and others read Dyrpe or Dirpe.

promission, that is the holy lande, with the helpe of
Christen men, and he shall do singe[1] a masse under that
tree, and the tree shall waxe grene and beare fruite and
leaves, and through that miracle many Sarasins and
Jewes shal be turned to the Christen fayth, and therefore
they do great worship therto, and kepe it right[2] basely.
And yet though it be dry, it beareth a great vertue, for
certainly he that hath a lyttle thereof about him, it
healeth a sicknesse called the falling evill, and hath
many other vertues also, and therefore it is holden right
precious.

CAP. XVII.

Fro Bethlehem.

FROM Ebron men go to Bethlehem in halfe a daye,
for it is but five myle, and it is a fayre waye &
thorow[3] woddes full pleasaunt.   Bethlem is but a little
citie long and narowe, and well walled, and enclosed
with a great diche and it was wont to be called Effrata
as holy wryte sayth *Ecce audivimus eum in Effrata* &c.,
That is to saye, Lo we herde him in Effrata.   And
toward the ende of the citie toward the East, is a ryght
fayre churche and a gracious and it hath many toures,
pinacles and kirnelles[4] full strongly made & within that
Church is xliiii great pyllers of marble & betwene this
church the field[5] florished, as ye shall here.

---

[1] Cause a mass to be sung.
[2] To keep it carefully.   [3] Through woods.
[4] Battlements.   [5] The flowered field.

CAP. XVIII.

Of a fayre mayden that should be put to death wrongfully.

THE cause is, for as much as a fayre maiden y' was blamed wyth wrong that she hadde done fornication, for the which cause she was demed[1] to dye and to bee brente[2] in that place to the which she was ledde. And as the woode began to brenne about hir, she made hir prayer to our Lorde as she was not gyltie of that thing, that he would helpe hir that it might be knowne to all men. And whan she had thus sayde, she entred the fyre and anone the fyre went out, and those braunches that were brenninge became red Roses and those

---

[1] Condemned.　　　[2] Burnt.

braunches that were not kindled became white Rosiers[1] full of white roses, and those were the fyrst roses and rosyers that any man sawe, and so was the mayden saved through the grace of God, and therefore is that felde called the feeld of God florished, for it was full of Roses. Also besyde the quire of that Church aforesayd at the right side as men come downwarde xii[2] grees[3] is the place where our Lorde was borne that is now full well dyght[4] of Marble & full rychely depaynted of golde, sylver and asure and other colours. And a lyttle thens by three paces is the crybe[5] of the Oxe and the Asse, and besyde y[t] is the place where the sterre[6] fell that lede the three Kinges Jasper, Melchior and Balthasar, but men of Grece call the Kinges thus, Galgalath, Saraphy, Malgalath. These three Kinges offered to our Lorde, Encence, Gold & Mirre and they came together through myracle of God, for they mette togither in a citie that men call Chasak, that is liii journeys from Bethleem, and there they were at Bethleem the fourth[7] daye after they hadde seene the sterre. And under the cloyster of this church xviii grees[3] at the righte syde is a great pytte where the bones of the Innocentes lie, and before that place where Chryst was borne is the tombe of Sainct Jerom that was a priest and a Cardinal that translated the Byble and the Sauter[9] from Hebrew into Latyn, and beside that church is a Church of Saynte Nycolas, where our Lady rested hir whan she was delivered of chyld, and for as much as she had so much mylke in hir pappes that it greved hir, she mylked it out uppon the redde stones of Marble, so that yet may the traces bee seene whyte

---

[1] Rose bushes.   [2] Other editions say 16.   [3] Steps.
[4] Adorned.   [5] Crib or Manger.   [6] Star.
[7] Other editions say "thirteenth."   [8] Paces   [9] Psalter.

uppon the stones. And ye shall understande that all
that dwell in Bethleem are Chrysten men, and there are
fayre vynes all aboute the citie and great plentie of
wine, for their booke that Mahomet betoke [1] them, the
which they call Alkaron and some call it Massap
and some call it Harme, forbiddeth them to drinke
any wyne, for in that booke Machomet curseth
all those that drynke of that wyne and all that
sell it, for some men saye that he onse slewe a good
hermite in his dronkennesse which [2] he loved much,
and therefore he cursed the wyne, and them that
drynke wyne, but his malyce is torned to hymselfe, as
holye writ sayth "*Et in verticem ipsius iniquitus ejus
descendit*," That is to say in Englyshe, His wickednesse
shall descende on his owne head. And also the Sarasins
bringeth forthe no geise,[3] ne they eate no swines fleshe,
for they say it is brother to manne and that is was forbidden in the olde lawe. Also in the lande of Palestine
ne in the lande of Egypte they eate but lyttle veale and
beefe but it be so olde that it may no more travayll[4] ne
werke, not that it is forbidden but they kepe them to
tylling of their lande. In this castell of Bethleem was
Kyng David borne and he had Lx wives and ccc lemmans. From Bethleem to Hierusalem is two myle, and
in the way of Hierusalem halfe a myle from Bethleem is
a Church where the aungell sayd to the shepherdes of
the bearing of Christ. In that waye is the tombe of
Rachel that was Josephs mother the Patryarke and she
dyed as soone as she hadde borne Benjamyn and there
she was buried, and Jacob hir husbande set xii great
stones upon hir in tokening that she had borne xii

---

[1] Gave.   [2] Whom.   [3] Breed no pigs.
[4] Plough or draw loads.

children.   In this way to Hierusalem are many Christen
churches by the which men go to Hierusalem.

CAP. XIX.

Of the citie of Hierusalem.

FOR to speake of Hierusalem, ye shall understande
that it standeth fayre among hylles, and there is
neither ryver nor well, but water commeth by conduit
from Ebron, and ye shall wete that men called it first
Jebus and sythen it was called Salem unto the time of
King David, and he set those two names togither and
called it Hierusalem and so it is called yet.   And aboute
Hierusalem is the Kingdome of Surry, & thereby is
the lande of Palestyne and Askalon, but Hierusalem is
in the lande of Jude, and it is called Judee, for Judas
Maccabeus was King of that lande, and also it marcheth
afterward on the Kingedome of Araby, on the South
side on the lande of Egipt, on the west side on the great
sea, on the north syde on the Kingdome of Surry and
the sea of Cipres.   About Hierusalem are these cities.
Ebrone at viii¹ myle, Jerico at vi myle Barsebe at viii
myle Askalon xviii² myle, Jaffa at xxv³ Ramatha at iiii⁴
mile.   At Bethlem towarde the South is a church of
saint Markerot,⁵ that was abbot there, for whom they
made much sorow when he should dy & it is painted
there how they made dole⁶ when he dyed, and it is a

¹ ² ³ Other editions say respectively 7, 17, 16.
⁴ Other editions say 3 miles.
⁵ Variously written, Markertot, Karitot, Karscati, and Mer-
caritot.
⁶ Grieved, from *Lat.* Dolor.

piteous thing to beholde. This lande of Hierusalem hath ben in dyvers nations hands, as Jewes, Cananens, Assyrians, Percians, Macedons, Grekes, Romayns & Chrysten men, Sarasins, Barbaryans, Turkes & many other nacions. For Chryste wyll not that it be long in the handes of traytours ne sinners be they Christen or other. And now hath the mistrowing[1] men holden that lande in theyre handes Lx yeare & more, but they shall not holde it long and if[2] God wyll.

[1] Unbelieving, or heathen.
[2] Unless it is God's pleasure.

CAP. XX.

Yet of the holy citie of Hierusalem.

A ND ye shall understand that whan men fyrst come
to Hierusalem, they go fyrste a pylgrimage to the
Church, where that the holy grave is, the whiche is

out of the citie on the North syde, but it is now closed
in with the wall of the towne, and there is a full fayre
church rounde, all open aboue, and well covered with

leede and on the west syde is a fayre toure and a strong
for belles.

And in the middes of the church is a Tabernacle
made like a little house, in maner of halfe a compasse,
ryght well and richly of gold and asure and other
coloures well dyght & on the ryght syde is the sepulchre
of. oure Lorde, and the tabernacle is viii foote long and
v fote wide and xi fote of height. And it is not longe
sythen the sepulchre was all open, y[t] men might kysse
it and touche it : but for men that came thether payned[1]
them to breake the stones in peces or pouder, therefore
the Soudan hath made a wall about the sepulchre that no
man may touch it. On the lefte syde is no wyndowe, but
therein is many lampes light, and there is a lampe that
hangeth before the sepulcre lyght brenning and on the
fryday it goeth oute by itselfe, and lyghteth againe by
itselfe at the houre that our Lorde rose from death to
life. And within that church upon that right side is the
mount Calvary, where our Lord was done on the crosse,
and the crosse was sette in a morteys[2] in the roche that
is white of coloure, and a lyttle redde medled[3] with, and
upon that roche dropped the bloude of the woundes of
our Lord whan he was pained on the crosse & that is
called Golgatha and men go up to that Golgatha upon
greces.[4] And in that mortays was Adams head founde
after Noyes flood, in token that the sinnes of Adam,
shoulde bee boughte in the same place, and aboue that
roche made Abraham sacryfice to our Lord, and there is
an auter,[5] and before that auter lyeth Godfry of Boleyn,[6]
Bawdewyn[7] and other that were Christen and kinges of
Hierusalem. And ther as our Lord was done[8] upon the

[1] Tried hard. [2] Mortise. [3] Mixed. [4] Steps.
[5] Altar. [6] Bouillon. [7] Baldwin. [8] Placed.

crosse, is thys wrytten in greke, *Otheos* [1] *basylon, ysmon persemas, ergaste sothyas oyos.* That is to say in latine, *Hic Deus Rex noster ante secula operatus est salutem in medio terræ,* That is to saye, This God our King before worldes, hath wrought healthe in the myddes of the earth. And also upon the roche where the crosse was fyxed is wrytten within the roche, *Eros* [2] *guyst basys, thou, pestes, thoy, thesmoysy.* That is to say in latin, *Quod vides est fundamentum totius mundi et hujus fidei.* And it is to saye, that thou seest, is grounde of all the world and of this faith. And ye shall understande that our Lorde whan he dyed was thyrty & two [3] yeare olde and three monethes and the prophecie of David sayth that he should haue xl yeares, when he saith thus. *Quadraginta annis proximus fui generatione huic,* that is to say, fourtie yeare was I neighbour to this kinde, and thus it should seme that prophecie were not sothe, [4] but it is. For in olde time men called yeares of ten monethes of the which Marche was the fyrst & December the last. But Cayus Cezar [5] that was Emperour of Rome dyd sette to these two moneths Januarie & Februarie and ordeyned the yere of xii months. That is to say ccc [6] dayes without lepe yere the proper course of the sonne and therefore after the accompting of x monethes to the yeare, he dyed in xl yeare and three moneths.

Also within mounte Calvary at the ryghte syde is there an aulter where the piller lyeth that our Lorde was

[1] Should read "Ο Θιὸς Βασιλιὸς ἡμῶν πρὸ αἰώνων ειργάσατο σωτηρίαν ἰν μίσῳ τῆς γῆς."
[2] Should read "Ο εἴδεις, ἱστὶ Βασις τῆς πίστιως ὕλης τοῦ κοσμου τούτου."
[3] Other editions have 33 years and 3 months.
[4] Sooth, true.   [5] Caius Julius Cæsar.
[6] Other editions give the proper number of days, *viz.,* 365.

bound to when he was scourged and thereby are three [1]
other pyllers that alwaye drop water, and some saye
that those pyllers weepe for our Lords death, and neare

this aulter in a place xlii grees [2] depe was founde the
verye crosse by the assent [3] of sainct Eleyne [4] under a
roch where the Jewes had hydde it and it was assayed,
for they founde three crosses, one of our Lorde and two
of theves. And Saint Elene assayed them on a dead
body that rose as sone as the very [5] crosse of our Lorde

[1] Other editions say four, which is the number represented in the
engraving.   [2] Paces.
[3] Perception, or sagacity. *Lat.*, sensus.
[4] Helena, mother of Constantine.
[5] True, veritable.

was laid on him.　And thereby, in the vale, is the place
where the foure nayles of our Lord were hyd, for he had
two nayles in his handes and two in his fete, and one of
those nailes the Emperour of Constantinople[1] dyde
make a bridell for his horse to beare him in bataile, for
by[2] the vertue that it had, he overcame his enimies,
and wan[3] all the land of Asye, Turky, Damasse the
more[4] and the lesse, Surrey and Hierusalem, Araby,
Percy, and Mesopotamy, the Kingdome of Alabe,[5] Egipt
the high and the lowe, and other kingdomes many full
nyghe all unto Ethyope the low, and also unto Inde the
lesse, that then was chrysten.　And there was in that
tyme many good men and holy hermits, of whome the
booke of[6] the fathers lyves speaketh, and they are now
in Paynims & Sarasins handes, but whan God will
righte[7] as these landes are lost through sinne of Christen
men, so shall they be won againe by christen me throygh
the helpe of God.　And in the myddes of this Church
is a compasse,[8] in the which Joseph of Armathy[9] layd
the body of our Lord whan he had taken him of[10] the
crosse & upon the same place dyd he wash the fete of
our Lorde, & that compasse men say is in the myddes
of the world.

　[1] Another is said to be incorporated in the so-called Iron Crown
of Lombardy.　Guisto Fontanini, Archbishop of Ancyra, gives a
list of twenty-three places claiming to have a nail—Venice having
three.　M. Rohault de Fleury gives six more—whilst, according to
tradition, Helena sent two to her son, and threw one in the sea to
still a storm, thus leaving but one to meet all demands.

　[2] Through.　　　　　　　　[3] Won or conquered.
　[4] Greater.　　　　　　　　[5] Aleppo.
　[6] The Vitæ Sanctorum Patrum, many old printed copies of which
exist.
　[7] When God thinks fit.　　　[8] A linen swathing-band.
　[9] Arimathæa.　　　　　　[10] Off.

CAP. XXI.

Of the church of the holy sepulchre.

IN that Churche of the sepulcre on the north syde is the place where our Lord was done[1] (*in*) prison, and there is a part of the cheyne with which he was bound, and there he appeared fyrst to Mary Magdeleyne when he was risen from death and she trowed[2] that he had bene a gardeiner. In the Church of the sepulcre was wont to be[3] Chanons of sainct Benet and they had a pryour ; but the Patryarke was theyr soveraigne.

And without the dores of the Churche on the righte syde as men go up xviii grees,[4] our Lorde sayde to his mother[5] *Ecce filius tuus.* That is to say, Woman beholde thy sonne *De inde dixit discipulo, Ecce mater tua.* That is to say, Then said he to his disciple, Behold thy mother.[6] And these wordes he sayde when he hanged upon the crosse. And upon these grees went our Lorde when he bare the crosse uppon his shoulder, and under these grees is a Chappell where the priestes synge, but not after our lawe, and alway they make theyr Sacrament of the aulter of bread, say *Pater noster* &c., and other prayers, as with the which thing they say the wordes of whome the sacrament is made, for they

---

[1] Put.   [2] Thought or believed.

[3] Were formerly Canons of the Order of St. Benedict.

[4] Should be *grees* or steps.

[5] The printer has omitted the word " *Mulier* ecce," &c.

[6] Gospel according to St. John, cap. 19, vv. 26, 27.

know not of the addicions that many Popes haue made
but they singe in good devocion. And nere there is the
stone wher our Lord rested him when he was wery for
bearing of the crosse. And ye shall understand that
before the Churche of the Sepulcre is the citie most
strong[1] for the great playne that is betwene the citie
& the church; on the East side without the walles of
the citie is the vale of Josaphat that commeth to the
walles. In that vale of Josaphat without the citie, is the
churche of sainct Stephen where he was stoned to death,

and thereby is the gate gylted that may not be opened.
Through this gate our Lord entred on palme Sonday
upon an asse, and the gate opened against him whan he
would go to the Temple, and yet are the steppes of the
asse sene in three places the which stand[2] in full harde

[1] *Pynson* says, "most wake" or weak, and other editions say,
"feeble."

[2] *Pynson* has this passage: "The wyche are full of harde
stones."

stones. Before the churche of the sepulcre two hundred paces, is a great hospitall of Sainct John, in the which hospytall are liiii pyllers made of stone.

And to go towarde the East from the hospitall is a righte fayre churche that men call our lady the greate, and then is there another church after that, that men call our lady of the latyn,[1] and there it was Mary Cleophe and Magdeleyne drew[2] theyr here whan oure Lord was put to death.

CAP. XXII.

Of the Temple of God.

AND from the churche of the sepulcre towarde the East at xviii[3] paces is *Templum Domini.* That is a fayre house and it is all rounde and ryghte high & covered with leed,[4] and it is well paved with white marble, but ye Sarasins wyl suffre no christen men ne Jewes to come therein, for they say that so[5] foule men should not come into that holye place, but I came therein and in other places where I woulde, for I had letters of the Soudan, wyth hys great seal, and, commonly, other men but have of his signet, and men beare hys letter with his seale before them hanginge on a speare, and men do great worship thereto, and kneele against[6] it as it were against God's body : for those men that it is sent to,

---

[1] *Pynson* says " Nostre dame de Vatyns."
[2] Tore.   [3] Other editions say 160 paces.
[4] Lead.   [5] Such unclean.   [6] Before.

before they take it, they encline[1] thereto & and then they
take it, and laye it upon their heads, and afterward they
kisse it, and then they reade it, all enclining with great
worship, and then they profer[2] them to do all that the
bringer will.   And in this Templum Domini were wont

to be Chanons regulers, and they had an Abbot to
whome they were obedient, in this Temple was Charle-
maine when the Aungell brought him the prepuis of
our Lorde when he was circumsised, and after King
Charles brought it to Acon[3] into our Ladies Chapell.

[1] Bow.   [2] Proffer or offer.
[3] *Pynson* and others say Paris.

CAP. XXIII.

Yet of the temple of God.

AND ye shall understande that this is not the temple
that Salomon made, for that temple lasted but a
thousand, an hundred and two yeare. For Titus, Ves-
pasianus Son, that was Emperour of Rome that layde
syege about Hierusalem for to discomfyte the Jewes, for
they hadde put Chryst to death without leave of the
Emperour, and when he had taken the citie he did
brenne the temple and caste it downe, and toke all the
Jewes and put to death CXIM and the other he put in
prison, and solde xxx for a peny for they sayd that they
bought Jesu Christ for xxx pence. And sithen[1] gave
Julian Apostata leve to ye Jewes to make the Temple
of Hierusalem againe for he hated christen men, and
yet he was Chrysten, but he forsoke his lawe. And whan
the Jewes hadde made the Temple, then came an earthe
quacke (as God woulde) and caste downe all that they
had made. Sythen Adryan the Emperour that was of
them of Troye made Hierusalem againe and the Temple
in that same maner that Salomon made it, and would
that no Jewe should dwell there but all christen men,
for if all it were[2] so that he was not chrystened, he loved
the christen men more than other men, save men of his
owne fayth. And this emperour dyd enclose and wall
the church of the holy sepulcre within the citie, that
before was farre without the citie, and he would have

----

[1] Since then.   [2] For even if he were not baptised.

chaunged the name of Hierusalem and called it Helyam,[1]
but that name lasted not longe. And ye shall wete[2]
that the Sarasins do greate worship to that Temple and
they saye that place is right holy, and when they go
therein they go bare foote and knele many times downe.
And when I and my felowes came therein, we did of[3]
our harnesse[4] and came bare foote into the Temple &
thought that we should doe as much or more than they
that were mistrowing.[5]   And this Temple is three score[6]
and three cubites of wydenesse and as much of length
and xxxii[7] cubites in height and covered with lead and
it is within full of pillers of Marble   And in the middes
of the Temple is a stage of twenty[8] and foure greces of
height and good pillers all about. This place called
of Jewes *Sancta Sanctorum.* That is to say Holy of
Holyest and in that place cometh none but their
prelate that maketh theyr sacrafyce, and the people
standeth all about in divers stages, after they are[9] of
dignitie and worshippe, and there be foure entrings into
that Temple and the dores are of Cipres well dighte,[10]
and within the East dore our Lord sayd, here is Hierusalem.   And on the northe syde within the dore is a
fountaine but it runneth not ; of the which holy writ
speaketh & saith thus—*Vidi aquam egredientem de
templo.* That is to saye, I saw water comming out of
the temple. And upon the other side is a roche that
men calle sometyme Moryach, but after it was called
Belet,[11] or the arke of God, with the reliques of the
Jewes. Thys arke did Titus cary with him to Rome

[1] Ælia.   [2] Know.   [3] Put off.   [4] Armour.
[5] Unbelieving.
[6][7][8] Other editions say, respectively, 64, 120, and 14.
[9] According to their dignity, &c.
[10] Finely ornamented.   [11] Bethel.

when he had discomfited all the Jewes. In that same
arke were the ten commandementes and Aarons rodde
and Moyses rodde with which he departed[1] the red sea,
when the people of Israell passed through on dryefoote
& with that rod he did many wonders, and there was the
vessell of gold ful of manna, & clothing & ornaments &
the tabernacle of Aaron, and a table square of golde
with twelve precious stones, & a box of Jasper graven
with four figures & eight names of our Lorde within,
& seven candlesticks of golde, & foure sensers of golde,
and an aulter also of fine gold & foure lions of gold,
uppon the which they had Cherubin of gold twelve
spanne long, & a tabernacle of golde & also twelve[2]
trumpets of silver & a table of sylver & seven barly
loves and all other reliques that were before the nativitie
of Jesu. Also upon this roch slept Jacob, when he sawe
Aungels go up and downe, and sayde, *Vere locus iste
sanctus est, et ego ignorabam,* That is to say Forsooth this
place is holy & I wist[3] it not. And there the Aungel
chaunged Jacob's name and called him Israell, And in
that same place David saw the aungell that slew the
people with a sworde, and put it all blody in the shethe.
And in this roch was saynct Symeon when he received
our Lorde into the temple, and on this roch he set him
when the Jewes would have stoned him and the roch
rived in two and in that refte[4] he hid him and after a
sterre came downe & gave him light. And on this roch
sat our Lady and learned hir sauter.[5] And there forgave our Lord the sinnes of the woman that was taken
and found in adoultry, and there was our Lorde Jesu
Christ circumcised, and there the Aungell denounced to

[1] Divided.   [2] Other editions say 2.
[3] Knew.   [4] Rift or cleft.   [5] Psalter.

Zachary the nativitie of sainct Jhon Baptist, and there offred fyrst Melchisedech bread and wine and water to our Lorde in tokening of the sacrament that was to come, and there fell Davyd, praying to our Lorde for mercy for him and for his people, when he sawe the Aungell slea[1] his people, and our Lorde anon herde his prayer, & therefore woulde he make the Temple in that place, but our Lorde Jesu Christ forbadde hym by an Aungell, for he had done treason when he did slea Euryas, a good knight, for to haue his wyfe. And therefore all that he had ordeined for to make the Temple he betoke[2] it to Salomon hys sonne, and he made it, and he prayed our Lorde, that all those that prayed in that place devoutly, and wyth good hearte, that he woulde heare theyr prayer and graunt that they asked ryght wysely, and our Lorde graunted it, and therefore Salomons son called it the Temple of counseyll and helpe of God. Wythout the dores of that Temple is an auter, where Jewes were wont to offer doves[3] and tur-tylles, and in that Temple was Zachary slayne, and on that pynacle the Jewes sette Sainct James that was the fyrst Byshoppe of Hierusalem. And a lyttle from this temple on the right syde, is a church covered with lead, that is called the scole[4] of Salomon. And toward the south is the temple of Salomon that is full fayre, and a greate place, and in this place dwell knightes y[t] are called Templars and that was the founder thereof and of theyr order and in that Templum Domini dwell Chanons. From this Temple towarde the East xxvi[5] paces in a corner of the citie, is the bathe of our Lorde,

[1] Slay.   [2] Bequeathed.
[3] Pigeons and turtle doves.   [4] School.
[5] Other editions say 120.

and (*in*) thys bath was wont to go[1] to Paradise & beside is our Ladies bed and nere there is the tombe of Saynt Symeon.   And without the Cloyster of the Temple towarde the North is a ryght fayre Churche of Sainct Anne our Ladies mother, & there was our ladye conceyved, and before that churche is a great tree that began to grow that same nighte. And as men go downe from y[t] Church xxii greces lieth Joachim our ladyes father, in a tombe of stone and there nere was layde sometyme sainct Anne, but saint Eleyne did translate hir to Constantinople.   In this churche is a well in maner of a cesterne that is called *Probatica piscina* that hath five entrings, and in that cesterne was wont an Aungell to discende and sterre the water, and what man that bathed him firste therein after the morning,[2] was made hole that was sicke, what sycknesse so euer he had, and there was the man of the palsye made hole, that was sicke xxxviii yeare and our Lorde sayde to him in this maner of wyse *Tolle grabatum tuum et ambula.*   That is to say, take thy bed and go.   And there besyde, was the house of Pylate and a little thence was the house of Kinge Herode that dyd slea the Innocentes

[1] Others say, "wont to come water *from* Paradise."
[2] *Pynson* has it "moving."

CAP. XXIIII.

Of Herod the King.

THIS King Herod was a full wycked man and a fell,[1] for he did firste and formost slea his wife which he loved full well, and for the greate love of hir, he went out of his witte,[2] and so was he a long time, and afterwarde he came againe to himselfe. And sythen he did slea his own children that he had gotten of that same wyfe, and after he made slea[3] the other, his second wife & a son that he had gotten of that same wyfe, and after he did slea his owne mother, & he wold also haue slaine his owne brother, but his brother died sodeinly, and thus he did all the yll that he might. And then he fell syke and when he sawe that he should dye, he sent for his sister, and all the great lordes of that countrie, and when they were there, he did put all the Lordes into a toure and sayde to his syster, he wist well that the men of the countrey should make no sorowe for him when he was deade, and therefore he made hir for to sweare unto him that she should [4] do smite of the heads of his lordes every one, after his death and then shoulde men of the countrey make sorowe for his death or else they woulde not sorowe and then he made his testament. But his

---

[1] Crafty.

[2] In *Pynson's* version it is "and for the greate love that he had to hir, whan she was dede, he behelde her, and want out of his wyt."

[3] Killed.   [4] Cause to be smitten off.

sister fulfylled it not as of that thing that pertayned unto the lordes, for, as sone as he was deade, she delyvered the lordes out of the toure, and sent every one home to theyr houses, and tolde them what hir brother would that she do unto them. And ye shall understande that in that tyme was three Herodes of great name. This of whome I speake, men called him Herode Ascolonite, and he that did smite of Saint John Baptist heade, was called Herode Antipa and the thirde was called Herode Agrypa that did sleay Saint James and put Saint Peter in prison.

CAP. XXV.

Of Saynte Salvators church.

A LYTTEL within the citie is saynct Salvatours
church & therein is Saint Jhon Crysostoms arme,
and the most part of Sainct Stephens head.

And on the other syde towarde the south as men go
to mount Syon is a fayre church of sainct James where
his head was smitten of, and there is mounte Syon
and there is a fayre church of God and of our Lady
where she was dwelling and dyed, and there was
sometime an Abbey of Chanons regulers and from that
place she was borne of the Apostles unto the Vale of
Josaphat. And there is the stone that ye aungel bare
to our ladye from mount Synay & it is of that colour
that the roche of Sainct Katheryne is of, and there

besyde is the gate where our Ladye when she was with
Childe went through to Bethlem. Also at the entrynge
of Mount Syon is a chappell and in that Chapell is that
stone greate and large, with which the Sepulcre was

covered when Christe was layde therein, the which stone
as it is wrytten yᵉ three Maryes saw turned upward when
they came to the sepulcre, and they found an Aungell
that sayd to them, that Christ was rysen from death to
lyfe. And there is a litle piller to the which our Lord
was bounde and scourged, and there was Anas house
that was bishop of the Jewes in that time, and in that
same place forsoke Saint Peter our Lord thrise before
the Cocke crewe. And there is a part of the table on
the which God made his maunde with his disciples & yet
is there the vessell with water out of the which his disciples feete were washed, and thereby is Sainct Stephens
grave and there is the Aulter where our Lady heard the
Aungels sing masse and there appeared Christ fyrst to
his disciples after his resurrection, and when the gates

were sperde,[1] and sayde *Pax vobiscum*.   That is to saye,
Peace be to you.   And on that Mount apeared Christ to
Sainct Thomas, and badde him assaye hys Wounde, and
that was the viii daye after his resurrection and then he
beleved perfectly & sayde *Dominus meus & deus meus*.
That is to say in English, My Lorde & my God.   In
that same Chappell behind the highe aulter were all
the Apostles on Witsonday, when the holy ghoste
descended on them in likenesse of fyre, and there made
God Paske [2] with his disciples, and there slepte Saynt
Jhon the Evangelyst on our Lordes breast and saw slep-
ing many privy things of heaven.   And mount Syon is
within the Citie, and it is a lyttle hygher than the other
syde of the Citie, and that Citie is stronger on that one
syde than on the other, for at the fote of mount Syon is

a fayre Castell & strong which the Soudan did cause to
be made there.   On mount Syon was King David buried

---

[1] Shut.   [2] . Kept the Passover.

and Salomon and many other Kings of Hierusalem, and here is the place where saint Peter wepte full tenderly when he had forsaken our Lorde, and a stones cast from that is another place where our Lord was judged, for that time was there Caiphas house & betwene that Temple (of) Salomon and Mount Sion is the place where Christ raysed the mayden from death to lyfe. Under mount Syon toward the vale of Josaphat is a well that men call Natatorium [1] Sylo, there was our Lord washed after he was baptized. And thereby is the tree on which Judas hanged himselfe for dispaire when he had soulde Christ. And thereby is the synagoge where the Bishops of Jewes and the Pharyses came to hold theyr counsel and there Judas cast the xxx pence before them & said *Peccavi tradens sanguinem justum.* That is to saye, I haue sinned in betraying the innocent bloude.

CAP. XXVI.

Of the feelde of Acheldemack [2] which was bought with the xxx pence.

ON the other syde of mount Syon towarde the South a stons Cast, is the feeld that was bought with those xxx pence for which Christe was sold, that men call Acheldemack, that is to say the feeld of bloude, in that feelde is many tombes of Chrysten men for there bee many pylgrims graven.[3] And also in Hierusalem toward the weast, is a fayre churche where the tree grew of which the crosse was made and thereby is a fayre

---

[1] The Pool of Siloah.   [2] Aceldama.   [3] Buried.

churche where our lady mette with Elizabeth when they were both with Chylde & sainct Jhon styrred in his mothers wombe and made worship to our Lord his maker, and under the aulter of the church is a place where Sainct Jhon was borne and thereby is the castell of Emax.[1]

CAP. XXVII.

Of mount Joye.

TWO myle from Hierusalem is the mounte Joye that is a fayre place and a liking, & there lieth Samuell the prophete in a fayre tombe, and it is called mount Joye for there many pylgrims se first Hierusalem. And in the middle of the Vale of Josaphat is a lyttle ryver that is called Torrens [2] Cedron, and over thwart this laye a tree, of the which the crosse was made, that men passed over on. Also in ye vale is a churche of our lady, and there is the sepulchre of our lady, and our lady was of age when she dyed, lxxii yeare. And there nere is the place where our Lorde forgaue Sainct Peter all his sinnes and mysdedes that he had done. And beside that is a chappell where Judas kissed our Lorde, that men call Getsemay,[3] and he was taken of the Jewes, and there lefte Christ his disciples before his passion, when he went to praye, and seyd, *Pater Si fieri potest, transeat a me calix iste*, that is to say in English, Father if it may be done, let this chalice go from me. Also thereby is a chapell where our Lord swet both bloud & water and there is the tombe of King Josaphat, of

[1] Emmaus. [2] The Brook Kedron. [3] Gethsemane.

whom the Vale had the name, and on the syde of that Vale is the mount Olivet, and it is called so for there groweth many Olive trees, and it is higher than Hierusalem & therefore from that hill men may see into the streetes of Hierusalem. And betwene that hill and the citie is nothing but the vale of Josaphat and that is not full large, and uppon that hyl stode our Lorde when he went into heaven, and yet semeth there the steppe[1] of his left foote in the stone. And there is an Abbey of black chanons that was great sometime, but now there is but a church. And but a little thence xviii paces is a chapell, and there is the stone on the which our Lord God sate and when he preched, and sayde thus, *Beati pauperes spiritu, quoniam ipsorum est regnum celorum.* That is to saye in English, Blessed be they that are poore in spirite, for theyrs is the Kingdome of heaven, and ther he taught his disciples theyr *Pater noster.* There also is a churche of that blessed woman Mary Egypcian, and there is she buryed. And uppon the other side towarde the East three bow shotes from thence, standeth Bethephage, where our Lorde Jesu Christ sente Sainct Peter and saynte James, for to fetch an asse on Palme Sonday.

[1] Footprint.

CAP. XXVIII.

Of the Castell Bethania.

THERE toward the East is a castel, that men call
Bethania and there dwelled Symon the lepruse,
that harborowed [1] our lord, and them that were Baptysed
of his disciples, and he was called Julyan and was made
Bishop and that is he that men call on for good har-
borow.[2]   In that same place our lord forgave Mary
Magdeleyne hir sinnes, and there she washed his fete
with teares & wiped them with hir here & there was
Lazarus raised that was foure dayes deade.

CAP. XXIX.

Of Jerico and other things.

IN the returning to mount Olivet, is the place where
oure Lorde wept uppon Hierusalem and thereby [3]
our Lady apeared to Sainct Thomas after hir assump-
tion and gave him hir gyrdell and thereby is the stone
on the which our Lorde sat often upon and preched and
thereon he shall syt at the day of Judgement, as himselfe
sayd.   And there is mount Galile where the appostels
were gathered when Mary Magdelein tolde them of
Christe's rising.   Betwene mount Olivet & mount

----

[1] Lodged.   [2] Protection.   [3] Close by.

Galile is a church, where the Aungell sayde to our Lady when she should die. And from Bethany to Jerico is fiue myle. Jerico was sometime a little citie but it was wasted, and now it is but a lyttle towne, that towne toke Josue through miracle of God, & bydding of the aungell, and destroyed it, & cursed all those that builded it againe. Of that citie was Raab that common woman, that received messengers of Israel & kept them from many perils of deth, & therefore she had a good rewarde, as holy writ sayth "*Quando accepit prophetum in nomine meo mercedem prophetæ accipiet.* That is to say, He that taketh a prophet in my name, he shall take mede of a prophet.[1]

CAP. XXX.

Of the holy place betwene Bethany and flom Jordane and other things.

ALSO from Bethany men go from Jordan thorow the Wildernesse and it is nere a daies journey betwene. Toward the East is a great hill where our Lord fasted XL dayes & upon this hill was Christ brought of the fende[2] of Hell, & sayd to him thus, *Dic ut lapides isti panis fiant.* That is to say, Commaund that these stones be made bread. And there is an Hermitage wher dwelled a maner of Christen men called Georgins[3] for sainct George converted them, and upon that hill

---

[1] Matt. x. 41, "He that receiveth a prophet in the name of a prophet, shall receive a prophet's reward."

[2] Fiend.   [3] Georgians.

dwelled Abraham a great whyle. Also as men go to
Jerico, in the way sate many sicke men crying, *Jesu fili
David, misere nobis.* That is to say, Jesu the sonne of
David have mercie upon us. And two myle from Jerico
is flom [1] Jordan & ye shall wete the dead sea departeth
the lande of Jude and of Araby and the water of the
sea is right bitter and this water casteth out a thinge
that men call *aspatum* [2] as great pieces as a horse. And
Hierusalem is cc furlonges from this sea, and it is called
the dead sea, for it runneth not, nor no man, ne beast,

that hath life, that is therein, may lyve, and that hath
bene proved many times, for they have cast therein men
that were judged to death, nor no man may drinke of
that water & if men cast yron therein it commeth up
againe, and if a man cast a fether therein it goeth to the
grounde, and that is against kinde.[3]

And there about grow trees that beare fruite of faire

[1] River. *Lat.,* Flumen.   [2] Asphaltum.   [3] Nature.

color and seme rype, but when a man breaketh them or
cut them, he findeth naught in them but coales or asshes,
in tokening that throughe the vengaunce of God these
cities were brent with the fyre of hell. And some men
call that lake the lake of Alphytedde,[1] and some call it
the flome of the divell, and some call it the stinking
flome, for the water thereof stynketh. There sanke
these five cities through the wrath of God, that is to
saye, Sodome, Gomor,[2] Aldema,[3] Solome,[4] and Segor, for
the sinne that raigned in them, but Segor through the
prayer of Loth, was saved a great while, for it sat on an
hyll, and yet apeareth much thereof above the water,
and men may see the walles in cleare weather. And in
this citie of Segor, Loth dwelled a great while .   .   .
.   .   .   . and at the ryght side
of this see dwelled Lothes wife in a stone of salt for that
she looked againe when the citie sanke downe.

CAP. XXXI.

Of Abraham and his generation.

AND ye shall understande that Lothe was Arons
sone, Abraham's brother, and Sara Abraham's wyfe
was Loths syster, and Sara was xc yere olde when she
gate Ysaac and Abraham had another son named Ismael
that he had gotten on his mayden Ager. And when
Ysaac was viii days olde he was circumcised and his
other son Ismaell was cyrcumcised the same day and
was xiiii yeare of age, therefore the Jewes that be of the

---

[1] Assa fœtida.　　[2] Gomorrah.　　[3] Aldama.　　[4] Seboym.

generation of Isaac do circumcyse them at the viii day
of theyr age and the Sarasyns that be of Ismaels kinde
doe cyrcumsise them at theyr xiii yeare of age.   And
into that dead sea aforesayde runneth flome Jordan and
maketh there an ende and this is within a myle of saint
Jhons church & a lyttle beneth that same church Westward, were the Christen men are wont to bath them & a
myle thence is the river Loth, through which Jacob went
when he came from Mesopotamye.

CAP. XXXII.

Of the river Jordan.

THIS flom Jordan is no great ryver nor depe, but
there is much good fishe therein, and it commeth
from mount Lybany from two welles, that men call Jor and
Dane and of them it taketh the name.   And upon the
one syde of that river is mount Gelboe,[1] and there is a
fayre playne.   And on that other syde men goe by
mount Lybany, to the desert of Pharon.[2]   These hylles
departe the kingdome of Surry and the countreys of
Phenys.[3]   On that hyll grow Cedres that beare longe
apples which are as muche as a mannes heade.   Thys
flom Jordan departeth Galily and the lande of Idumea
and the lande of Botron[4] & it runneth into a playne
that men call Meldam[5] in Sarasyns language, and in
Englyshe, fayre, because ofte tymes bee there kepte

[1] Gilboa.   [2] Pharan.   [3] Phœnicia.   [4] Betron.
[5] In all probability the same as the Arabic word *Multamin*,
which means a congregation of visitors.

great fayres, and in the playne is the tombe of Job.   In
this flom Jordane our Lord was baptised, and there was
the voice of the Father hearde saying, *Hic est filius meus
dilectus, in quo mihi bene complacui, ipsum audite.*   That
is to saye in English, Here is my sonne that I love, in
whome I am well pleased, heare him.   And the holy
ghost descended on him in lykenesse of a doue & so was
there in thys baptysing all the Trinitie.   And through

the flome Jordan passed the children of Israell all dry,
and they sette stones in the myddest of the water, in
token of great myracle.   And also in that flome Naaman
of Surry bathed him, that was mesel, and he was made
hole, and a lyttle from thence is the citie of Hay, the
which Josue assayled and toke.   And about flom Jordan
are many churches where Christen men dwel, also by
flom Jordan, is the vale of Mambre that is a fayre vale
& a plenteous.

CAP. XXXIII.

Of many other mervailes.

AND ye shall understande, that for to go from the
dead sea afterward out of the marche of the land
of promissions, is a stronge Castell that men call Carran [1]
in Sermoys, that is to saye, the kinges hyll in English.
This castell did a King of Fraunce make, that men call
Baudewin, that had conquered all that lande, and put it
into Christen mens handes to kepe, and under that castell is a fayre towne that men call Sabaoth, and there
about dwell many Christen men under tribute.   And
then go men to Nazareth, of the which our Lord had
his name.   And from Nazareth unto Hierusalem is
three dayes journey.   Also men go through the province
of Galyle, through Romacha,[2] through Sophyn,[3] and
through the hygh hill of Effrayne,[4] where Anna that
was Samuells mother the prophet dwelled, & there was
the prophete borne and after his deathe was buried at
mount Joye as I have sayde.   And after come men to
Sybula,[5] where the Arke of God was kepte under Helye[6]
the Prophete.   And there made the people of Israell[7]
theyr sacrafyce unto our Lorde   Also there spake our
Lorde fyrst unto Samuell and there mynistered God the
sacrament.   Also nere there at the lefte side is Gabaon[8]

[1] In some other editions called Carak.   [2] Ramoth.
[3] Sodom.   [4] Ephraim.   [5] Shiloh.
[6] Eli.   [7] Hebron.   [8] Gibeon.

and Rama[1] & Benjamin of the which holy writ speaketh.
After that come men to Sychem, that some men call
Sycar and this is in the province of Samaritanes, and
sometime there was a Church, but it is all wasted, and it
a faire vale and plenteous, and there is a good citie that
men call Neople,[2] and from thence it is a dayes journey

unto Hierusalem. And there is the well where oure
Lorde spake to the woman of Samaritane, and Sechen
is ten myle from Hierusalem and it is called Neople,
that is to saye, the new towne. And there is the Temple
of Joseph, Jacobs sonne, that governed Egipte, and

---

[1] Ramah.   [2] Neapolis.

from thence were his bones brought and layde in the
temple, and thyther came Jewes often in pilgrimage
with great devotion, and in that citie was Jacob's
daughter Diana ravished, for whom hir brethren slewe
many men, and thereby is the citie of Garysim[1] where
the Samaritanes make their sacrifyce.

On this hill wold Abraham haue sacryfised his sonne
Isaac and there nere is the vale Dotaym,[2] and there is
the cesterne that Josephe was cast in of his bretherne
before that they solde him, and it is two myle to Sichar,
and fro thence men come to Samary,[3] that men call
Sabaste, and that is the chiefe citie of that countrey,
and in that citie was the seat of the twelve Kynges of
Israell, but it is not so great as it was.   And there was
saint John Baptist buried betwene two prophetes Helyas[4]
and Abdon,[5] but he was beheaded in the castell of
Makaryn besyde the dead sea and he was translated[6] of
his disciples and buried at Samary, but there dyd Julius
apostata take hys bones and brente[7] them, for he was that
tyme Emperour, but that finger with whiche hee shewed
our Lord saying, *Ecce Agnus dei*,   That is to say,
Beholde the lamb of God, and that finger might not bee
brent, and sainct Tecla[8] the Virgin did bring this finger
under the Alphen,[9] that be mountaynes, where they do
it great worshippe.   And there was sainct Jhon Baptist
head closed in a wall, but the Emperour Theodosius did
take it out, and found it lapped in a clothe all bloudie,
and bare it to Constantinople, and there is yet the one

[1] Gerizim.   [2] Dothan.   [3] Samaria.
[4] Elisha.   [5] Abdias.
[6] Carried away   [7] Burnt.
[8] Was an English woman, and was invited by St. Boniface into
Germany, where she was made Abbess of Kissengen, near Wurtz-
burg in Bavaria.   [9] Alps.

halfe of the head, and the other is at Rome in Saint
Sylvesters church, & the vessell wherein his head was
layde when it was smitten of is at Geene,[1] and they do
it great worship. Some saye that Sainct Jhons hedde is
at Amiens in Pycardy, and some say it is saincte Johns
head the byshop. I wot not but to God it is knowne.

CAP. XXXIIII.

Of the Samaritanes.

FROM Sebasten to Hierusalem is xii myle and betwene the hylles of this countrey is a well, that
men call *fons Jacob*, That is to say Jacobs well, that
chaungeth foure times in the yeare his coloure, for some-

[1] Genoa.

G

tyme it is redde, sometymes cleare, sometime grene and
sometyme thycke, and men that dwell there are called
Samarytanes, & they were converted through the
Apostles and theyr law varieth from Christen law and
Sarasins lawe and also from Jewes & Paynims.   They
beleve well in one God that all shall deme,[1] and beleve
the Byble after the lettre, and they lappe theyr heads in
redde linnen cloth, for difference of other, for Sarasins
wrap theyr heads in white cloth & christen men that
dwell there in blew cloth, and Jewes in yelow, and in
this country dwell many Jewes paying tribute as Christen
men doth.

CAP. XXXV.

Of Galyle.

FROM this countrey that I have spoken of, men go
to the playne of Galyle and leave the hyll on the
one side and Galyle is of the province of the lande of
promyssion and in that province is the lande of Naym
and Capharnaym and Corasaym and at Bethsayda was
Saint Peter & Saint Andrew borne.   At Carasaym shall
Antechrist be borne, and as some men say he shall be
borne in Babilon therefore sayd the Prophet, *De babilonia
Coluber exiet, qui totum mundum devorabit,*   That is to
say, Of Babilon shall come a serpent that shall devoure
all the worlde.   And this Antechrist shall be nourished
in Bethsayde and shall raign in Corasaym, therefore sayth
holy writ, *Ve tibi Corasaim Ve tibi Bethsayda,* that is to
say, Wo be to the Corasaim, Wo be to the Bethsayda.

---

[1] Regard, consider, or suppose.

And the cave of Galyle is foure myle from Nazareth. Of that citie was the woman of Cananee, of whome the Gospell speaketh, and there our Lorde did the fyrst myracle at the wedding at the Archedeclyne[1] when he turned water into wine. And from thence men go unto Nazareth that was sometime a great Citie, but now there is but a lyttle towne and it is not walled, and there was our Lady borne, the name toke our Lorde of this Citie, but our Ladie was gotten at Hierusalem. At Nazareth Joseph toke our lady to wyfe whan she was fourtene yeare of age, and there the aungell saluted hir sayinge, *Ave gratia plena Dominus tecum*, That is to saye, Hayll full of grace the Lord be with thee. And there was sometime a great Church, and now is there but a lyttle closet to receive the offryngs of the Pylgrymes, and there is the well of Gabryell where our Lorde was wont to bathe him in wan he was lyttle. At Nazareth was our Lord nouryshed, and Nazareth is to say floure of gardeyn & it may be well called so, for there was nourished the floure of lyfe, that was our lorde Jesu Christ. At halfe a myle from Nazareth is the bloude[2] of our Lorde, for the Jewes ledde him upon an hyghe roche to cast him downe & slea him, but Jesu Christ passed them and lepte on a roche where his steps be yet sene, & therefore some when they dreade them of theves or else of enemies, say thus, *Jesus autem transiens per medium illorum ibat*. And they say also these verses of the Psalter three tymes, *Irruat super eos formido & pavor in magnitudine brachii tui Domine Fiant immobiles quasi lapis, donec per transeat populus tuus domine, & populus iste quem redemisti.* And

[1] *Pynson* says Archetryclyne. Ἀρχι τρίκλινος, the president of a banquet.
[2] Should be *leap*.

so when all this is sayd, a man may go without any let-
tyng.[1]   Also ye shall understande and know that our
blessed Lady bare hir chylde whan she was xv yeare of
age, and she lived with hym xxxii[2] yeare and three
monethes, and after his passion she lived xxii[2] yeare.

CAP. XXXVI.

The way of Nazareth to the mount or hyll of Tabor.

AND from Nazareth to the mounte Tabor is thre[3]
myle, and there our Lord transfygured hym before
sainct Peter, sainct Jhon & sainct James.   And there
they saw ghostly[4] our Lorde and Moyses and Helye the
prophetes. And therefore Sainct Peter sayde, *Bonum est
nos hic esse, faciamus tria tabernacula*, That is to say, It
is good to us to be here, make we three tabernacles.
And our lord Jesu Chryste bad them that they should
say it to no man, unto the time that he was rysen from
death to lyfe.   And uppon the same hyll shall foure
aungels sowne[5] theyr trompets, and rayse all men that
are dead to lyfe, and then shall they come in bodie and
Soule to the Judgement, but the Judgement shall be in
the Vale of Josaphat on Easterday, at the same tyme as
our Lorde rose from death to lyfe.   And also a myle
from mounte Tabor is mount Hermon, and ther was
the citie of Namy,[6] before the gates of the Citie our

---

[1] Hindrance.
[2] Other editions say 33 and 24, which would make the Virgin's
age 72 when she died (see *ante*, p. 70).
[3] Others say 4.   [4] In a spiritual shape.   [5] Sound.
[6] Nain.

Lord raysed the wydowes sone, that had no more
Chyldren.

CAP. XXXVII.

Of the sea of Galyle.

AND from thence men go to a citie that men call **Tybe-**
ryen,[1] that sitteth[2] on the sea of Galyle, it is no
sea ne arme of the sea, for it is but a staumble[3] of fresh
water, and it is no more than an hundred furlongs long
and XL brode, and therein is many good fyshes.   And by
that same sea, standeth many good cities, and therefore
thys sea chaungeth often his name after the cities that
stande thereupon, but it is all one water or sea and upon
this sea, our Lorde went dry fote and there sayde he to
Peter when he came on the water, & was nere drowned,
Modice fidei quare dubitasti ?   That is to saye, Thou of
lyttle fayth, why hadst thou doubte.

CAP. XXXVIII.

Of the table whereon Christ eat after his resurrection.

IN this citie of Tiberyen is the table that Christ eat on
with his disciples after his resurrection & they knew
him in breaking of bread (as holy writ saith) *Et cognove-*
runt eum in fractione Panis.   That is to say, they knew

---

[1] Tiberias.   [2] On the borders of.   [3] A pool or lake.

him in breaking of bread.   And aboute the hyll of Tiberien is the citie where our Lord fed v thousand people with five Barly loves and two fishes, and in that same citie did men cast in anger a fierbrand or burning stick after our Lord, but the same burning sticke did fall on the earth, and incontinent grew out of the same sticke a tree, and is waxen a bigge tree, and groweth yet, and the scales of the tree be all blacke.   And ye shall under-

stand that flom Jordan beginneth under the hill of Libany, & there beginneth the lande of promission, and it lasteth under Barsabe [1] of length, & from the North part to the South, it holdeth ix score myle and of breadth from Jerico to Jaffe it is XL mile, and ye shall understande that the lande of promission beginneth at the Kingdome of Surry and lasteth unto the wildernesse of Araby.

[1] Beersheba.

CAP. XXXIX.

Of straunge maners and divers.

AND in this countrey & in many other landes over the sea, it is a maner when they have warre and cities or castels beseged so strongly that they may send no messages to any lordes for socour then they write their letters & binde them about the neckes of doves and let them flie their wayes, bicause the dove is of that

nature that he will returne againe to the place where he is brought up, and thus they do commonly in that countrey. And ye shal wete that among the Sarasins in many places dwel christen men under tribute and they are of divers maners, and divers maners of monkes, and

they are all christened and have divers lawes, but they
all beleve well in our Lord God, the father, the sonne, &
in the Holy ghost, but yet they fayle in the articles of
our faith, and they are called Jacobyns.   For sainct

James converted theym to the fayth, and sainct John
baptised them, and they say that men shall onely shryve[1]
them unto God, & not unto man for they saye that God
bad not man shryve him unto another man.   And therefore saith David in the Psalter in this maner of wise,
Confitebor tibi, domine in toto Corde meo, &c.   That is to
saye, Lord I shall shrive me unto thee in all my hart.
And in another place he saith thus, *Delictum meum tibi
cognitum feci.*   That is to saye, My trespasse I have
made knowne unto thee.   And in another place, *Deus
meus es tu & confitebor tibi.*   That is to saye, Thou art
my god and I shall be shriven to thee.   And in another
place *Quoniam cogitatio hominis confitebitur tibi*, &c.

[1] Confess.

That is to say, The thought of man shal be shriven to
thee, and they knowe well the Bible and Psalter but
they say it not in latin, but in their owne language, and
they saye that David and other prophetes have sayde it.
But Sainct Austyn and Saynct Gregory say, *Qui scelera
sua cogitat, & conversus fecerit, veniam sibi credat*, That
is to say, Who so knowith his syn and turneth, he may
beleve to have forgivenesse. And Sainct Gregory sayth
thus, *Dominus potius mentem, quam verbum considerat*,
That is to saye, Our Lord taketh more kepe[1] to thought,
than to worde, and Sainct Hilarius sayth, *Longorum tem-
porum crimina, ictu oculi pereunt, si cordis nata fuerit
compunctio*, That is to say, Synnes that are done of olde
tyme perysh in twinkling of an eye, if despising of them
be born in a mans heart. And therefore say they, men
shal shrive them onely to God, by these authorities,
& this (*it*) was the Apostles, & popes that came sithen

[1] Heed.

haue ordeyned, that men shall shrive them to priestes
& men as they are, & the cause is this, for they saye that
a man that hath a sicknesse, men may giue him no good
medecines but they know yᵗ kinde of the sicknesse, also
they say a man may give no covenable [1] penaunce but if
he know yᵉ sin.   For there is a maner of synne that is
grevouser to one man than it is to another, and therefore
it is nedefull that a man should know and understande
the kinde of sinne.   And there be also other men that
men call Surryens and they hold halfe our faith, and
halfe the faith of the Grekes and they have longe berdes
as the Grekes have.

And there ben [2] other that men call Georgiens, whome
sainct George converted, and they doe more worship to
halowes [3] of heaven than other doe, and they haue their
crownes shaven, the clerkes haue rounde crowns, and the
lewde [4] have crownes square, & they holde the Grekes

[1] Convenient.   [2] Be.   [3] Saints.   [4] Common people.

lawe. And there be other that men call christen men of gyrding,[1] for as much as they were gyrdels underneth, some other men call Nestoryens, some Aryens, some Nubyens, some Gregours, and some Indiens that are of Prester Johns lande, and euery one of those haue some artycles of our belefe. But eche of them varye from other, and of their varyaunce it were to muche to declare.[2]

CAP. XL.

For to turne on this syde of Galyle.

NOW sythen I haue tolde you of many maners of men, that dwell in the countreys before said, now will I tourne againe to my waye for to tourne uppon this side. Now he that will tourne from the lande of Galyle, that I spake of, to come on this syde, he shall go through Damas that is a fayre citie & full of good marchaundises, and it is three Journeys from the sea and five journeis from Hierusalem, but they cary marchaundises upon camels, mules, horses and dromedaries and other maner of beastes. This citie of Damas founded Helyzeus, that was Abrahams servaunte before Ysaac was borne, and he thought to haue bene Abrahams heyre and therefore he named that citie Damas. And in that place slew

---

[1] This arose from a curious ordinance in A.D. 856 of the Khalif Molawakkel, who ordered both Jews & Christians to wear leather girdles; hence those Christians who lived in Syria were called "Christians of the girdle."

[2] Tell.

Cayne his brother Abel, and besyde Damas is yᵉ mount
of Syry, and in yᵗ Citie is many a Phisicion & yᵗ holy man
S. Paule was a phisicion to saue mens bodys before yᵗ he
was Converted, and after, he was a phisicyon of soules.
And from Damas men come by a place called our Lady

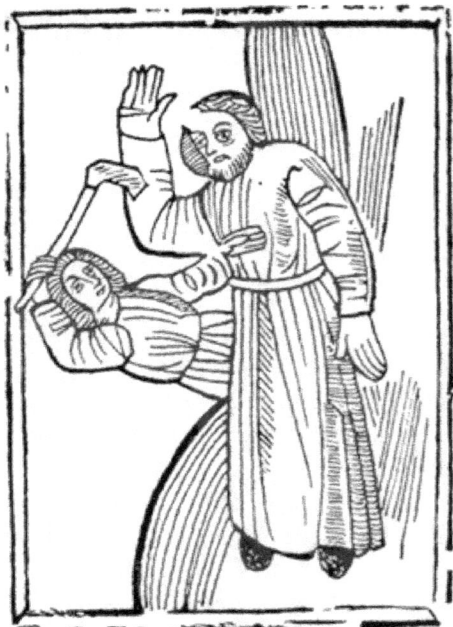

of Sardmarch,[1] that is fiue myle from Damas & it is on
a roch & there is a fayre churche and there dwell Monkes
& Nunnes, crysten, in the church, behynde the high
auter is a table of tree,[2] on the whiche table the ymage
of our lady was depainted that many tymes was turned
into fleshe, but the ymage is now sene but a lyttle, but

---

[1] Others say Sardenak.   [2] On wood panel.

evermore through grace of God, the table droppeth oyle,
as it were an Olyfe, & there is a vessell of marble under
the table to receive the oyle, thereof they giue to Pyl-
grimes, for it maketh whole many sicknesses, and he that
kepeth it clenely a year, after a yeare, it turneth to fleshe
and bloud.   Betwene the citie of Darke and the citie of
Raphane is a ryver that men call Sabatory, for on the
Saterday it runneth fast, and all the weeke else it standeth
styll and runneth not or little.   And there is another
ryver that in the night freseth fast and upon the day no
frost is seene.   And so men go by a citie that men call
Berugh,¹ and there men go into the sea that will go into
Cipres and they aryve at a porte of Sur or of Thyrry² &
then men go to Cipres, or else men go or may goe from
the porte of Thyry ryght, and come not to Cypres and
arryve at some haven of Grece & there come men into
those countreys by ways that I haue spoken of before.

CAP. XLI.

*How a man may go furdest and longest in those countreys
as heare are rehersed.*

NOWE have I tolde you of wayes by the whiche men
goe furthest and longeste, as by Babylon and
mount Synay, and other places many, through the which
landes men turne againe to the lande of promission.
Now will I tell you the way of Hierusalem, for some men
will not passe it, some for they have no company³ and

¹ Others say Beruthe.   ² Tyre.
³ *i.e.*, it was unsafe to go alone.

many other causes resonable and therefore I shall tell
you shortely how a man may go with lyttle coste and
short tyme.

A man that commeth from the lande of the Weast,
he goeth through Fraunce, Burgoyn,[1] Lumberdy & to
Venys or to Geen[2] or some other haven of those marches,
and take there a ship and go to the yle Gryffe,[3] and so
arryveth he in Grece, or else at port Myrock,[4] or Valon
or Duras or some other haven of those marches, and to
go lande for to reste hym, and goeth againe to the sea
and arryveth at Cypres and commeth not in the yle of
Rodes and arriveth at Famagost that is the Chiefe haven
of Cypres or else at Lamaton, And then enter shyppe
againe, and passe besyde the haven of Tyre and come
not to lande, and so passeth by all the havens of the
coste, untill he come to Jaffe, that is the next hauen to
Hierusalem, for it is xxviii[5] myle betwene.   And from
Jaffe men go to the Citie of Ramos[6] & that is but little
thence, & it is a fayre citie & beside Ramos is a fayre
churche of our lady, where our lord shewed hym unto
hir in three shadowes, that betokeneth the trinitie, and
there nere is a church of Sainct George where his head
was smitten of, and then to the Castell of Emaux, and
then to the mount Joye & from thence pilgrimes see
Hierusalem, and then to mount Modyn & then go to
Hierusalem.   At mount Modyn lyeth the prophet Mac-
habe,[7] and over Ramatha[8] is the towne of Donke, whereof
Amos the prophet was.

---

[1] Burgundy.   [2] Genoa.
[3] In some editions Gryffh, Grif, or Gresse, probably Crete.
[4] In other editions Moroche or Myroche.   [5] Others say 27.
[6] Rames, Ramla.   [7] Maccabeus.   [8] Ramah Gibeon.

CAP. XLII.

Of othar wayes for to go by lande unto Hierusalem.

FOR as muche, as many men may not suffer the savour of the sea, & better it is to go by lande even if it be more payne, and a man shall go to one of the havens of Lumberdy as Venys or another, and he shall passe into Grece to port Myroche, or another and shall goe to Constantinople, and shall passe the water that is called the brache of Saynt George that is an arme of the sea. And from thence ye shall come to Pulveral, and then to the castel of Synople. And from thence shall ye go unto Capadoce, that is a great countrey, wherein is many great hylles and he shall go thorow Turky, and to the citie of Nike, the which they wan from the Emperour of Constantinople, and it is a faire citie and well walled, and there is a river that men call the Lay, and there go men by the Alpes of Mormaunt, & through the vales of Malebrynes and the vale of Ernax, and so to Antioche lesser, that sitteth on the river richly, and there is about many good hills & fayre and many fayre woddes and wild beastes. And he that will go another way, he goeth by ye plaine of the Romain [1] Coste and the Romaine sea. On that coste is a fayre castell that men call Florage, and when a man is oute of the hilles, he passeth through the citie of Moryach and Artose, where there is a great bridge upon the river of

---

[1] Roumanian.

Ferne, that men call Fassor,[1] & it is a great river bering
ships, and beside the citie of Damas, is the river that
cometh from the mount of Libany, and that men call
Alban,[2] at the passing of this river Sainct Eustache lost
his two sonnes when he had lost his wife. And it goeth
through the playne of Archades, & to the red sea, and
then men go to the citie of Fermyne, and so to the citie
of Ferne, and then to Antioche & that is a fayre citie
and well walled, for it is two myle long, and there is a
bridge over the river, that hath at eche pillar, a good
tower, and is the best citie of the Kingdome of Surrey.
From Antioche, men go to the citie of Locuth[3] and so
to Geble[4] and to Tortouse,[5] & thereby is the lande of
Lambre & a strong castell, that men call Mambeke.
And from Tortouse, men go to Trypelle[6] on the sea, and
upon the sea men go to Dacres,[7] and there is two wayes
to Hierusalem, on the lefte way men go first unto Damas
by flom Jordan, and on the right syde men go throughe
the lande Flagme and so to the citie of Cayphas,[8] in
which citie Cayphas was lorde, & some call it the castell
Pelleryus and from thence it is foure dayes journey to
Hierusalem & they go throughe Cesarye Phylyp,[9] and
Jaffe, and Ramas, Eumaux, & so forth to Hierusalem.

[1] ? Pharphar of the Scriptures.   [2] ? Abana.
[3] Latakijah.   [4] Jebili.   [5] Tortosa.   [6] Tripoli.
[7] Acre.   [8] Caiffa.   [9] Philippi.

CAP. XLIII.

Yet another way by lande toward the lande of promission.

NOW haue I tolde you some wayes by land and by
water how men may go to Hierusalem. And if
it be so that there be many other wayes that men go by,
after the countreys that they come from, neverthelesse
they tourne all to one ende, yet is there a way all by
land to Hierusalem, & passe no sea from Fraunce or
Flaunders, but that way is full longe and perylous & of
great travaile, & therefore few go that way, he that goeth
that way, he goeth through Almayn & Pruse and so to
Tartary, this Tartary is holden of the great Cane,[1] of
whome I shall speake afterwarde, for thether lasteth[2]
his lordeshippe, and all the lords of Tartary yelde to him
tribute. Tartary is a full evill land, sandy and a lytle
fruite bearing, for there groweth but little corne or fruyte,
but bestes are there great plentie, and therefore eate
they but fleshe without breade, and they sup the broth,
and they drynke mylke of all maner of bestes, they eat
Cattes, and all maner of wyld bestes, rattes & myce, and
they haue but lyttle wodde,[3] and therefore they dyght[4]
theyr meate with horse dounge & other bestes doung,
when it is dry. Princes and other lordes eate but ones
in the day, and ryght lyttle, and they be ryght foule
folke, and of evyll lyking, and in somer there is many
tempests and thonders, that sleaeth many men & bestes

---

[1] Khan.   [2] For his dominions extend as far.
[3] Wood.   [4] Cook.

H

(*sodainly it is*) right colde, and sodainly it is right hot.
The Prince that governeth that land they call him Roco
and he dwelleth at a Citie that men call Orda, and forsoth there is no man that will dwell in that lande, for it
is good to sow in thornes & wedes, other good is there
none, as I herd say, for I was not that way, but I have
bene in other lordes landes marching thereon, and the
land of Rossye and Nyflonde & the Kingedome of Grecon[1]
and Lectowe, and the kingdome of Grasten[2] & in many
other places, but I went neuer that way to Hierusalem
& therefore I may not tell it, for I haue understande,
that men may not well go that way but in winter, when
the waters and marys[3] that be in that lande be
frosen and covered with snow, so that men may passe
thereon, for were not the snow, there might no man go
in that lande but he wer lost.   And ye shall understande
that a man shall go three days journey from Pruse to
passe this waye, tyll he come to the lande of Sarasyns,
that men dwell in.   And if by fortune any christen men
passe that way, as once a yeare they doe, they cary theyr
vitale with them, for they shoulde finde nothing there
but a maner of things that they call Syleys, and they
cary theyr vytales upon the yce on sleddes[4] and charyottes
without wheles, and as long as theyr vitayles laste, they
may dwell there, but no longer.   And when spyes of the
countrey see christen men come, they runne to the towns
and castels and cry right loude, Kera, Kera, Kera, and
as sone as they haue cryed, then dothe the people arme
them.   And ye shall understande that the yse there is
harder than it is here, and euery man hath a stew[5] in
his house, and therein they eat and do all things that

---

[1] Cracow.

[2] Darestan, or Silistria.

[3] Marais or marshes, meres.

[4] Sledges.   [5] Stove.

them nedeth. And that is at the North part of the world, where it is commonly colde, for the Sonne cometh ne shineth but a little in that countrey, and that lande is in some places so colde, that there may no man dwel therein, and on the South side of the world it is in some places so hote, that there can no man dwel, the son giveth so great heate in those countreys.

CAP. XLIIII.

INASMUCH as I haue told you of the Sarasins and of other landes, if ye will I shall tell you a parte of theyr law, and of theyr beleve, after as theyr boke sayeth, that they call Alkaron,[1] and some call that boke Mysap,[2] some call it Harme[3] in diverse language of countreys, which booke Machomet gave them, in yᵉ which boke he wrote among other things as I have often red and sene, that they that are good shall goe to Paradise, and the evill folkes to hell, and that beleeve all the Sarasyns. And if a man aske of what Paradise they meane, they say it is a place of delytes, where a man shall finde all maner of fruites at all times, and waters, and rivers running with milke & hony, wine and fresh water, and they shall have faire houses & good as they have deserved, and those houses are made of precious stones, gold & sylver & every man shall haue ten[4] wives and all maydens. Also they speake often & beleve of the Virgin Mary and tell of the Incarnation, that Mary was learned[5]

1 The Koran.
2 Some say Meshaf. Mishaf means written sheets of paper.
3 Harme is "Haram," *sacred*. 4 Some say 80.
5 Taught by.

of Aungels and that Gabriel sayd to hir that she
was chosen before all other from the beginning of
the world, and that wytnesseth well theyr booke, &
Gabriel tolde hir of the incarnation of Jesu Christ, and
that she shoulde conceive and beare a childe and they
saye that Christ was a holy prophet in word & dede, and
also meke & rightwise to all men, and without any
blame worthy.   And they saye that when the Aungell
tolde hir of the incarnation, she hadde great dread,
for she was righte younge, and there was one in the
countrey that medled with sorcery, that men called
Takina,[1] that with enchauntements could make him lyke
an Aungell and he went often and lay with maidens, and
therefore was Mary the more aferde[2] of the Aungell, and
thought in hir mynde that it had bene Takina that went
to maydens, and she conjured him that he should tell
hir if he were the same Takina, and the Aungell bad hir
have no dreade for he was for certayne a true messenger
of Jesu Christ.   Also theyr booke of Alkaron saith, that
she had a child under a palme tree, then was she greatly
ashamed and sayde that she woulde she had bene dead.
As sone as hir childe was borne, he spake and comforted
hir and sayd, *Ne timeas Maria*, That is to say, Be not
afraide Mary.   And in many other places, sayth theyr
booke Alkaron, that Jesu Christ spake as sone as he was
borne, & the booke sayth that Jesu Christ was sent of
Almighty God to be ensample to all men, and that God
shall deme[3] all men, the good to heaven and the wicked
to hell & that Jesu Christ is the best prophete of all
other and nexte to God and that he was a holy prophet,
for he gave to the blynde theyr sight, and heled Mesels[4]

---

[1] Other editions have Taknia.   [2] Afraid.
[3] Judge.   [4] Lepers.

& raysed men and went all quick[1] to heaven. And if
they may finde a boke with gospels, namely, *Missus est
Angelus*, they doe it great worship, they fast a moneth in
the yere & they eate but in the night, and they kepe
them from theyr wyves, but they that are syke are not
Constrayned to that.   And that booke Alkaron speaketh
of Jewes and sayth, they are wicked people for they will
not beleve that Jesu Christ is of God.   And they say, y^t
the Jewes lye on our Lady and hir sonne Jesu Christ,
saying that they did him not on the crosse, for Sarasyns
beleve so nere our fayth, that they are lightly converted
when men preche the lawe of Jesu Christ, and they saye
that they wote well by theyr prophicies, that theyr lawe
of Machomet shall fayll as doth the law of Jews and that
Christen mens laws shall last unto the worlds ende. And
if a man aske them wherein they beleve they say that
they beleve in god almightie, that is the maker of heaven
and earth and all other things and without him is nothing
done and at the day of Judgement when euery man
shall be rewarded after his deserving, & that all things
is soth[2] that Christ said through the mouthes of his
prophetes.

CAP. XLV.

Yet it treateth more of Machomet.

ALSO Machomet badde in his boke Alkaron, that
euery man shoulde haue two wives or three or
foure, but now they take nine and as many lemmans as
them liketh, & if any of their wives doe amisse against

----

[1] Alive.   [2] True.

their husbandes, he may driue hir out of his house, and
take another, but he must giue to hir part of his goodes.
Also when men speake of the Father, and the Sonne, and
holy Ghost, they saye they are three persons, but not
one God, for their boke Alkoran speaketh not thereof,
nor of the trinitie, but they say that God spake or else
he was dumb, and that God hath a ghost,[1] or else he
were not alive, & they say Gods word hath great strength,
and so saith theyr Alkaron & they say that Abraham
and Moyses were greatly in favor with God, for they
spake with him, & Machomet was right messenger of
God.   And they haue many good articles of our faith
and some understand the scriptures, profites, gospels, and
the Bible, for they haue them written in theyr language,
in this maner they knowe holy writ, but they understande
it not, but after the letter and so do the Jewes, for they
understande it not, but after their letter ghostly, and
therefore saith Sainct Paule, *Litera occidit: Spiritus vivi-
ficat*—that is to say, Letter dieth, and ghost maketh
quicke.   And the Sarasins say y[t] Jewes are wicked, for
they kepe not y[e] lawe of Moyses the which he toke to
them, & also chrysten men are yll, for they kepe not the
commaundments of the gospels that Jesu Christ sent
unto them & therefore I shall tell you what the Soudan
tolde me upon a daye in his chamber, voiding[2] out all
other men, as Lordes, Knightes & other, for he woulde
speke with me in counsel, and then asked he me how
christen men governed them in our countrey and I
aunswered him & sayd, right well thankes be to God ;
& he sayd, secretly nay, for he sayd that our priestes
made no force of gods service, for they shoulde giue good
example to men, to doe well, and they giue ill example,

---

[1] Spirit.   [2] Turning.

and therefore when the people should go on the holy
daies to church to serve God they go to the taverne to
sin in glotony both day and nighte, and eate and drink
as bestes, that wot not when they haue had ynough, and
also Christen men he sayde, inforced them to fight
together & eche to begile other and they are so proude,
that they wot not how they may cloth them, now short,
now long, now straite now wyde, of all manner of fas-
sions. They shoulde be simple, meke and softe, and doe
theyr almes as Jesu Christe dyd, in whome they beleve,
and he sayde they are so covetouse, that for a lyttle
money they sell theyr children, theyr systers, and theyr
wyves, and one taketh another mans wife, and none
holdeth his fayth to other, therefore sayde he, for theyr
sinnes hath God given these landes to our handes, and
not through our strength, but all for your synnes. For
we wot well, that when that ye serve well your god,
that he wyll helpe you, so that no man shall winne of
you, if that ye serve your god as ye oughte to doe, but
while they lyve so sinfully as they doe, we have no
dread[1] on them, for theyr God shall not helpe them.
And then I asked him how that he knew the state of
Chrysten men in that maner, & he sayde that he knewe
well both of lordes and of commons, by his messengers
which he sent through all the countreys as it were mer-
chants with precious stones & other marchandise to know
the manner of euery countrey. And then he did call
againe all the lordes into his chamber to us & then
shewed he unto me iiii persons that were great lordes of
that countrey, that shewed me the maner of my countrey,
and of all Christendome, as though they had bene men
borne in the same partes, and they speak french right

[1] Fear of.

well and the Soudain also, and then I had greate marvaile of this slaunder of our faith and so they that should
bee turned by our good examples to the fayth of Jesu
Christe, they are drawen away through our evyl living,
and therefore it is no wonder if that they call us evyll,
for they saye soth, but the Sarasins are true for they
kepe truly the commaundements of their Alkaron that
God sent them by his messenger Machomet, to whome
they say, Gabryell the Aungell spake often, and tolde to
him the will of God.

CAP. XLVI.

Of the byrth of Machomet.

A ND ye shall understande y* Machomet was borne in
Araby, and that he was first a pore drudge & kept
horse & went after marchaundise. And so he came once
into Egipt with marchaundise & Egipt was the same
time Christen, & there was a chappell besyde Araby, &
there was an hermite & when he came to the chappell y*
was but a lyttle house and a lowe, as sone as he entered,
it began to be as great as it were of a palas gate and
that was the first miracle that the Sarasyns saye that he
did in his youth. After began Machomet to be wise and
rich and became a great Astronomer, and sithen was he
keper of the lande of the prince Corodan and governed
it full well, in such maner that when the prince was dead
he maryed the lady y* men call Quadryge.[1]   And
Mahomet fell often in the falling evill,[2] wherefore the

---

[1] Kadijah.   [2] Had epileptic fits.

lady was wroth that she had taken him unto hir husband, & he made hir to understande that every tyme that he fell so, he said that Gabriel the aungell spake to him, and for the great brightnesse of the aungell he fell downe. This Machomet raigned in Araby the yeare of our Lord, vi hundred and xx[1] and he was of the kinde of Ismael that was Abrahams son that he begat of Agar, and other are called Sarasins of Sara, but some are called Moabites and some Amenites after the two sons of Loth. And also Machomet loved well a good man an hermite that dwelled in the wildernesse a myle from Mounte Sinay in the way as men go from Araby to Caldee, and a dayes journey fro the sea where marchaunts of Venice come, and Machomet went so often to this hermyte that all his men were wroth, for he harde[2] gladly the hermit preach, and his men did walke all the night & thought they would this hermyte were dead. So it befell on a night that Machomet was full dronken of good wine, and he fell in a slepe, and his men toke Machomets sworde out of his sheath whyles he lay and slept, and therewith they slew the Hermit, and afterwarde they put up the sword againe all bloudy, and upon the morow when that he founde the Hermite thus dead, he was in his mynde verye angry, and right wroth, and woulde haue done his men unto the death, but they all with one accorde, and with one will sayde that he himselfe hadde slaine hym when he was dronken, and they shewed his own swerd all bluddy & then he beleved that they sayde soth, & then cursed the wine & all those that drank it. And therefore Sarasins that are devout drinke

---

[1] Other editions have it 610, but it was A.D. 611 when Mahomet professed to have received his call.

[2] Heard.

no wine openly, else they should be reprouued but they
drynke good beverage & sweete & nourishing that is
made of Calamelles, and thereof is suger made.

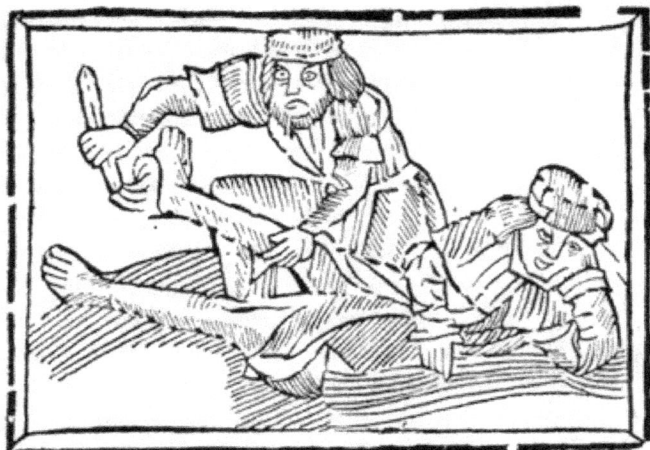

And it befel [1] sometime, y[t] christen men became Sarasins, either through povertie, simplenesse, or wickednesse
& therefore theyr Archbishop when he received them,
sayd thus,[2] *Laeles ella Machomet roses ella* That is to
say, there is no God but one, and Machomet is his mes-
sengere.   And sithern [3] I have told you a part of theyr
law, and of theyr customes, now I shall tell you of theyr
letters that they haue with theyr names. First they have
for A- almoy, B. bethath, c- cathi, d- delphoy, e- ephoti,
f- forthy, g- garophin, h- hechum, i- iocchi, k- kattu, l-
lothum, m- malach, n- nahalgt, o- orthy, p- choziri, q-

---

[1] *Pynson* says "befalleth."
[2] The Mahometan Confession of Faith is Lá iláha illá 'lláh
Muhammadun rasúlu 'lláh.
[3] Since.

zothii, r- rucholat, s- routhi, t- solathy, v- chorimus, x-yrithom, y- mazot, z-alepin & ioheten- com—these are the names.   These foure letters have they yet more for diversitie of their language, for as much as they speake so in their throtes, as we have in our language and speake in England.   Two letters may they then have in theyr A. B. C that is to say, y &, the which are called thorne- and zowx.

CAP. XLVII.

Of the yles and divers maner of people and of marvaylous beastes.

AND sithen I have devised before of the holy land and countreys there about, and many wayes thether, and to mount Synay, and to Babilon, and other divers places which I have spoken of, now will I tell & speake of iles and of divers bestes, and divers folke and countreys that be departed[1] by the flouds that came out of Paradise terrestre.   For Mesopotame and the kingdome of Calde and Araby are between two floddes, Tigre and Eufrace, and the kingedome of Media and Perce are betwene two flouds Tigre and Nyle, & the kingdome of Surrey, Palestine and Femines[2] are betweene Eufrace and the sea Mediterranean, it is of length from Marroch on the sea of Spaine, unto the great sea, and so lasteth it beyonde Constantinople three M and xx[3] myle of Lombardy and to the Occean sea.   In Inde is the kingdome of Sichem,[4] that is all closed among hils, and beside

[1] Parted.   [2] Phœnicia.
[3] Others say 3,040.   [4] Scythia

Sichem is the lande of Amazony, wherein dwell none but women.

And thereby is the kingdome of Albany, which is a great lande and it is called so bicause that men are more whiter there than in other places, & in this countrey are great houndes and stronge, so that they overcome Lions and slay them.   And ye shall understande that to those countreys are many iles and landes, of the which were too long to tell, but of some I will speake more plainly afterwarde.

CAP. XLVIII.

Of the haven Gene, for to go by the sea into divers countreys.

FOR he that wyll goe to Tartary, Percy, Caldee or Inde, he entreth the sea at Gene or at Venyce, or at any other haven, and so passeth by the sea, and arriveth at Topasonde,[1] that is a good citie, that sometime men call the haven of bridge, and there is the haven of Perce, of Medes, and of other marches.[2] In this citie lieth saint Athanasius, that was bishop of Alexandry, that made the Psalme, *Quicunque vult salvus esse.* This man was a great doctour of divinitie, and of the godheade, he was accused unto the Pope of Rome that he was an heritike, and the pope sent for hym and put him in prison, and while he was in that prison he made this Psalme and sent it unto the Pope & sayde if that he were an heretyke, then that was heresie, for y[t] was his faith and his belefe : and when the Pope saw that he had sayde therein was all our faith, then anon he did deliver him out of prison, and he commaunded that Psalme to be sayd every day at prime, & so he held Athanasius for a good christen man, but he never would after goe to his bishoprych for they accused him of heresie.

Topasond was some tyme holden of the Emperour of Constantinople, but a great man that he sent to help

---

[1] Trebizond.   [2] Neighbouring countries.

that countrey against the Turkes, did holde it to himselfe, & called himself Emperour of Topasonde.

And from thence men go through lyttle Armony,[1] &
in that countrey is an olde castell that is on a rock, y[t]
men call the castell of Spirys, & there men finde an
hawke sitting upon a perch right well made & a faire
lady of Fayry that keepeth it, & he that will wake[2] this
same hawke seven days and seven nightes, and some say
that it is not but three days and three nightes, alone
without any company and without slepe, this faire ladie
shall come unto him at the vii dayes or iii dayes ende
& shall graunte unto him the first thing that he will
aske of worldly things, and that hath often ben proved.
And so uppon a time it befell that a man which that
tyme was Kinge of Armonye that was a righte doughty[3]

[1] Armenia.   [2] Watch.   [3] Brave.
[3] In the old Romance of Melusina, which was written by Jean
d'Arras, Secretary to the Duc de Berri, brother to Charles V. of

man waked uppon a tyme, and at the seven dayes ende
the lady came to him and bade him aske what he would
for he had wel done his devoure,[1] and the king aunswered
and sayde that he was a great lorde and in good peace,
and he was riche, so that he would aske nothing but all
onely the body of the fayre lady, or to haue his will of
hir. Then this fayre lady aunswered and sayde unto
him, that he was a foole, for he wist not what he asked,
for he might not have hir, for he shoulde not haue asked
hir but worldly thinges & she was not worldly. And
the king sayde he woulde nought else, and she said sith

France—in 1387 (at the command of his master) is the legend of
the Lady of the Sparrow Hawk, which shows how current it was at
the time. According to his version, a fairy, named Presine, married
King Helmas, and made him vow that he would never go near her
at the time of childbirth. She bore him three daughters—Melusina, Melior, and Palestine—and at the birth of the latter the king
broke his vow. When his children grew up they learnt this fact,
and were very indignant at their father's conduct, to punish which
(being gifted with supernatural power) they enclosed him in an en-
chanted mountain until he died. Presine was powerless to undo
this deed, but she visited their unnatural conduct severely upon her
daughters. Melusina was to become half serpent, half woman, every
Saturday ; Palestine was ever to watch their father's treasure on
the top of a mountain in Arragon ; while Melior's fate is thus told
by the chronicler :—

"And thou Melyor to the I gyve a Castel in the grette Armenye,
whyche is fayre and riche, wher thou shalt kepe a Sperschak unto
the tyme that the grett maister shall hold his Jugement. And al
noble and worthy knyghts, descended and come of noble lynee,
that wil you watche there the day byfore the even, and th' even also
of Saint Johan Baptiste, whiche is on the xx day of Juny, without
any slep, shal have a geft of the of suche thinges, without to demande thy body, ne thy love, by maryage, nor other wise. And al
thos that shal demande the without cesse, and that wol not forbere,
and absteyn them not, shal be infortunat unto the IX lynee, and
shal be put from theire prosperytees."

[1] Devoir, duty.

he would aske nought else, she should graunt him three thinges and all that came after hym, and saydę unto him, Sir kinge you shall haue warre without peace unto the ix degree, and you shall be in subjection of your enemies, and you shall have greate nede of good and cattell, and sithen that tyme all the Kynges of Armonye have been in warre and nedefull [1] and under trybute of the Sarasyns.   Also a poore mannes sonne as he waked on a tyme, and asked the lady that he might be rych and happy in marchaundise and the ladye graunted him, but she sayde to him that he hadde asked his undoynge for great pryde that he shoulde haue thereof.   And this became so greate a marchaunte bothe by sea and lande, that he was so ryche that he knew not the thousande parte of hys goods.   Also a Knight of the Templers waked likewise and when he had done, he desired to haue a purse full of golde and what soever he tooke thereof it shoulde ever be full againe and the ladye graunted it hym, but she tolde him that hee had desyred his destruc- tion for great mistrowing that hee shoulde have of the same purse, and so it befell.   But he that shal wake hath great nede for to kepe him from slepe, for if he sleepe he is lost that he shall neuer bee sene, but that is not the righte way, but for the mervaile.   And from Topasonde men go to greate Armony to a citie that men call Artyron [2] that was wont to be a great Citie, but Turkes have destroyed it, for there neyther groweth no wyne nor fruyt.   From this Artyron men go to an hyll that is called Sabissacol & there nere is another hil that men call Arath, [3] but the Jewes call it Thano where Archa Noe [4] rested after the diluvie, [5] & yet it is on that

---

[1] Poor, needy.   [2] Erzeroum.   [3] Ararat.
[4] Noah's Ark.   [5] Flood.

hyll, a man may se it from ferre in cleare wether, & the hilles be xii[1] myle of height & some saye they haue bene there & put theyr fingers in the holes where the fende[2] went out when Noe sayde in this maner of wyse *Benedicite.* But they note well, for none may go on that hyll for snowe, that is alwaye uppon that hyll bothe wynter and somer, that no man may go by and never yode[3] syth Noe was, but a monke, through the grace of God, broughte a planke that yet is at the Abbey, at the

hyll foote, and he had great desyre to go uppon that hyll, and aforced him thereto, and when he was at the thyrde part upwarde he was so wery that he might goe no further, and he rested him & slept and when he was awake he was downe at the hyll foote, and then prayed he to God devoutly that he would suffer him to go upon

[1] Others say seven.   [2] Fiend.
[3] Never went there.

I

the hill, and the Aungell sayd that he should go upon
the hil, and so he dyd, and since that tyme no man came
there.   And therefore men shoulde not beleve such
wordes.

And from thence men go to a citie that men call Tan-
ziro [1] and that is a fayre citie & good.   Besyde that citie
is an hyll of salte, and thereof every man taketh what
he wyll and there dwelled many Christen men under

tribute to the Sarasyns.   From thence men go through
many cities, townes, and castels towarde Inde, and then
come to a citie that men call Cassaye that is a fayre
citie, and in that citie is aboundance of corne wynes,
and all maner of goods, and there met the three kynges
togither that wente to make theyr offeryng to our Lord
in Bethlehem.   From that citie men go to a citie that
men call Cardabago, and paynims say y[t] Christen men

[1] Tabreez or Tabriz.

SYR JOHN MAUNDEVILLE, KNIGHT.   115

may not dwell there, by [1] they dye sone and they know
not the cause. And from thence men go through many
countreys, cities & townes, that it were to long to tell, &
to the citie of Carnaa, that was wont to be so great, that
the wall about was of xxv myle, the wall sheweth yet,
but it is not inhabited now with men, and there endeth
the land of the Emperour of Perce.

CAP. XLIX.

Of the countrey of Job, and of the Kingedome of Caldee.

ON the other side of the citie of Carnaa men enter
into the land of Job, that is a good lande & great
plentie of all fruites & men call that land of Swere.[2] In
this lande is the citie of Thomar. Job was a Paynim
& also he was Cofraas son & he helde that lande as
prince thereof, & he was so riche that he knew not the
hondreth parte of his good, and after his povertie God
made him richer than ever he was before, for after he
was Kinge of Idumea after the death of King Esau, &
when he was king he was called Joab, and in that kingedome he lived c yeare and lxx so that he was of age when
he dyed cc yeare and xlviii. And in this lande of Job
is no defaute [3] of nothing that is nedefull to mans body.
There are hilles where men finde manna, and manna is
called Aungell's bread that is a whit thing right sweete
& much sweter than suger or hony, and that commeth
of the dew of heaven that falleth on the herbes, and

---

¹ For.   ² Susiana.   ³ Want of anything.

there it congeled and waxeth white and men doe it in medecines for riche men.

This lande marcheth to the lande of Caldee that is a great land, & there is full faire folke & well apparaited & they go richly araied with cloth of gold & with perls & other precious stones. But the women are righte foule & evill clad & go bare fote & bare an ill cote, large, wide, & short, unto theyr knees, & haue long sleves down to the fote, & they haue great black here long hanging about theyr shoulders & they are right foule for to loke upon that I dare not tell it all bicause that I am worthy for to haue a great reward for my praising of them.   In this land of Caldee aforesayde is a citie that men call Hur & in yᵗ citie was Abraham yᵉ patriark born.

CAP. L.

Of the Kingedome of Amazony whereas dwelleth none but women.

AFTER the lande of Caldée is the lande of Amazony
that is a land where there is no man but all women
as men say, for they wil suffer no men to lyve among
them nor to haue lordeshippe over them. For sometyme
was a kinge in that lande and men were dwelling there
as did in other countreys, and had wives, & it befell that
the kynge had great warre with them of Sychy, he was
called Colopius and hee was slaine in bataill and all the
good bloude of his lande. And this queene when she herd
that, & other ladies of that land, that the king and the

lordes were slaine, they gathered them togither and killed all the men that were lefte in their lande among them, and sithen that time dwelled no man among them.

And when they will have any man they sende for them in a countrey that is nere theyr lande, and the men come and are ther viii dayes or as the woman lyketh, & then go they againe, and if they have men children they send them to theyr fathers when they can eate & go, and if they have maide chyldren they kepe them, and if they bee of gentill bloud they brene [1] the left pappe [2] away for bearing of a shelde, and if they be of little bloud they brene the ryght pappe away for shoting.   For those women of that countrey are good warriours and are often in soudy [3] with other lordes, and the queene of that lande governeth well that lande, this lande is all environed with water.   Beside Amazony is the lande of Termagute that is a good lande, King Alexander did make a citie ther that men call Alexandry.

[1] Burn.   [2] Breast.   [3] War.

CAP. LI.

Of the lande of Ethiope.

O N the other side of Calde toward the south side is
Ethyope a great lande. In this lande on the
south are the folke right blacke. In that side is a well
that in the daye the water is so colde that no man may
drinke thereof, & in the nighte it is so hote that no man
may suffer to put his hand in it. In this lande the rivers

and all the waters are troublous and some dele salte for
the great hete, and men of y^t lande are lightly dronken
& haue little appetite to meate, and they haue commonly
the flixe of body and they live not long. In Ethiope [1]

---

[1] Like many other marvellous stories related by Sir John Man-

are such men that have but one foote, and they go so
fast y' it is a great marvaill, & that is a large fote that
the shadow thereof covereth y^e body from son or rayne
when they lye uppon their backes, and when their

children be first borne they loke like russet, and when
they waxe olde then they be all blacke. In Ethiope is
the lande of Saba, of the which one of the three Kings
that sought our Lorde at Bethleem was King.

deville, they were told by Pliny, in his Natural History, nearly 1200
years previously. For instance, in Book 7, chap. ii., devoted to
Man, he quotes Ctesias as saying that in India is another race of
men, who are known as Monscoli, who have only one leg, but are
able to leap with surprising agility. The same people are also
called Sciapodœ, because they are in the habit of lying on their
backs during the time of extreme heat and protect themselves from
the sun by the shade of their feet. For other types of these " peculiar people" see Appendix.

CAP. LII.

*Of Inde the more, & **Inde** the lesse, & of diamonds, **and** small people, & other things.*

FROM Ethyope men go into Inde through many dyverse countreys, and it is called Inde the more, and it is departed in three parties, that is to say, Inde the more that is a full hote lande, & Inde the lesse is a temperate land, and the thyrde part that is toward the north there it is right cold, so that for greate colde, frost & yce, the water becommeth Cristal & upon that groweth the good diamondes y[t] is like a trouble [1] colour, & that Diamonde is so harde that no man may breake it. Other Diamonds men finde in Araby that are not so good for they are more softer and some are in Cipres and in Macedony men also finde diamondes but the best are in Inde & some are founde many times in a masse that cometh oute where men fynde golde from the myne when men breake the masse in pyeces, and sometyme men finde some of greatnesse of a pese, [2] and some lesse, and those are as harde as those of Inde, and all if it be that men fynde good dyamondes in Indie upon the Roch of Crystall, also menne finde good dyamondes upon the Roch of Adamante [3] in the sea and on hilles, as it were haysell noutes, [4] and they are all square and poynted of theyre owne

---

[1] Prismatic.   [2] Pea.
[3] Rocks of Magnetic Loadstone were then firmly believed in.
[4] Hazel nuts.

kynde, and they grow both togither, male and female,
and are noryshed with the dewe of heaven, and they
engendre commonly & bring forth small children that
multiply & growe all the yeare.   I haue many times
assayed that if a man kepe them with a lyttle of the
roche, and wette them with many dewes oft times, they
shal grow euery yeare, and the small shall waxe greate.
And a manne shall bere the Diamonde in his left side,
and then it is of more vertue, for the strength of theyr
growing is toward the North, that is on the lefte side as
men of those countreys say.   To him that beareth the
diamond upon him it giveth him hardinesse, it kepeth
his lims of his body hole, it giveth victory of [1] enimies if
a mans cause be ryght, and hym that bereth it in good
will, it kepeth him from strife, from ryote, ill dreames,
and sorcerys, and enchauntements, and no wylde beste
shall greve him nor assaile him.   And also the Dya-
monde shoulde be given freely without covetyse and
bying, & then it is of more vertue, it healeth him that is
lunatyke, and he that is travailed with a divell, and if
venym or poyson be brought in the presence of the
Diamonde so soon it moysteth and beginneth to sweate,
and men may well polyce [2] them to make men beleve
that they may not be polyshed.   But men may assaye
them well in this maner, fyrst cut with them an diverse
precious stones, as Saphyrs or other uppon Crystall and
then men take a stone that is called Adamande, lay a
nedell before that Adamande and if the Diamond is
good & vertuous the Adamande draweth not the nedell
to him whiles the Diamonde is there.   And this is the
proof that they make beyonde the sea.   But it falleth
sometime that the good diamond loseth his vertue

[1] Over.   [2] Polish.

through him that wereth it, and therefore it is nedefull for to make it to recover his virtue againe, or else it is lyttle of value.[1]

CAP. LIII.

Of diverse countreys & Kingdomes & yles of the lande of Inde.

M ANY diverse countreys & Kingdoms are in Inde, and it is called Inde of a river that runneth through it, which is called Inde also & there are many precious stones in that river Inde.   And in that ryver men finde Eles of xxx foote long & men y^t dwell nere that river are of evill colour, yelowe & grene.   In Inde

---

[1] This description of the diamond is largely taken from Pliny, book 37, chap. iv.

is more than fyve thousande yles that men dwell in
good and great, beside those that men dwel not in.
And in eche one of those is great plenty of cities and
muche people, for men of Inde are of that condicion that
they passe not out of theyr lande commonly, for they
dwell under a planet that is called Saturne, & that planet
maketh his course by the xii signes in xxx [1] yeare and
the Mone passeth through the xii signes in a moneth
and for that Saturne is of so late sterying, [2] therefore men
that dwell under him, & in that clymate have no good
will to be much sterying aboute.   And in our countrey
is it contrary, for we are in a climate that is of the mone,
& of light stering and that is the planet of way, & therefore it giveth us will to much moving & steryng and to

*   *   *   *   *

go into diverse countreys of the world, for it goeth about
the worlde more lyghtly than any other planet dothe.

[1] *Pynson* says 20 years.   [2] Slow motion.

Also men passe through Inde by many countreys unto
the great Occean Sea. And then they fynde the yle of
Hermes where marchaunts of Venis and of Gene and of
other diverse partes of christendome come for to by
them marchaundise.

In this lande men and women lye all naked in the
ryvers and waters, from undren [1] or heate of the day tyll
it be past none, and they ly all in the water but the face,
for the great heat that is there, and the women be not
ashamed for the men. In that yle are the ships without
nayles of yron, or bond, for roches of Adamand [2] that
are in the sea would draw shippes to them. From this
yle men go by the sea to the yle of Lana where is great

plenty of corne, and the King of this yle was sometime
so mighty that he helde war against King Alexander

---

[1] An early hour before noon. A Latin edition has it :—" _A diei
hora tertia, usq : ad nonam._"

[2] Loadstone rocks.

with great strength.   Men of this yle have many maner
beleves and faithe & have also diverse lawes, for some do
worship the Sunne, some the fyre, some the trees, & some
the serpents, or any other thinge that they fyrst meete in
the morning, and some doe worship simulacres [1] and
Idoles, but betwene symulacres & ydoles is no [2] difference, and that is to understande, ymages made to what
lykenesse of thing that man may invent, for some ymage
hath an head lyke an Oxe, some haue three or foure
heddes, on of a man or an hors or Oxe or any other best
that no man hath seene.   And ye shall understande
that they that worship symulacres they worship them as
for worthy men that were sometime, as Hercules, and
other that dyd many mervayles in theyr tymes.   For
they saye they know well that they are not god of
kynde [3] that made all thinges, but that they are wel [4]
with god for the mervayles that they did, and therefore
they worship them.   And so say they of the sonne, for
it chaungeth oft tymes, for it giueth sometime great
heate for to nourych [5] all things on earth, & bicause it
is of so greate profyte they knowe well that it is not God
but it is well with God & that God loveth it more than
any other thing, and for this cause they worshippe it.
And also they saye theyr reasons of other planettes, and
of fyre also, for it is profitable, and nedefull.   And of
ydolls they say the Oxe is the holyest that they may
finde here in earthe, and more profitable than any other,
for he doth much good, and none ille, and they knowe
well that it maye not bee without the speciall grace of

[1] Images.
[2] Other editions have "a gret difference," which the context
shows should be the right reading.
[3] Similar to Him that made, &c.
[4] They were helped by God in the marvels, &c.   [5] Nourish.

God, and therefore they make theyr God of an Oxe, the
one halfe, and the other halfe a man, for man is the
fairest and the best creature of the worlde.   And they
doe worship to serpentes, and other beastes that they
fyrste meete with in the morninge, and namely those
bestes that have good, meting after whome they speake [1]
well all the day after, the which they have proved of
long time, & therefore they say that this meting cometh
of Gods grace, and therefore they doe make ymages lyke
unto those things that they may worship them before
they meete anythinges else. And there are some christen
men that say that some bestes are better for to meet

than some, for hares, swine, and other bestes are ill to
meete first, as they saye.   In this yle of Cana is many
wilde bestes, & rattes in that countrey are as great as
houndes here, and they take them with mastifes, for
cattes may not take them.   Fro thence men come to a

[1] Speed, *i.e.* have good luck.

citie that men call Sarchys, and it is a faire and a goode
citie and there dwell many christen men of Gods faith,
and there be men of religion.   From thence men come
to the land of Lombe & in that lande groweth peper in
a forest that men call Tomber & it groweth in none other
place more in all the worlde than in that forest, and that
forest is well L[1] daies journey.   And there by the lande
of Lombe is the Citie of Polomes,[2] and under that Citie
is an hyll that men call Polombe and thereof taketh the
citie his name.   And so at the fote of the same hill is a
right faire and a clere well, that hath a full good and
sweete savoure, and it smelleth of all maner of sortes of
spyces, and also at eche houre of the daye it changeth
his savour diversly, and who drinketh thries on the daye
of that well, he is made hole of all maner (*of*) sicke-
nesse that he hathe.   I have sometime dronke of that
well, and methinketh yet that I fare the better; some
call it the well of youth, for they that drinke thereof
seme to be yong alway, and live without great sicknesse,
and they saye this well, cometh from Paradise terrestre,
for it is so vertuous, and in this lande groweth ginger,
and thither come many good marchauntes for spyces.
In this countrey men worship the Oxe for his great simplenesse and mekenesse, and the profite that is in him,
for they make the Oxe to travaile vi or vii yere and then
men do eate him.   And the Kinge of that land hath
euermore one Oxe with him, and he that kepeth him
euery day taketh hys fees for the keping.   And also
euery daye he gathereth his uryne and his dong in a
vessell of gold, and bereth it to the prelate that they call,
Archi porta papaton[3] and the prelate bereth it to the

---

[1] Other editions say 18.   [2] Quilon, on the Malabar Coast.
[3] Archi proto papaton.

King, and maketh thereupon a great blessing and then
the King putteth his hande therein, and they call it gaule
and hee anoynteth his fronte, and his breste therewith,
and they doe it great worship, and saye he shall be fulfilled with the vertu of the Oxe before sayde, and that
he is halowed through vertue of that holy thinge as they
saye.   And when the Kinge hath this done, then doe it
other lordes, and after them other men after theyr
degree, if they may haue any of the remenaunt.[1]   In
thys countrey theyr ydoles are halfe men and halfe oxe,
as the figure sheweth in the seconde lefe here before, and
out of these ydolles the wycked ghost[2] speaketh unto
them, and giveth them aunswere of what thing that they
aske him, and before these ydolles they many times
sleay theyr children, and sprinkle the blood on the
ydoles, and so make they sacrifice.   And if any man die
in that countrey, they brene them in tokening of penaunce that he should suffer no penance if he were layd
in the earth for eating of wormes.   And if his wife haue
no children then they burne hir with him, and they saye
that is good reason that she keepe him company in the
other worlde, as she dyd in this, & if she haue children
she may liue with them and [3] she will ; and if the wyfe
dye before, she shall be burnt, & hir husbande also, if he
will.   In this countrey groweth good wine, & women
drink wine & men none, and women shaue theyr berds
& not men.

[1] Remnant.   [2] Wicked spirit.   [3] An, if.

K

CAP. LIIII.

Of the Kingedome of Mabaron.

FROM this lande men go many journeys to a countrey that men call Mabaron,[1] and this is a greate
Kingdome, therein is many fayre cities & townes.   In
this lande lyeth Sainct Thomas in a fayre tombe, in

fleshe and bones, in the Citie of Calamy, and the arme
and hande that hee put in our Lordes syde after his
resurrection, when Christ sayde unto hym, *Noli esse in-
credulus sed fidelis :*, that is to saye, Be not of vaine hope

---

[1] Identical with the Maabav of Marco Polo, book 3, cap. xvi.,
where he gives a very interesting account of the place. It was what
we call the Coromandel Coast.

but beleve ; that same hande lyeth yet without the
tombe bare, and with this hande they giue theyr domes[1]
in that countrey, to mete[2] who saith righte, and who
doeth not, for, if any stryfe be betwene two parties, they
write their names, & put them into the hand, & then
incontinently the hande casteth away the byll[3] of him
that hath wronge and holdeth the other still that hathe
righte, and therefore they come from farre countreys to
have Judgementes of causes that are in doubte.   In this
church of Saint Thomas is a great image, y^t is a simulacre, & it is richly beset with precious stons & perles,
to that image men come in pilgrimage from farre countreys, with great devocion, as Christen men go to Saint
James, & there come some pilgrims y^t beare sharp knives
in theyr handes, & as they go by the waye they shere[4]
theyr shankes & thyghes, that the bloude may come out
for the love of that ydoll and they saye that he is holy
that will dye for that ydols sake.   And there is some
that for the time that they go out of their houses at eche
third pace they knele till that they come to this idole.
And when they come there they have ensence[5] or such
other thing for to ensence the ydole, as we would do to
Gods body.   And there before that mynster or church of
this ydol, is a river full of water, & in that river pilgrims
cast gold, silver, perles & other precious stones without
number, in stede of offerings, and therefore, when y^e
maister of the minster hath any neede of helping, as sone
they go the river & take thereout as much as they haue
neede to helping of ye minster.   And ye shall understande when that any greate festes come of ye Idol, as
the dedication day of the church, or of the throning of

---

[1] Judgments.   [2] Find out.   [3] Paper.
[4] Cut their legs.   [5] Incense.

the Idol, all the countrey there about assemble them
there togither and then men set this Idoll with great
reverence & worship in a chaire well dressed with cloth
of gold, and other tapistry, & so they carry him with
great reverence & worship, rounde about the citie, and
before the chaire goeth firste in procession all the maidens
of the countrey two & two togither, & so after them go
the pilgrimes that are come fro far countreys, of the which

pilgrims some fall downe before the chaire, & letteth all
go over them and so are they slaine, and some haue
theyr armes broken & leggs,[1] and this they doe for love
of the Idol, and they beleve the more paine that they
suffer here for their Idol the more joy shall they haue in
y⁰ other world, & a man shall finde few Christen men
will suffer so much penaunce for our Lordes sake as
they do for the ydoll.   And nighe before the chaire go

[1] Mandeville probably describes the Car of Juggernaut.

all the mynstrels of the countrey, as it were without nomber with many divers melodyes. And when they are come againe to the Church they sette up the ydol againe in his throne, and for worship of the ydoll two or three [1] are slaine with sharpe knives with their good will.

And also a man thinketh in our countrey that he hath a great worshippe to haue an holy man in his kyn, lyke-wise they saye that those that are there slayne are holye men and sayntes & they are wrytten in their letany, and when they are thus dead theyr frendes brene theyr bodies & they take the ashes, and those are kepte as relykes, and they say it is an holy thing, & that they doubte of no perill when they haue of those ashes.

[1] Other editions have it " two or three hundred."

CAP. LV.

Of a great countrey called Lamory, where the people go all naked & other things.

FROM this countrey LII journeys is a countrey that
men call Lamory,[1] and in that lande is greate
heate, and it is the custome there, that men and women
go al naked and they scorne all them that are clade, for
they say that God made Adam & Eve all naked, and
that men shoulde haue no shame of that God made, &
they beleve in the same God that made Adam & Eve
and all the world, and there is no woman wedded, but

[1] Sumatra.

women are all common there, and they forsake no man.
And they say that God commaunded to Adam & Eve
and all that come of them saying, *Crescite & multiplica-*
mini, & replete Terram. That is to say in English,
Encrease & multiply and fyll the earth, and no man
may say there, This is my wife, & no woman may say,
this is my husbande.   And when they haue any children
they give them to whom they will of men that haue
medled with them.   Also the lande is all common, for

every man taketh what he will, for that one man hath in
one yere now, an other man hath another yeare.   Also
all the goods, as corne, beastes and all maner thing of
that countrey are all in common.   For there is nothing
under locke, and as riche is one man as an other, but
they haue an evill custome in eating of fleshe, for they
eate gladlier mans fleshe than other.   Neverthelesse in
that lande is abundaunce of corne, of fleshe, of fishe, of
golde of silver and all maner of goods.   And thether

doeth the marchauntes bring their children for to sell, and those that are fatte they eate them, & those that be lean, they kepe them tyll they befatte, & then are they eaten.   And besyde this yle of Lamory, is another yle that men call Somober,[1] and is a good yle, men of that yle do marke them in the visage with an hot yron, bothe men & women for great nobility & to be knowen from

other, for they hold themselfe the worthiest of y° world and they haue warre evermore with those men that are naked that I spake of before.   Also there are many other yles and diverse maner of men, of the which it were overmuch for to speake of all.

[1] ? Sumatra.   One or other, Lamory or Somober, is evidently this island.

CAP. LVI.

Of the countrey and yle named Java, which is a mighty lande.

A ND there is also a great yle that men call Java &
the kinge of that countrey hath under hym seven
kinges, for he is a full mightie prince. In this yle
groweth all maner of spyces more plenteously than in

any other place, as ginger, clowes, canell[1] nutmyge[2] and
other, and ye shall understande that the nutmyge beareth
the maces, & of all thing therein is plenty savinge wine.
The King of this lande hath a riche palace and the best

---

[1] Cinnamon.   [2] Nutmeg.

that is in the worlde, for all the greces of his hall and
chambres are all made one of gold & another of silver,
& all the walls are plated with fine gold and silver, &
on those plates are written stories of knightes, and
batayles, and the pavimente of the hall and chambres is
of golde and silver, and there is no man that woulde
beleve this riches that is there except hee had sene it,
and the Kynge of this yle is so mightie, that he hath
many times overcom the great Caane of Cathay which
is the myghtiest Emperour that is in all the worlde, for
there is often warre amonge them, for the great Caane
would make hym hold his land of him.

CAP. LVII.

*Of the Kingdome of Pathen or Salmasse, which is a
goodly lande.*

AND for to go forth by the sea, there is an yle that
is called Pater, and some call it Salmasse, for it is
a great kingedome with many faire cities. In this lande
groweth trees that beare meale, of which men make faire
bread & white & of good savour, and it seemeth lyke as
it were of wheate. And there be other trees that beare
venym,[1] againe the which is no medicine but one, that is
to take of the leaves of the same tree and stampe them,
and tempre them with water and drinke it, or else he
shall dye sodainly, for Treacle may not helpe. And if
you will know how this tree beare meale, I shall tell you,

---

[1] Poison, *i.e.*, are poisonous.

men hew with a hatchet aboute the rote of the tree by the earth, and they perce him in many sundry places, and then cometh out a lycoure the which they take in a vessell, and sette in the sonne and dry it, and when it is dry, they cary it unto the mille to grynde, and so it is faire meale and white.   Also hony wyne, and venym are drawen out of other trees in the same maner, and they

put it in vessels to keepe. In that yle is a dead sea, which is a water that hath no grounde and if anythinge fall therein it shall never be founde, besyde that sea groweth great canes and under theyr rootes men finde precious stones of great vertue, for he that beareth one of those stones uppon him, there may no yron greve[1] him nor drawe blood on hym, and therefore they y' have those stones fyght full hardely, for there may no quarell[2] nor such thing greve them, therefore they that knowe the maner make their quarell without yron & so they sleay them.

[1] Wound or hurt.   [2] Arrow.

CAP. LVIII.

*Of the Kingdome of Talonach, the king thereof hath
many wyves.*

THEN is there another yle that men call Talonach,
that is a greate lande, and plenteous of goods &
fyshes, as you shall hereafter heare.   And the King of

the lande hath as many wives as he will, a thousande &
mo, and lyeth never by one of them but once, and that
lande hath a marvayle that is in no other land, for all
maner of fyshes of the sea cometh there once a yeare,
one after another, and lyeth him nere the lande, sometime on the lande, and so lye three dayes, and men of
that lande come thither and take of them what he will,

and then go those fyshes awaye and another sorte
commeth, and lyeth also three dayes and men take of

them, and doe thus all maner of fyshes tyll all haue
bene there, and menne have taken what they wyll.   And

menne wot[1] not the cause why it is so. But they of that countrey saye, that those fyshes come so thyther to do worship to theyr king, for they say he is the most worthiest king of the worlde for he hath so many wives and geateth so many children of them. And that same kinge that XIIII M Olyfauntes or mo which be all tame, and they be all fedde of the men his countrey, for his pleasure bicause that he may haue them redy to his hande when he hath any warre against any kyng or prince, and then he doth put uppon theyr backs castels & men of warre as the use is of the lande, and lykewyse do other kyngs and princes thereabout.

[1] Know.

CAP. LIX.

Of the ylande called Raso[1] *where men be hanged as sone as they are sicke.*

A ND from this yle menne go unto another yle that men call Raso, and menne of this yle when that theyr friendes are sicke & that they beleve surely that they shal dye, they take them & hange them al quick on a tree, and say that it is better that byrdes, that are aungels of God, eate them, than wormes of the earthe. Fro thence men go to an yle where the men are of ill kinde, for they nourishe houndes for to strangle men. And when theyr friendes are sicke that they hope they

[1] *Pynson* and others say Gaffolo or Caffolos.

shal dye, then do those houndes strangle them, for they
wyll not that they dye a kyndely death, for then shoulde
they suffre to great paine as they say, & when they are
thus dead they eate theyre flesh for venison.

CAP. LX.

Of the ylande of Melke wherein dwelleth evill people.

FROM thence menne go through many yles by sea
unto an yle that men call Melke, and there be full
yll people, for they haue none other delyte but to fyght
and slee men, for they drinke gladly mans blood, which
blood they call good, and they that maye most sleay is
of moste name amonge them.   And if two men there be
at stryfe and after bee made at one, it behoveth them to
drink eyther others blood, or else the accorde is nought.

From this yle men go to an yle that is called Tracota
where all men are as beastes & not reasonable, they
dwell in caves, for they haue not wyt to make them
houses, they eate adders [1] and they speake not, but they

make such a noyse as adders doe one to another, and
they make no force of ryches but of a stone that hath
forty colours, and it is called Traconyt after that yle,
they know not the vertue thereof but they covete it for
the great fayreness.

[1] Pliny speaks (Book 7, cap. 2) of adder-eating people in India
and elsewhere, but he says they live to the age of four hundred
years, which is supposed to be owing to the flesh of vipers, which
they use as food, in consequence of which they are free from all
noxious animals, both in their hair and their garments. In book
29, c. 38, he also gives directions for the preparation of viper's flesh
for food.

L

CAP. LXI.

Of an yland named Macumeran, whereas the people haue heads lyke houndes.[1]

FROM that yle menne go to an yle that is called Macumeran, whiche is a greate yle and a fayre and the men and women of the countrey haue heads like

houndes, they are reasonable & worship an oxe for their god, they go all naked but a little clothe before them,

[1] Again in Book 7, cap. 2, Pliny speaks of *Cynocephali*, or dog-headed people, for he says that on many of the mountains there is a tribe of men, who have the heads of dogs, and clothe themselves with the skins of wild beasts. Instead of speaking, they bark ; and, furnished with claws, they live by hunting and catching birds.

they are good men to fighte, & they beare a great target
with which they couer all the body and a speare in theyr
hande, and if they take any man in batayle they sende
him to theyr King which is a great lorde & devoute in
his faith, for he hath about his necke on a cord thre
hondred pearles great & orient,[1] in maner of Pater noster,
and as we saye Pater noster, and Ave maria, Right so
ye King saith euery day three hundred prayers to his
god before he eate, & he beareth also about hys necke a

ruby, oryent, fine & good, that is neer a foote & five
fingers long. For when they chuse theyr Kyng they
giue to him that Ruby to beare in his hande, and then
they lead him riding about the citie, and then euer after
are they subjecte to him, and therefore he beareth that
Ruby alway about his necke, for if he beareth not the
Ruby, they woulde no longer holde hym for kynge. The

[1] Oriental,—coming from the East.

greate Caane of Cathay hath much coveted this Ruby :
but he might never haue it, neither for war nor for other
catell,[1] and this Kinge is a full true & a righteous man,
for men may go safely & surely through his lande &
beare y[t] he will, for there is no man so hardy to let[2]
them.   And from thence men go to an ile that is called
Silo, this ile is more than a hundred[3] myle about and

therein be many serpents which are great with yelow
stripes & they haue foure feete, with short leggs & great
claws, some be five fadome[4] of length & some of viii &
some of x & some more and some lesse & be called
Cocodrylles & there are also many wylde beasts & Olyfants.[5]   Also in this yle & in many yles thereabout are
many wyld geese with two heads, and there be also in
y[t] countrey white lyons and many other dyverse mer-

---

[1] Nor in exchange.   [2] Hinder.   [3] Others say 800.
[4] A fathom is 6 feet.   [5] Elephants.

vaylous beastes, & if I should tell it all it should be to long.

CAP. LXII.

Of a great yland called Dodyn, where are many diverse men of evill conditions.

THEN there is another yle that men call Dodyn, &
it is a great yle. In this yle are maner diverse
maner of men y᷑ haue evyll maners, for the father eateth
the son & the son the father the husband his wyfe and
the wyfe hir husbande. And if it so be that the father
be sicke, or the mother, or any frend, the sonne goeth
soone to the priest of the law & prayeth him that he will
aske of the ydoll if his father shall dye of that sicknesse
or not. And then the priest and the son kneele downe

before the ydole devoutly & asketh him, and he aun-
swereth to them, and if he say that he shall lyve, then
they kepe him wel, and if he say that he shall dye, then
commeth the priest with the son or with the wyfe or
what frende that it be unto him y' is sicke, and they lay
their hands over his mouth to stop his breath, and so
they sley him & then they smite all the body into peces
& praieth all his frendes for to come and eate of him that
is dead, and they make a great feste thereof and haue
many minstrels there, and eate him with great melody.
And so when they haue eaten al y^e flesh, then they take
the bones and bury them all singing with great worship,

and all those that are of his friendes that were not there
at the eating of him haue great shame and vylany, so
that they shall never more be taken as frends. And the
King of this yle is a great lord and mightie, & he hath
under him LIIII grete Yles and eche of them hath a King,

and in one of these yles are men that haue but one eye,
& that is in the middest of theyr front and they eate not

flesh & fishe all rawe.   And in another yle dwell men
that haue no heads & theyr eyen are in theyr shoulders

& theyr mouth is on theyr breste.[1] In another yle are men
that haue no head ne eyen and theyr mouth is in theyr
shoulders.   And in another yle are men that haue flatte
faces without nose and without eyen, but they haue two
small round holes in stede of eyen, and they haue a flatte
mouth without lippes.   And in that yle are men also
that haue their faces all flat without eyen, without mouth
& without nose, but they haue their eyen and their mouth
behinde on their shoulders.   And in an other yle are
foule men that haue the lippes aboute the mouth so

greate that when they sleepe in the sonne, they cover all
theyr face with the lippe.   And in another yle are lyttle
men as dwarfes, and haue no mouth but a lyttle rounde
hole & through that hole they eate their meat with a

---

[1] Here again Pliny says in his 7th book, cap. 2 :—" These people
dwell not very far from the Troglodytæ (*dwellers in caves*) to the
west, of whom again there is a tribe who are without necks, and
have eyes in their shoulders."

pipe, & they haue no tongue & they speake not but they blow & whistle and so make signes one to another. And in another yle are men with hanging eares unto their shoulders.[1] And in another yle are wild men with hanging eares & haue feete lyke an hors & they run faste & they take wild beastes and eate them. And in another yle are men that go on theyr handes & feete lyke beasts & are all rough and will leape upon a tree like cattes or apes. And in an other yle are men that go euer uppon theyr knees mervaylosly, and haue on euery foote viii Toes.[2] Many other maner of folke bee in the sea in yles thereabout, of whome it were to longe to tell all.

CAP. LXIII.

Of the Kingedome named Mancy which is the best kinge-dome of the worlde.

TO go from this yle toward the east many journies a man shall finde a kingdome that is called Mancy[3] & this is in Inde the more, & it is ye most delectable and plenty of goods of all the worlde. In this lande dwell christen men and Sarasins, for it is a great lande, and therein are II M great cities & many other townes. In this lande no man goeth a begging, for there is no

---

[1] See Appendix.

[2] Here a paragraph is omitted, not being suitable for general readers.

[3] Or Manzi, that part of China south of the river Hoang-ho.

pore man, and there men haue beardes of heare[1] as it
were cattes.   In this lande are faire women, and therefore some men call that lande Albany, for the white
folke, and there is a citie that men call Latorim and is
more[2] than Paris, and in that land are birdes twise
greater than they be here and there is all maner of
vytayles good cheape.[3]   In this countrey are whyte
hennes, and they beare no feathers but woll[4] as shepe

doe in our lande ; and women of that countrey that are
wedded beare crownes uppon theyr heads that they may

[1] *Pynson* has " berdes *thynne* of here, as it were cattes."
[2] Larger.
[3] *Pynson* here has, " and there is plenty of great neddres (*adders*)
of whyche they make a greate fest and ete theym at great solem-
nytees.   For, if a man make a greate fest, and had gyven them all
the mete that he myght gete, and he give theym no neddres, he
hath no thanke for all that he doth."
[4] Wool.

be knowne by.   In this countrey they take a beast that
is called Loyres, and they keepe it to goe in to waters
or ryvers, and straighte waye hee bringeth out of the
water great fishes, and thus they take fishe as longe as
they will, and as them nedeth.   Fro this citie men go
by many journeys to an other citie that is called Cassay,[1]
that is the fayrest citie of the worlde, and that citie is
fifty myle about and there is in that citie mo than xii[2]
principall gates without.   From thence within three myle
is an other great citie, and within this citie are more
than xii thousand bridges and upon eche bridge is a
stronge toure where the kepers dwell to kepe it against
the great Caane, for it marcheth[3] on his land.   And on
one side of the citie runneth a great river, and there
dwell christen men & other for it is a good countrey and
plentious, & there groweth right good wine.   In this
noble citie the King of Mancy was wont to dwell and
there dwell religious men, as fryers.   And men go vpon
the river till they come to an Abbey of Monkes a lyttle
from the citie & in y' Abbey is a great gardeine, and
therein is many maner of trees of divers fruites, in that
gardein are divers kindes of beastes, as Baboyns,[4] Apes,
Marmosets and other, & when the covent[5] haue eaten, a
monke taketh the reliefe[6] & beareth it into the gardein,
& smiteth once with a bell of silver which he holdeth in
his hand, anone come out these beastes that I speake of
and many nere II or III thousand,[7] and he giveth them

[1] Hangchow-fu.
[2] *Pynson* says, " There is in y' citie mo than VII thousand gates
and each of III gate is a good toure where the kepers dwell," &c.
[3] Borders.   [4] Baboons.   [5] Convent.
[6] What is left over.
[7] *Pynson* says III Thousand or IIII Thousand.

to eate of[1] faire vessels of silver, & when they haue
eaten he smyteth the bell againe and they go away, and
the monke sayth that those beasts are soules of men
that are dead, and those beastes that are fayre are soules
of Lordes and other rich men, & those that are foule
beastes are soules of other commons, and I asked them
if it had not been better to give that relife to pore men,
& they sayde there is no pore men in ye countrey and if
there were yet were it more almes to give it to those
soules y^t suffer there their penaunce & may go no farther
to get their meat, than to men that haue wit & may
travail for theyr meat.   Then come men to a citie y^t is
called Chibens & there was the first sege[2] of the King
of Mancy.   In this citie are LX brydges of stone as
fayre as they may be.

CAP. LXIIII.

*Of the lande of Pygmen,[3] wherein dwell but smal people of
three spanne long.*

WHEN men passe from that citie of Chibens, they
passe over a great river of freshe water, and it
is nere IIII mile brode & then men enter into the lande
of the great Caan.   This river goeth through the land
of Pigmeens, and there men are of little stature for they

---

[1] Off.   [2] Seat or settlement.

[3] Pigmies, dwarfs.   Homer, in the third book of the Iliad, has
immortalized the Pigmies and their battles with the Cranes.   (See
Appendix for a curious engraving.)   Pliny, in his 7th Book, cap. 2,
speaks thus of them : " Beyond these people, and at the very ex-

are but three span long, and they are right fayre bothe
men and women, though they bee little, and they are
wedded when they are halfe a yere olde, and they live
but viii[1] yeare, and he that liveth viii yeare is holden
right olde, and these small men are the best workemen
in sylke and of cotton in all maner of thing that are in
the worlde, and these smal men travail not nor tyl land
but they haue amonge them great men, as we are, to
travaill for them & they haue great scorne of those great
men, as we would haue of giaunts or of them if they
were among us.

tremity of the mountains, the Trispithami (*from* τρεῖς, *three, and*
πιθαμί, *spans*), and the Pigmies are said to exist; two races that
are but three spans in height—that is to say, twenty-seven inches
only.   They enjoy a salubrious atmosphere and a perpetual spring,
being sheltered by the mountains from the northern blasts: it is
these people that Homer has mentioned as being waged war upon
by cranes.   It is said that they are in the habit of going down,
every spring, to the sea shore in a large body, seated on the backs
of rams and goats, and armed with arrows, and there destroy the
eggs and the young of those birds; that this expedition occupies
them for the space of three months, and that otherwise it would be
impossible for them to withstand the increasing multitudes of the
cranes.   Their cabins, it is said, are built of mud, mixed with
feathers and egg-shells.   Aristotle, indeed, says that they dwell in
caves; but, in other respects, he gives the same details as other
writers."

   [1] Other editions say six or seven years.

CAP. LXV.

Of the citie of Menke where is a great navy.

FROM this land men go through many countreys
cities & towns, till they come to a citie that men
call Menke.   In that citie is a great navy of ships and
they are as white as snow of the kind of the wod that
they are made of & they are made as it were great
houses with halles and chambres and other easements.[1]

CAP. LXVI.

Of the land named Cathay and of the great riches thereof

AND from thence men go uppon a river that men
call Ceremosan, and this river goeth throughe
Cathay[2] & doth many times harme when it waxeth
great.   Cathay is a faire countrey & rich, ful of goods
and merchandises, thether come marchauntes everye
yeare for to fetch spices and other marchandises more
commonly than they do in other countreys.   And ye
shall understand that marchaunts that come from Venice
or from Gene or from other places of Lombardy, or of
Italy, they go by sea and land, xi monthes and more or
they may come to Cathay.

---

[1] Conveniences.   [2] Northern China.

CAP. LXVII.

Of a great citie named Cadon therein is the great Caanes palaice and sege.

IN the province of Cathay towards the East, is an olde citie & beside that citie the Tartariens have made an other citie that men call Cadon,[1] y[e] hathe xii[2] gates, and betwene eche two gates is a great myle, so those two cities the olde and the new is round about xx myle.   In this citie is the palaice and sege of y[e] great Caane in a full faire place and great, of which the wals about is two myle, and within that are many fayre places, and in the gardeyne of that palaice is a right greate hill on the which is an other palaice, and it is the fayrest that may bee founde in any place, and all about that hyll are many trees berynge divers fruites, and about that hyll is a great dyche, and there nere are many rivers on eche syde, and in those are many wylde foules that he may take and not go out of the palayce.   Within y[e] hall of that palaice are xxiiii pillers of gold and all the walks are covered with rych skynnes of beastes that men call Panthera.

Those are fayre beastes and well smelling and of the smell of those skynnes, none evyll smell may come to the palayce, those skynnes are as redde as bloude, and they shine so against the Sonne that a man can scarcely

---

[1] Others call it Sugarmago or Eugarmago.
[2] *Pynson* says seven.

beholde them and those skynnes are estemed there as much as golde.

In the myddest of the palace is a place made that they call the Monture[1] for the great Caane, that is well made with precious stones and great hanging about, and at the foure corners of that Montour are foure nedders[2] of golde, & under that mountour and about are conduites of bevrage that they drink in the Emperour's courte. And the hall of that palayce is richly dight and wel, and firste at the upper ende of the hall is the throne of the Emperour right hie where he sitteth at meate (*at a*) table that is well bordered with gold and that bordure is full of precious stones and great pearles, and the greces on which he goeth up are of diverse precious stones bordred with golde.

At the left syde of his throne is the sege of his wife a degree lower than he sitteth and that is of Jasper bordred with gold and the sege of his seconde wife is a degree lower than the fyrste, and that is also of good Jasper bordred with golde and the sege of the thyrd wife is a degree lower than the seconde for alwaye he hathe three wives with him wheresoeuer he is, besyde these wives on the same side setteth other ladies of his kin eche one lower than other, as they are of degree, and all those that are wedded, haue a counterfaite[3] of a man's foote uppon their heads a cubite long and all made with precious stones, & about they are made with shining fethers of pecockes or such other in tokening that they are in subjection to man & under men's feete, & they

---

[1] This is a curious term, which can scarcely be translated. A French edition has *Mountaynette*, which *Cotgrave* says is a little mountain. A Latin edition says *Ascensorium*.

[2] Serpents.   [3] Representation.

that are not wedded haue none such.   On the right side
of the Emperour sitteth fyrste his sonne the which shall
be Emperour after him, and he sitteth also a degree
lower than the Emperour in such maner of seges as the
Emperour sitteth, and by him sitteth other lordes of his
kyn, eche one lower than other as they are of degree.
And the Emperour hath his table by himselfe alone that
is made of golde and precious stones, or of white Crystal
or yelowe, bordred with golde, and eche one of his wyves
hath a table by hirselfe.   And under the Emperours
table sitteth foure clerkes at his feete that wryteth all
that the Emperour sayth be it good or ylle.   And at
great feastes about the Emperours table, and all other
tables in the hall is a vine made of gold that goeth all
about the hall, and it hath many braunches of grapes
lyke to grapes of the vine, some are white, some are
yelowe, some red, some grene, and some blacke, all the
red are of rubies of cremes [1] or allabonce, the white are
of cristall or byrall,[2] the yelowe are of topaces, the grene
are of Emeraudes & Crysolytes, and the blacke are of
Quickes and Gerandes, & this vyne is made thus of
precious stones so properly that it seemeth that it were
a vyne growinge.   And before the borde of the Emperour standeth great lordes and no man is so hardy to
speke unto hym, except it be musicians for to solace the
Emperour.   And all the vessell that is served in his hall
or chambres, are of precious stones and namely at tables

---

[1] I have up to the present failed in finding equivalents for these
two words, also for Quickes (spelt in *Pynson* Onichez, which may
probably mean onyxes,) and Gerandes.   This latter word is spelt
in one MS. *Garantez*, and may mean garnet. Cotgrave gives
Alabandique, "a kinde of blacke stone mingled with purple."
[2] Beryl.

M

where great lordes eate, that is to say, of Jasper, crystall, amatyst, or fyne golde, and the cuppes are of
Emeraudes, saphyres, topaces, and many other maner of
stones ; and (of) silver haue they no vessell, for they
praise silver but little to make vessell of, but they make
of silver greces, pylers & paviments of halles & chambres.
And ye shall understande that my felaw & I were in
wages with him xvi moneths against the Kinge of
Mancy,[1] uppon whome he made warre, and the cause
was we had so great desire to see the nobilitye of his
his court, if it were suche as we heard speake of, and
forsoth we founde it more richer & solempne than ever
we harde speake of, and we should neuer haue beleved
it, had we not seene it. But ye shall understande the
meat and drinke is more honest among us than it is in
those countreys, for all the comons eate upon skines of
beastes on theyr knees and eate but fleshe of all maner
of beastes, & when they haue all eate they wipe theyr
handes on their skirtes & they eate but once in the day
& eate but little bread but the maner of the lordes is
full noble and richly.

[1] *Marco Polo* gives a graphic description of the invasion and
subjection of Manzi, or Southern China, in the year 1268, by
Kublai's great general *Bayan* (great or noble) *Hundred eyes.* If,
therefore, there is any truth in Mandeville, he and his "felaw"
may have helped to put down an insurrection in the kingdom of
Manzi.

CAP. LXVIII.

Wherefore that the Emperour of Cathay is called the great Caane.

AND ye shall understande why he is called y⁰ great Caane, ye knowe y⁻ all the worlde was destroied with Noes floud but Noe his wife & children.   Noe had three sons, Sem, Cham & Japhet.   Cham when he saw his father naked when he slept, scorned him & therefore he was cursed and Japhet covered him againe.   These three brethrene hadde all the land.   Cham toke the best parte eastward that is called Asia.   Sem toke Afryke and Japhet toke Europe.   Cham was the mightiest and richest of his bretherne and of him are come the Paynim folke & divers maner of men of the yles, some head-lesse, and other men disfigured, and for this Cham the Emperour there called him Cham and Lord of all.   But ye shall understande that the Emperour of Cathay is called Caane, and not Cham, & for this cause, it is not long ago that all Tartary was in subjection and thrall to other nations about, and they were made herdemen to kepe beastes, and among them was vii linages¹ or kindes, the firste was called Tartary that is the best, the second linage is called Tamghot,² the third **Furace,**³ the fourth Valaire, the fifth Semoth,⁴ the sixth Menchy,⁵ the seventh Sobeth.⁶   These are all holding of the great Caane of

¹ People or tribes.
² Tangut, or Tanghút, is the name given to certain tribes of Thibetan extraction, who lived on the north-west frontier of China.
³ ⁴ ⁵ ⁶ Called variously Eurache, Semoche, Megly and Coboghe, whose relative positions can scarcely now be defined accurately.

Cathay. Now it befell so that the first linage was an
olde man & hee was not ryche and men called him
Chanius. This man lay and slept on a nighte in his
bedde, and there came to him a knighte, all white, sitting
uppon a white hors, and sayde to him, Caane slepeste
thou? God that is almighty sent me to thee, & it is
his will that thou saye to the vii linages y' thou shalt be
theyr Emperour, for ye shall conquere all the lande about
you, and they shall be in your subjection as you have bene
in theirs. And when morow came he rose up and sayde it
to the vii linages, and they scorned him and sayde he
was a fole, and the next night the same knighte came to
the vii linages and bad them of gods behalfe to make
Chanius their Emperour, and they shold be out of all
subjection. And on the morow they chose Chanius to
be Emperour, and dyd him all worship that they might
do, & called him Caane as the white knighte called him,
and they sayde they would doe as he badde them. Then
he made many statutes and lawes, the which he called
Ysakan.[1] The firste statute was, that they shoulde be
obedient to God almyghtie, and beleve that he should
deliver them out of thraldome, and that they shoulde
call on him in all their workes. Another statute was, y'
all men that might beare armes shoulde be nombred, and
to eche x shoulde be a master, and to a hundred a master,
and to a thousand a master. Then he commaunded to
all the greatest and principallest of the vii linages, that
they should forsake all that they had in heritage or
lordship, and that they should hold them payed of that
he wold give them of his grace, and they did so. And
also he bad them y' eche man should bringe his eldest

[1] Others write it Ysya-Chan.

sonne before him, and sleay his owne sonne with his owne
handes, and smyte of their heads, and as sone they did
his bidding.   And when he saw they made no letting [1]
of what he bad them, then bad he them folow his baner,
and then he put in subjection all the landes about him.

CAP. LXIX.

*How the great Caane was hid under a tree, and so escaped
his enimies bicause of a byrd.*

AND it befell on a day that the Caane rode with a
fewe men to see the lande that he had wonne, and
he met with a greate multitude of his enimies and there
he was caste downe of his horse, and his horse slayne,
and when his men saw him at y[e] earth [2] they went [3] he
had been deade, and fledde, & the ennimies folowed after,
and when he sawe his ennimies were fer, [4] he hid him in
a bushe, for the wod was thicke there, and when they
were come againe from the chace, they went to seke
among the wood if any were hid there, and they founde
many, and as they came to the place where he was, they
saw a birde sitte uppon a tree, the which byrd men call
an Oule, and then sayd they, that there was no man, for
the birde sat there, and so went they away, and thus was
the Caane saved from death, & so he went awaye on a
night to his owne men, which were glad of his comming,
and from that time hitherwardes men of that countrey

---

[1] Hindrance.   [2] On the ground.
[3] Weened—supposed, imagined.   [4] Far away.

haue that byrde in great reverence, and for that cause
they worship that byrd aboue all other birds of the
worlde. And incontinent he assembled all his men, rode
uppon his enimies and destroyed them, and when he had
won all the landes that were aboute him, he helde them
in subjection. And when the Caane had won all the
lordes to mounte Belyan, the white knighte came to him
in a vision againe, and said unto him, Caan the will of
God is, that thou passe the mounte Belyan, and thou
shalt win many landes, and for thou shalt find no passage,
go thou to mount Belian that is upon the sea side and
knele ix times thereon against the east in the worship of
God, & he shall shew thee a way how thou shalt passe,
and Caan did so, & anon the sea that touched the hil,
withdrew him, & shewed him a faire way of ix foote
brode betwene the hill and the sea, & so he passed right
wel with al his men, & then he wan the land of Cathay
that is the best land and the greatest of all the worlde,
and for those ix knelings and the ix foote of way, Caane
and the men of Tartary have the number of ix in great
worship.

CAP. LXX.

Of the great Caanes letters and the wryting about his seale.

NOW when he had wonne the lande of Cathay he
dyed, and then raigned after Cythoco [1] the eldest

---

[1] In other editions Ecchecha. In reality, Ok-lar-Khan, who
succeeded his father in 1229, and reigned over the Tartars till 1241.

sonne of Caane, & his other brothers went to winne them landes in other countreys, and they wan the land of Pruisse, and of Russy & they dyd cal themselfe Caane, but he of Cathay is the greatest lorde of all the worlde and so he called him in his letters and sayth thus, *Caane filius dei excelsi, universam terram coulentium summus imperator, & dominus dominantium* That is to say, Caane Gods son, Emperour of all those that tyll all the lande, and Lorde of all lordes. And the writing about his great seale is, *Deus in celo & Caane super terram ejus fortitudo omnium hominum imperatoris sigillum* That is to say, God in heaven, Caan uppon earth, his strength the seale of the Emperor of all men. And the wryting about his privy seale is, *Dei fortitudo omnium hominum imperatoris sigillum* That is to say, The strength of God, seale of the Emperour of all men. And if it be so that they be not christen, yet the Emperour and the Tartarins beleve in God Almightie.

CAP. LXXI.

Of the governaunce of the countrey of the great Caane.

NOW haue I tolde you why he is called the great Caane, now shall I tell you of the governinge of his courte when they make great feastes, and he kepeth foure principall feastes in the yeare, the fyrste of his byrth, the seconde when he is borne to the Temple to be circumcised, the third is of his ydoles when they begin to speake, and the fourth when the ydole beginneth fyrst to do myracles, & at those tymes he hath men well

arayed by thousands and by hundreds and eche one
wote well what he shal do.   For there is fyrst ordeined
4000 rich barons and mighty for to ordeine the feast &
to serve the Emperour & all these barons haue crowns
of gold well dight with precious stones and pearles,
and they are clad in clothes of golde & camathas [1] as
richly as they may bee made & they may well have
suche clothes for they are there of lesse pryce than
wollen cloth is here.   And these foure thousande barons
are departed in foure parties, & eche company is clad in
diverse colour ryght richely, and when the first thousand
is passed and hath shewed them, then come the seconde
thousande, and then the thirde thousande & then the
fourth, and none of them speketh a word.   And on the
one side of the Emperours table sitteth many phylo-
sophers of many sciences, some of Astronomie, Nygro-
mancie [2] Geometry, Pyromacy,[3] & many other sciences,
and some haue before them Astrolabes [4] of golde or of
precious stones full of sande or of coles brenning, some
haue horologes [5] well dight and richly, and many other
instruments after their sciences.   And at a certaine
houre when they see time, they say to men that stand
before them, make peace, and then saye those men with
a loude voyce to all the hall, now be styll awhile, and
then saith one of the philosophers, eche man make
reverence and encline to the Emperour, that is Gods
sonne, and lorde of the worlde, for now is time and
houre, and then all men enclyne to him, and knele on

[1] A rich silken or thread stuff.
[2] Necromancy, or foretelling events by pretended communion
with the dead.
[3] Divination by fire.   [4] An astronomical instrument.
[5] Timepieces.

the earth, and then the Phylosopher biddeth them rise
up againe. And at another houre another philosopher
biddeth them put their fingers in theyr eares and they
do so, and at another houre another philosopher biddeth
that all men shall laye their hande on their heads, and
they do so, and then he biddeth them take them away and
they doe so, and thus from houre to houre they bid divers
thinges. And I asked privily what it shoulde meane and
one of the masters said that the enclining and the
kneling on the earth at that time hath this token, that
all those men that kneled so shall evermore be true to
the Emperour, that for no gift nor thretning they shal
never be traitours nor false to him and the putting of
the finger in the eare hath this token, that none of those
shall here any yll spoken of the Emperour or his coun-
sayll. And ye shall understande that men dight nothing,
as clothes, bread, drinke nor no such things to the
Emperour but at certaine hours that the Philosophers
tell, and if any man reyse war against the Emperour in
what countrey so ever it bee these Philosophers know it
sone, & tell ye Emperour or his counsail and he sendeth
men thether, for he hath many men.   Also he hath many
men that kepeth birdes, as gerfaukons[1] sperhaukes,[2]
faucons,[3] gentils,[4] lavers, sacres,[5] popyniayes[6] that can
speake, and many other, ten thousande olyphants,
baboynes marmosets and other and he hath ever aboute
him many Physicions more than two hundred that are
Christen men & xx sarasyns, but yet he trusteth more
to Christen men than in Sarasyns.   And there is in that
countrey many Sarasins and other Servaunts that are

[1] Girfalcons.   [2] Sparrowhawks.   [3] Falcons.
[4] Gentles.   [5] Sakers or Peregrine hawks.
[6] Parrots.

Christen and converted to the faith, through preching of good Christen men that dwel there, but there are many that will not that men [1] wete that they are Christen.

CAP. LXXII.

Of the great ryches of the Emperour and of his dispending.

THIS Emperour is a great lorde, for he may dispend what he will without nombre, bicause he spendeth nother sylver nor golde & maketh no money but of lether or skynnes, and this same money goeth through all his lande, and of the sylver & gold buylded he his palaces.   And he hath in his chambre a piller of golde in the which is a Ruby, and carbuncle of a foote [2] long, the which lighteth all his chambre by night & he hath many other precious stones & rubies, but this is the most.[3]   This Emperour dwelleth in the sommer towardes the North in a citie that men call Saydus and there it is colde enoughe, and in the winter he dwelleth in a citie that men call Camalach, and there it is right hot, but for the most part is he at Cadon, that is not farre thence.

---

[1] Will not let men know.

[2] Others say half a foot.   There were always rumours in the East of wonderful rubies, especially one belonging to the King of Ceylon, which Kublai Khan is reported to have coveted, and wished to purchase.

[3] The greatest.

CAP. LXXIII.

Of the ordynaunce of the lordes of the Emperour when he rideth from one countrey to another to warre.

AND when this great Caane shall ryde from one countrey to another they ordeyne foure hostes of people, of which the fyrst goeth before a daies journey; for that hoste lyeth at even where the Emperour shall lye on the morow, and there is plenty of vitailes. And another host commeth at the right side of hym and an other at the left side, and in eche hoste is muche folke. And then commeth the fourth hoste behind hym a bowe draught, and there is more men in that than in any of the other. And ye shall understande that the Emperour rideth on no horse, but when hee will go to any seacrete place with a privy meyny[1] where he will not be knowne, but he rideth in a chariot with four wheles & there uppon is a chamber made of a tree that men call *Lignum aloes* that commeth out of Paradise terrestre, & that chamber is covered with plates of fyne gold, and precious stones and perles, and foure Olyfants & foure Oxen all white go therein, and five or sixe great lordes ride about him, so that none other men shal come nigh him, except the Emperour call any, and in the same manner with a chariot & such hostes rideth the Empres by another side, and the Emperours eldest sonne in that same aray, and they haue so much people that it is a great marvaile for to see.

[1] Private retinue.

CAP. LXXIIII.

How the empyre of the great Caane is departed[1] into xii provinces & how that they do cast ensence in the fyre where the great Caane passeth through the cities & townes in worship of the Emperour.

THE land of the great Caane is departed in xii provinces, and euery province hath more than two thousande cities and townes. And when the Emperour rideth through the countrey, & he passeth through cities & townes, eche man maketh a fyre before his house, & caste therein ensence & other things that giue good smell to the Emperour. And if any man of relygion that are Christen men dwel nere as the Emperour cometh they mete him with procession, with crosse and holye water, and they singe, *Veni creator spiritus* with a loude voyce, and when he seeth them comming he commaundeth the lordes that they ride nere to him to make way that the religious men may come to him, and when he seeth the crosse, he doeth[2] of his hat that is made of precious stones and greate perles, & that hat is so riche that it is marvaile to tel, and then he enclineth to the crosse, & the prelate of the religious men sayth orisons before him and giveth him the benison[3] with the crosse, and he enclineth to the benison ful devoutly, and then the prelate giveth him some fruite to the number of ix in a platter of gold,[4] peares or apples or other fruite, &

---

[1] Partitioned.   [2] Taketh off.   [3] Blessing.
[4] Others say silver.

then the Emperour taketh one thereof and the other he
giueth to his lordes, for the maner is such there, that no
strange man shall come before the Emperour but he
giue him somewhat, after the olde law that sayth, *Non
accedat in conspectu meo manis* [1]   That is to say, No man
come into my sight idle.   And then ye Emperour biddeth these religious men that they shall goe forth, so
that the men of his hoste defyle them not, and those
relygious men that dwell where the Empresse or the
Emperours sonne cometh, they do in the same maner.

CAP. LXXV.

How the great Caan is the mightiest lord of all the worlde.

THIS great Caane is the myghtiest lorde of the
worlde, for prester [2] John is not so great a lorde as
he, nor the Sowdan of Babilon, ne ye Emperour of Percy.
In this lande a man hath a hundred wiues & some xi, [3]
some more some lesse, & they take of their kin to wiues,
all saue their sisters, their mothers & daughters and they
take also wel theyr stepmother if their father be dead,
and men & women haue all one maner of clothing, so
that they may not bee knowne, but y^t women that are

---

[1] Misprint for *vacuus*, empty-handed.

[2] In the 12th and 13th centuries there was a firm belief that
ruling over a vast population in the far East was a most wealthy
and powerful monarch of that name, who claimed to be descended
from one of the three kings who adored the infant Christ.

[3] Others say 60.

wedded beare a token on theyr heads, & they dwell not
with their housbandes, but he may lye by which he will.
They have plenty of all maner of beastes save swine,
and forsoth they wyll (*have*) none, and they beleve well
in God that made all thing, & yet have they ydoles of
golde and sylver, and to those Idols they offer theyr fyrst
mylke of beastes.

CAP. LXXVI.

Of other maners of this countrey.

THIS Emperour the great Caane hath three wives,
and the principall wife was Prester Johns daughter.
And the people of this countrey begin to doe all theyr
thinges in the newe Moone, and they worshippe muche
the Sonne and the Moone, those men ryde commonly
without spoores, & they holde it a great sinne to breake
one bone [1] with another, and to spyll mylke on the
grounde, or any other lycour y' men may drinke.[2]   And
when they haue eaten they wipe their handes uppon
theyr skyrts, for they haue no table clothes except it be
right great lordes, and when they haue all eaten they
put their dishes or platters not washed in the pot or
cauldron with flesh that is left when they haue eaten,
until they will eate another time, & rich men drink milke
of mares, of asses, or other beastes, and other beverage that
is made of milke and water togither, for they haue neither
beere nor wine.   And when they go to warre, they warre
full wysely, and eche man of them bereth two or three

---

[1] A bone.   [2] A passage is here omitted.

bowes and many arowes and a great hatchet, gentilmen
haue short swords,[1] and he that flyeth in batayle they
sleay him, & they are ever in purpose to bring all the
land in subjection to them, for they say prophecies say
that they shall be overcome by shot of archers, and that
they shall turne them to their law, but they wot not
what men they shall be, and it is great peril to pursue
the Tartaries when they flee, for they will shoot behinde
and slea men as well as before, and they have small
eyen[2] as little birdes, and they are commonly false for
they holde not their promise.   And when a man shal
die among them, they stick a speare in the earth beside
him, and when he draweth to the death, they go out of
the house till he dead, and then they put him in the
earth in the fielde.

CAP. LXXVII.

How the Emperour is brought unto his grave when he is
dead.

AND when the Emperour is dead, they set him into
a carte[3] in the middes of his tente, and they set
before him a table covered with a cloth, & there upon
they set flesh and other meat & a cup full of milke of a
mare, and they set a mare with a colte by him, & a
horse sadled & bridled, and they lay upon the horse
golde & silver, and all about him they make a greate
grave, and with all the things they put him therein, as

---

[1] Other editions say spears.   [2] Eyes.
[3] Other editions say a chair.

the tente, hors, golde & silver, and all that is aboute him
& they say, when he cometh in to another worlde he
shall not be without an house, nor hors, ne silver nor
gold, and the mare shall give him milke & bringe forth
more horses till he be well stored in the other worlde, &
one of his chamberlaines or servants is put with him in
the earth for to doe him service in the other worlde, for
they belieue that when hee is dead he shall go to another
world, and be a greater lord there than here ; & when
that he is laid in the earth no man shal be so hardy [1] for
to speake of him before his frendes.

CAP. LXXVIII.

When the Emperour is dead how they chose and make an other.

AND then when the Emperour is dead the seauen
linages gather them togither, and they touch his
son or the next of his blood, & they say thus, We wyll,
and we ordeyne, and we pray thee that thou wilt be our
lord & Emperour, and he enquireth of them and sayth,
if ye will that I raigne upon you, then must ye doe all
that I bidde you to doe. And if he bid that any shal
be slaine, he shal be slaine, & they aunswere all with one
voyce, y[t] ye bid shall be done. Then saith ye Emperour,
fro henceforth, my word shal cut as my sword, and then
they set him in a chaire, & crowne him, & then all the
good townes thereabout send to him presents, so much

---

[1] *I.e.*, his name is never mentioned.

that he shall haue more than a C Camelles [1] laden with
gold and silver, beside other Jewels y[t] he shall haue of
lords, of precious stones & gold without number &
horse, & riche clothes of Camacas [2] and Tarins,[3] & such
other.

CAP. LXXIX.

*What countreys and kingdomes lye next to the land of
Cathay and the frontes thereof.*

THIS lande of Cathay is in Asia the depe,[4] and this
same lande marcheth toward the west upon the
kingdome of Sercy,[5] the which was sometyme to one of
the three kings that went to seke our Lord in Bethlem
and all those that come of his kin are christen men.
These men of Tartary drinke no wine. In y[e] land of
Corosaym,[6] y[t] is at the north side of Cathay is right
great plenty of goods, but no wine, the which hath at
the east side a great wildernesse, that lasteth more than
an hundred journeys, and the best citie of that land is
called Corasaym, & after the name of that citie is the
lande called after, and men of this lande are good war-
riors and hardy, and thereby is the Kingedome of
Comayne, this is the most & the greatest kingedome of
the world, but it is not all inhabited, for in one place of the

[1] Other editions say 60 chariots.
[2] See footnote, *ante*, p. 168.
[3] Tartarins, a kind of silken fabric.   [4] Lower Asia.
[5] Others write it Tharse.   [6] ? Khorassan.

lande is so great cold, that no man may dwel ther for colde, and in an other place is so great heat, that no man may dwell there, & there are so many faithes[1] that a man wot not on what side hee may turne him, & in this lande are fewe trees bering fruite. In thys lande men ly in tentes, and they burne donge[2] of beastes for defaut of wood. This lande descendeth toward Pruse & Rossy & through this land runneth the river Echell,[3] that is one of the greatest rivers in ye world & it is frosen so hard euery yeare that men fight thereupon in great battayles on horse and footemen more than a C.M[4] at once. And a lyttle from ye river is the great sea of Occyan, that they cal Maure[5] and betwene this Maure & Caspy[6] is a full straight passage to go towarde Inde and therefore King Alexander did make there a citie y^t men call Alexander, for to kepe that passage, so that no man may passe but if he haue leave, & now is that citie called Port de fear,[7] and the principall citie of Comayne is called Sarachis,[8] this is one of the thre ways to go to Inde, but through this way may not many men go but if it be in winter, & this passage is called Berbent.[9] And another way is to go from ye land of Turkescon[10] through

---

[1] A misprint for flies.

[2] The usual fuel in an unwooded Asiatic country.

[3] Volga.   [4] Others say 200,000.   [5] The Black Sea.

[6] The Caspian Sea.

[7] Port de Fer, or Iron Gate. Other editions have it "Gate of Hell."

[8] Sarai, or Sara, on the Volga. Chaucer, in "Cambuscan," speaks of it thus :—

> " At *Sarra* in the Londe of Tartarie
> There dwelt a King that werrièd Russie."

[9] The Pass of Derbend, still called in Turkish *Demir Kapi*, or the Iron Gate.   [10] Turkestan.

Percy, & in this way are many journeys in wildernesse.
And ye third way is that cometh from Cosmane & goeth
through ye great citie & through ye Kingedome of
Abachare.[1]   And ye shall understand y^t all these kingedomes & lords unto Percy are holden of ye great Caan
& many other & therefore he is a great lorde of men &
of lande.

CAP. LXXX.

*Of other wayes comming from Cathay toward the Grekes
sea & also of the emperour of Percy.*

NOW I haue devysed you the landes towardes the
North, to come from the lands of Cathay to the
lands of Pruse & Rossy where Christen men dwel.
Now shall I devise unto you other lands & kingdoms, in comming down from Cathay to the Grekes
sea wher Christen men dwell, and for as muche as
next the great Caane of Cathay the Emperour of
Percy is the greatest lorde, therefore I shall speake
of him, & ye shall understande that he hath two kingdomes, the one beginneth eastward and it is the kingdome of Turkescon & it lasteth westward to the sea of
Caspy & southward to the lande of Inde.   This lande
is good & playne and well manned,[2] with good cities but
two most principal, ye which are called Bacirida &
Sormagaunt.[3]   The other is the kingedome of Percy, and
lasteth from the river of Phison[4] unto great Armony,[5] &

---

[1] Variously written Abcaz or Abkhas.   [2] Peopled.
[3] Bokhara and Samarcand.   [4] Pison.   [5] Armenia

northward unto the sea of Caspy & southward to the land of Inde & this is a full plenteous countrey and good. In this lande are three principall cities Nessabor, Saphan, & Sermesse.[1]

CAP. LXXXI.

Of the lande of Armony, which is a good land & of the lande of Middy.[2]

THEN is the lande of Armony, in the which was sometime three kingdomes, this is a good land and a plentious, & it beginneth at Percy, & lasteth westward to Turkey of length, and in breadth lasteth from the citie of Alexander (that is now called Port de fear) unto the lande of Myddy.   In this Armony are many fayre cities, but Cauryssy[3] is most of name.   Then is the land of Myddy, and it is full long and not brode & beginneth eastward at the land of Percy, & Inde the lesse, and lasteth westward to the kingdome of Calde,[4] & northward to little Armony.   In this Myddy are many great hyls, & little (of) plaines & ther dwel Sarasins & other maner of men, that men call Cordines.[5]

[1] Otherwise spelt Messabor, Caphon, and Sarmassane.
[2] Media.
[3] Other editions have it Taurizo—in all probability the modern *Tabriz* is meant.
[4] Chaldæa.   [5] Kurds.

CAP. LXXXII.

Of the Kingdome of George & Abcan, and many marvayles.

THEN next is the kingdome of George,[1] that beginneth eastward at a great hil that men call Abiorz,[2]
this land lasteth to Turkey to the great sea, & to the
land of Myddy, and great Armony & in this land are
two kynges, one of Abcan, and another of George but
he of George is in subjection of the great Caane, but he
of Abcan hath a strong countrey, and defendeth him
well against his enimies, & in this land of Abcan is
a great marvaile, for there is a countrey in this land that
is nere III dayes long and about, & is called Hanison,
and that countrey is all covered with darknesse, so that
it hath no light that no man may see there, and no man
dare go into that countrey for darkenes.   And neverthelesse men of that countrey thereby say that they may
sometime heare therein the voyce of man and horse
crying, and cocks crow, and they know wel that men
dwel there, but they know not what maner of men, and
they saye this darknesse came through miracle of God
that he dyd for Christen men there.   For there was a
wicked Emperour y[t] was of Poy[3] & was called Saures,
& he pursued sometime all Christen men to destroy them,

---

[1] Georgia.
[2] Probably Mount Elburz, one of the Caucasian range.
[3] Misprint for Persia.

and did make them do sacrifice to their false gods, & in
that countrey dwelled many Christen men ye which left
al their goods & catel, and riches, and wold go to Grece,
and when they were all in a great plain y^t is called
Megon the Emperour and his men came to sley the
Christen men, & then the christen men kneled down &
prayed to God, and anon came a thick cloude and covered
the Emperour and al his host, so that he might not go
away, and so dweled they in darkness, and they neuer
came out after, and ye Christen men went there as they
would, and therefore they might say thus, *A domino
factum est istud, & est mirabile in oculis nostris*, that is to
say, of our Lord is this done, & it is wonderful in our
eyes.   Out of this lande cometh a river y^t men may se
by good tokens y^t men dwel therein.

CAP. LXXXIII.

*Of the land of the land of Turky & divers other countreys
and of the land of Mesopotamy.*

THEN next is the land of Turky, that marcheth to
Great Armony and therein are many countreys as
Capadoce, Saure,[1] Bryke Quecion, Patan & Genethe, in
eche one of the countreys are many good cities, and it
is a plaine land, & few hills and few rivers, and then is
the kingdome of Mesopotamy that beginneth eastwarde
at flom of Tygre[2] at a citie that men call Mosell,[3] and
it lasteth westwarde to the flom of Euphraten, to a citie

[1] Otherwise written Brique, Quesiton, Pytan, and Cemethe.
[2] The river Tigris.   [3] Mosul.

that men call Rochaym [1] & westwarde from high Armony
unto the wildernesse of Inde the lesse, and it is a good
land and playne, but there is few rivers, and there is but
two hils in that lande, the one is called Simar, and the
other Lison, & it marcheth unto the lande of Caldee,
and ye shall understande that the land of Ethyope
marcheth eastward to the great wildernesse westwarde
to the land of Nuby,[2] southwarde to the lande of
Maratan [3] and northward to the redde sea & then is the
Maritan that lasteth from the hilles of Ethiope unto
Liby,[4] the high, and the low that lasteth to the great sea
of Spayne.[5]

CAP. LXXXIIII.

*Of divers countreys kingedomes & yles, and marvayles
beyond the land of Cathay.*

NOW haue I sayd and spoken of many things on
this side of the great Kingedome of Cathay, of
whome many are obeysant [6] to the great Caane. Now
shall I tell of some landes, countreys & yles that
are beyond the lande of Cathay. Whoso goeth from
Cathay to Inde the high and the low, he shal go through
a kingdome that men call Cadissen [7] & it is a great lande,
there groweth a maner of fruite as it were gourdes, &
when it is ripe men cut it a sonder, and men fynde

---

[1] Otherwise Roiantz.   [2] Nubia.   [3] Mauritania.
[4] Lybia.   [5] The Mediterranean.
[6] Obedient, or under the rule of.
[7] Other editions say Caldithe.

therein a beast as it were of fleshe and bone and bloud,
as it were a lyttle lambe without wolle, and men eate
the beast & fruite also, and sure it semeth very strange.
Neverthelesse I sayd to them that I held y^t for no marvayle, for I sayd that in my countrey are trees y^t beare
fruit y^t become byrds flying, and they are good to eate,
& that that falleth on the water liveth & that that falleth
on earth dyeth, & they marvailed much thereat.   In
this countrey & many other thereabout are trees that
beareth cloves, & nutmigs and canel [1] and many other
spyces, & there be vines that beare so great grapes that
a strong man shall enough to beare a cluster of grapes.
In that same lande are the hils of Caspy that men cal
Uber & amonge those hilles are the Jewes of the x

kindes [2] enclosed therein, that men call Gog & Magog &
they may not come out on no syde. There were inclosed

[1] Cinnamon.   [2] Tribes.

xxii kynges with theyr folke that dwelled betwene y^e
hills of Syche,[1] and King Alexander chased them thither
among those hilles, for hee trusting for to haue enclosed
them there through the working of men, but he might
not, and when he saw he might not, he prayed to God
that he woulde fulfyll that which hee had begun. God
heard his prayer and enclosed the hilles all about them
but[2] at the one side, and there is the sea of Caspy.
Here some men mighte aske, there is a sea on one side,
why go they not out there, for thereto aunswered I that
all if it be called a sea, it is not a sea, but a stange[3]
standing among hyls, and it is the greatest stange of all
the world, and all if they went over the sea, they wot
not wher to arive, for they can no speach[4] but their own.
And ye shall understand that the Jewes haue no law[5] of
their owne in all the world, but they dwell in those hils,
and yet they pay tribute for their land to the quene of
Armony[6] & sometime it is so that some of the Jewes
go over the hils but many men may not passe there
togither, for the hils are so great and high. Neverthelesse men say in that countrey therby, that in the time
of Antechrist they shall doe much harme to Christen
men and therefore all the Jewes that dwell in diverse
partes of the worlde lerne for to speake Ebrew, for they
hope that the Jewes that dwel among the hils aforesayde,
shall come out of the hils and speake all Ebrew and
nought else, & then shall these Jewes speake Ebrew to
them and lede them into Christendome for to destroye
Christen men. For these Jewes say they know by their

[1] Scythia.   [2] Except.   [3] Lake or pool.
[4] Can only speak their own language.
[5] Misprint for *land*.
[6] Other editions say Amazony.

prophecies that those Jewes y^t are among those hils of
Caspy shall come out, and Christen men shall be in their
subjection, as they bee under christen men. And if ye
wyll know how they shall finde the passage out, as I
have understand I shall tell you. In the time of Ante-
christe a foxe shall make his denne in the same place
wher King Alexander dyd make the gates & he shall
dyg in the earth so long til he pearce it through and
come among the Jewes, and when they see the Foxe,
they shall haue great marvaile[1] of him, for they saw
neuer such a beast, for other beastes have they among
them many, and they shall chase this foxe and pursue
him until y^t he be fled againe to his hole that he came
from, & then shall they dig after him untill they come to
ye gates y^t Alexander did make of great stones well
dight[2] with siment, then shall they brake these gates,
and they shall find the issue.

CAP. LXXXV.

Of the land of Bactry, and of many Griffons and other beastes.

FROM this land men shal go unto the land of Bactry,[3]
where are many wicked men & fell,[4] in that land
are trees that beare wol,[5] as it were shepe, of which they
make cloth. In this land are ypotains[6] that dwel sometime on land, sometime on water, and are halfe a man

[1] Be astonished at him.   [2] Well cemented.
[3] Bactria.   [4] Crafty.
[5] Wool.   [6] Hippopotamuses.

and halfe a horse, and they eate not but men, when they
may get them.   In this land are many gryffons, more
than in other places, and some say they haue the body
before as an Egle, and behinde as a Lyon, and it is
trouth, for they be made so ; but the Griffen hath a body
greater than viii Lyons and stall worthier [1] than a hundred Egles.   For certainly he wyl beare to his nest
flying, a horse and a man upon his back, or two Oxen
yoked togither as they go at plowgh, for he hath longe
nayles on hys fete, as great as it were hornes of Oxen,[2]
and of those they make cups there to drynke of, and of
his rybes [3] they make bowes to shoote with.

CAP. LXXXVI.

*Of the way for to go to prester Johns land which is
Emperour of Inde.*

FROM this lande of Bactry men goe many dayes
Jorneyes to the lande of Prester John, that is a
great Emperour of Inde, and men call his lande the yle
of Pantoroze.[4]   This Emperour Prester John holdeth

[1] Stouter, braver.

[2] The editor of the edition of 1827 says, in a footnote, p. 325:
" One 4 foot long, in the Cotton Library, has a Silver Hoop about
the end, whereon on is engraven *Griphi Unguis, Divo Cuthberto
Dunelmensi sacer.*   Another, about an Ell long, is mentioned by
Dr. Greis, in his History of the Rarities of the Royal Society, p.
26 ; tho' the Doctor there supposes it rather the horn of a Rock
Buck, or of the *Ibex mas.*"   Such was science a little over fifty
years since !

[3] Ribs.   [4] Other editions say Pentexoire.

great land, & many good cities, and good townes, in his
kingedome is many great yles & large for this land of
Ynde is departed in yles because of great flods that
come out of Paradise, and also in the sea are many great
yles, the best citie that is in the yle of Pantoroze is called
Nile,[1] that is a noble citie & a rich.   Prester John hath
under him many kings and many diverse people, and
his land is good & rych, but not so rich as the land of
the great Caane, for marchaunts come not so much
thyther as they do unto the lande of the greate Caane,
for it is so long a journey.   And also they finde in the
yle of Cathay all thing that they haue nede of, as spy-
cery, clothes of gold, and other riches, and all if they
might haue better cheape in the lande of Prester John
than in the land of Cathay, and more finer, neverthelesse they would let[2] it, for the long waye and great
perils on the sea, for there are many places in the sea
where are many roches of a stone that is called Adamand, the which of its own kinde, draweth to him all
maner of yron, & therefore there may no ships that hath
yron nayles passe, but it draweth them to him, and
therefore they dare not go into that countrey with ships
for dread of the Adamand.   I went once into that sea
& sawe along as it had bene a great yle of trees, stockes
& braunches growinge, and the shipmen told me that
those were of great shippes that abode there, through
the vertue of the Adamandes and of things that were
in the ships, whereof those trees sprong and waxed.
And such roches are there many in diverse places of
that sea & therefore dare there no shypman passe that
waye.   And another thing also that they dread the

---

[1] Nyse in other copies.   [2] Would not go that.

long way, and therefore they go moste to Cathay, and
that is nerer unto them.   And yet it is not so nere, but
then behoveth [1] for Venice or Gene be in ye sea toward
Cathay xi or xii moneths.   The land of Prester John is
long, & marchaunts passe thither through the lande of
Persy, and come unto a citie that men cal Hermes,[2] for
a Philosopher that was called Hermes founded it, and
they passe an arme of the sea, & come to another citie
that men call Saboth,[3] & there fynde they all marchaundises, & popiniayes, as great plentie as larkes [4] in
our countrey.   In this countrey is little wheat or barly,
and therefore they eate ryce mylk and chese, & other
fruits.   This Emperour Prester John weddeth commonly
the daughter of the greate Caane, and the great Caane
his daughter.   In the land of Prester John is many
divers things, and many precious stones so great & so
large that they make of them vessels, platters, and
cuppes, and many other things of which it were to long
to tell, but somewhat of his law and of his faith I shall
tell you.

[1] This must be a misprint, and the text must read that travellers
from Venice or Genoa to Cathay must make a voyage lasting 11 or
12 months.

[2] Ormuz.   [3] Other editions say Colbache.

[4] Others say *geese*.

CAP. LXXXVII.

*Of the faith and belyfe of Prester John, but he hath not
all the full beliefe as we haue.*

THIS Emperour prester John is christen & a great
part of his lande also, but they haue not all the
articles of our fayth, but they beleve well in the Father,
the Sonne, & the Holy Ghost, & they are full devout
and true to one another, & they make no force of Catal,[1]
and he hath under him Lxxii provinces and countries,
and in eche one is a king, & those kings haue other
kinges under them.   And in this lande are many marvailes, for in that lande is the gravely sea, that is of
sande and gravaile and no drop of water, and ebbeth
and floweth with righte great waves as another sea doth,
and it is never standing still, nor never in rest, and no
man may passe that land beyond it   And al if it so be
that there bee no water in the sea, yet men may finde
therein right good fishe, and of other fashion & shape
than is in any other seas, and also they are of full good
savour & swete, and good to eat.   And three jorneys
from that sea are many greate hills, through which runneth a great floud that cometh from Paradise, and it is
full of precious stones, and no drop of water, and it runneth with great waves into the gravely sea.   And this
floud runneth three dayes in the weke so fast, & stirreth
great stones of the roches with him that make muche

----

[1] They care not for property.

noise, and as sone as they come into the gravely sea,
they are no more sene, and in those three dayes when it
runneth thus, no man dare come in it, but the other
dayes men go therein where they will. And also beyond
that floud towards that wildernesse is a great plaine all
sandy and gravely among hills, & in that plain grow
trees that at the rising of the Son ech day begin to
grow, and so grow they to midday, and beare fruit, but
no man dare eate of that fruite, for it is a maner of
yron,[1] and after myddaye it turneth againe to the earth,
so that when the Sonne goeth downe it is nothinge seene,
and so doeth it every day. And there is in y^t wildernesse many wild men with horns on their heads righte
hidious, and they speke not but rout[2] as swine & in y^t
countrey are many popiniayes, y^t they call in theyr language (pistak) & they speke through their own kind as
a part as a man, & those that speake well haue long
tonges and large & on every fote five toes, but there are
som that haue but three toes but those speake nought
and very ill.

CAP. LXXXVIII.

Of an other ylande where also dwelleth good people therein,
and is called Sinople.

THEN is there an other yland that is called Synople,
wherein also are good people and true, & full of
good faith, & they are much lyke in their living to y^r

---

[1] In other editions it is "for it is a thing of Fayrye," or Magic.
[2] Root like hogs.

men before sayd, and they go all naked.   Into that
Iland came King Alexander, & when he saw their good
faith and trouth, and theyr good belefe, he said that he
wold do them no harme and bad them aske of him
riches and nought[1] else, and they shoulde haue it.   And
they aunswered, that they had richesse ynough, when
they had meat & drinke to sustaine their bodies, & they
sayde also that richesse of this world is nought worth,
but if it were so that he might graunt them that they
should never dye, that would they pray him.   And
Alexander said that might he not do, for he was mortal
and shold die as they shold.   Then sayd they, why
art ye so proude & woldest win all the world, and
haue it in thy subjection as it were a god & hast no
terme[2] of thy life, & thou will haue all riches of y^e
world, the which shall forsake thee or thou forsake it, &
thou shalt beare nothing with thee, but it shal dwel to
other, but as thou were borne naked, so shalt thou bee
done in earth.   And Alexander was greatly astonied of
this aunswere, & if it be so that they haue not the
articles of our faithe, neverthelesse I beleve that God
loveth their service to gree,[3] as he did of Job that was a
Paynim, the which he held for his true servant and many
other.   I beeleve well that God loveth al those that love
him and serve him mekely and truely, and that despise
the vaine glory of the world as these men doe, and as
Job did, and therefore saide our Lorde through the
mouth of the holy prophet Isay,[4] *Ponam eis multiplices
Leges meas*, That is to say, I will put my laws to them
in many maners, & the gospell saith thus, *Alias oves*

---

[1] Misprint for *aught*, anything.   [2] End, termination.
[3] Pleasure, " please Him."   [4] Others say Hosea.

habeo, que non sunt ex hoc ovili, That is to say I haue
other shepe that are not of this folde, and thereto
accordeth the vision that saint Peter saw at Jaffe how
the aungell came from heaven, & brought with him of
all maner of beastes, as serpents and divers foules, and
said to sainct Peter, Take and eat.   And sainct Peter
aunswered, I eat never of uncleane beste.   And the
aungell sayde to him, *Non dicas inmunda, que Deus mun-
davit.*   That is to saye, Call thou not those things uncleane that God hath clened.   This was done in token
that men sholde not haue many men in despite for their
divers lawes, for we wot never whom God loveth & whom
God hateth.

CAP. LXXXIX.

*Of two other iles, the one is called Pitan where in be little
men that eate no meat, and in that other ile are the men
all rough of fethers.*

THERE is another yle that men call Pitan, men of
this lande till no lande, for they eate nought and
they are smal, but not so smal as Pigmes.   These men
liue with smell of wild aples,[1] & when they go far out

---

[1] Pliny (book 7, cap. 2) says : "At the very extremity of India,
on the eastern side, near the source of the River Ganges, there is
the nation of the Astonei, a people who have no mouths ; their
bodies are rough and hairy, and they cover themselves with a down
plucked from the leaves of trees (*probably cotton*).   These people
subsist only by breathing and by the odours which they inhale
through the nostrils.   They support themselves upon neither meat
nor drink : when they go upon a long journey they only carry with

O

of the countrey, they beare apples with them, for anon
as they lose that savour of apples they dye, they are not
reasonable but as wyld beastes. And there is another
yle where the people are all fethers,[1] but the face and
the palmes of theyr handes, these men go as well about
the sea as on the lande, and they eate fleshe & fish all
raw, in this yle is a great river that is two mile brode &
a halfe that men call Renemar.

CAP. XC.

Of a rich man in Prester Johan's lande named Catolo-napes and of his gardeine.

IN an yle of Prester Johans land y[t] men call Miscorach,
there was a rich man y[t] was called Catolonapes, he
was ful rich & had a fair castel on a hil & strong, & he
made a wal all about ye hill right strong & fayre, within
he had a faire gardeine wherein were many trees bearing
all maner of fruits y[t] he might find, & he had planted
therein al maner of herbes of good smel and that bare
flowers, & ther wer many faire wels, & by them was
made many hals & chambers wel dight with gold &
asure, & he had made there dyverse stories of beastes
and birds y[t] song & turned by engin and orbage[2] as they

them various oderiferous roots & flowers, and wild apples, that they
may not be without something to smell at.   But an odour which is
a little more powerful than usual easily destroys them."

[1] Other editions read, *rough hair.*

[2] This word is very puzzling. It seems to me that it probably
means *wheel work*, from Lat. *orbis*, a circle ; but Rd. Braithwaite,
in his *Arcadian Princesse*, says : " In the lowest border of the

had been quick,[1] & he had in his gardeine al thing that
might be to man solace & comfort, he had also in that
gardeine maydens within ye age of xv yeare, ye fairest
y^t he myght find, & men children of the same age, &
they were clothed with clothes of gold, & he sayd that
they were aungels and he caused to be made certain
hils,[2] & enclosed them about with precious stones of
Jaspy & christal & set in gold & pearls and other maner
of stones, and he had made a coundute[3] under ye earth,
so that when he wold ye walls[4] ran somtime with milke,
somtime with wine, somtime honey, & this place is called
Paradise & when any yong bacheler of ye countrey,
knight or sqyer, cometh to him for solace and disport,
he ledeth him into his paradise & sheweth them these
things, as the songs of birds & his damosels and wels,
& he did strike diverse Instruments of musyke, in a
high tower that might be sene, and sayde they were the
aungels of God, & that place was Paradise, that God
hath graunted to those that beleved, when hee sayde thus,
Dabo vobis terram fluentam lac & mel. That is to say, I
shall giue you land flowing with mylk and hony. And
then this rych man dyd[5] these men drinke a maner of
drinke, of which they were dronken, & he said to them
if they wold dye for his sake & when they were dead
they shold come to his paradise, and they should be of
the age of those maydens, and shold dwell alway with
them, and he shold put them in a fayrer paradise where
they shold se god in his joy, and in his majesty & then

---

garden, I might see a curious *orbell*, all of touch, wherein the Syra-
cusan tyrants were no lesse artfully portrayed, than their severall
cruelties to life displayed."

[1] As if they had been alive.   [2] Misprint for Wells.
[3] Conduit.   [4] Wells.   [5] Made.

they graunted to do that he wold, and he bad them go
and sleay such a lord, or a man of the countrey that he
was wroth with, and that they should haue no dread of
no man and if they were slaine themselfe for his sake,
he shold put them in his paradise when they were dead.
And so went those bachelers to sleay great lordes of the
countrey, & were slaine themselfe in hope to haue that
Paradise, and thus was he avenged of his enimies through
his desert,[1] and when rich men of the countrey perceived
this cautell[2] and malice and the will of this Catolonapes,
they gathered them to gither & assayled the castel &
slew hym & destroyed all his goods and his faire places
and riches that were in his paradise, and the place of the
wales[3] are there yet, and it is not long ago since it was
destroyed.

CAP. XCI.

Of a marvelous vale that is beside the river of Physon.

AND a lyttle from that place, on the left syde besyde
the river of Physon is a great marvaile.   There is
a vale betwene two hils, and that is foure myle longe, and
some men call it the valay enchaunted, some y[e] valey of
Divels, some the valey perylous,[4] and in that valey are
many tempests & a great noyse very hydeous bothe day
& night & sound as it were a noise of Taburines[5] of
nakers[6] & of trumpets as it were a great feast.   This

---

[1] Deceit.   [2] Ill intent, evil mind.   [3] Wells.
[4] Perilous.   [5] Tambourines.
[6] A kind of drum, probably a kettledrum.

valey is all full of devils, and hath ben alway, and men
say thereby yᵗ it is a enter¹ to hell.   In this valey is
muche golde & silver, wherefore many Christen men &
other go thether for covetise of that golde and silver, but
few of them come out againe, for they are anon strangled
with divels.   And in the middes of that vale on a roche
is a visage, & the head of a fiend bodely, right hideous
and dreadfull to see, and there is nothing sene but the
head to yᵉ shoulders, but there is no christen men in yᵉ
world nor other so hardy but yᵗ he should be greatly afraide
to beholde it, for he beholdeth eche man so sharply &
felly² & his eyes are so staring & so sprinkling³ as fyre
& he chaungeth so often his countenaunce that no man
dare come nere for all the worlde, and out of his mouth
& his nose cometh great plenty of fyer of divers colours,
& sometime is the fyer so stynking, that no man may
suffer it, but alway a good christen man, and one that is
stedfast in the fayth may go therein without harme, if
they shrive them well and blesse them with the token of
the crosse, then shall the divels haue no power over them.
And ye shall understande that when my felowes & I
were in that valey, we had full great dought⁴ if we shold
put our bodies in a venture to go through it, & some of
my felows agreed therto, & some wold not, and there
were in our company two friers minours of Lombardy &
sayd if any of us wold go in, they wold also, as they had
sayd so, and upon trust of them we sayd that we wold
go, & we dyd sing a masse and were shriven & houseled,⁵
and we went in xiiii men & when we came out we were
but xᵈ & we wist not whether our felowes were loste

---

¹ Entrance.   ² Evilly.   ³ Sparkling.
⁴ Doubt.   ⁵ Received the Sacrament.
⁶ Others say 9.

there, or that they turned againe, but we saw no more of
them, others of our felowes that would not go in with us,
went about another way for to be before us, and so they
were.   And we went through the valey and saw there
many marvailous things, gold silver precious stones &
jewels great plenty, as we thought, whether it were so or
no, I know not, for divels are so subtill & false, that they
make many times a thinge to seme y^t is not, for to
deceive men, and therefore I wold touch nothing for
dread of enimies that I saw there in many likenesses,
and of dead bodies that I saw lye in the valey, but I
dare not saye that they were all bodies, but they were
bodies through making of divels.   And we were often
cast down to the earth by winde, thunder & tempest, but
God helped alway, and so passed we through that valey
without peryl or harme thankes be to God.

CAP. XCII.

Of an yland wherein dwell people as great as giants of
xxviii or xxx fote of length & other things.

A ND beyond that valey is a great yle, where people
as great as giaunts of xxviii fote long & they haue
no clothinge but beasts skyns that hang on them, & they
eate no bread but flesh raw and they drink milke, &
they haue no houses, & they eat gladlyer fleshe of men,
than other, & men saye to us, that beyond that yle is a
yle where are greater giaunts as xlv or L fote long, &
some sayd L cubits long, but I saw not them, and among
those giaunts are great shepe, as it were young oxen,

and they beare great wolle, these shepe haue I sene
many times.   An other yle is there northward where are
many evill and fell women and they haue precious stones
in their eies, & they haue suche kinde y' if they beholde
any man with wrath, they sley them of the beholding as
the Basalysk doeth.[1]

CAP. XCIII.

*Of women which make great sorow as theyr children are
borne & great joy when they are dead.*

A N other yle there is, where women make great sorow
when theyr children be borne & when they are
dead they make great joy and caste them in a great fier
and burne them, and they that loue well theyr husbands,
when they are dead they cast them in a fyer to burn
them, for they say that fyer shall make them clean of
all filth & vices & they shall be cleane in another world,
and the cause why they wepe when their children are
borne, and y' they joye at their death, they say a child
when he is borne cometh into this world to haue travaile,
sorow & heavinesse, & when they are dead they go to
Paradise where rivers are of mylke and honey, & there
is lyfe & joy and plenty of goods without travaile or
sorow.   In thys yle they make their kings by chosing, &
they chose him not for his riches and noblenesse, but
him that is of good conditions and most righteous and
trew that judgeth euery man truely, little & much after

[1] Here a passage is omitted.

their trespasse, and ye king may judge no man to death without counsel of his barons, & that they all assent. And if it so be y' the king do a great trespasse, as sley a man or such lyke, he shall dye also, but he shall not be slaine, but they shall defend and forbid that no man be so hardy to beare him company, nor to speake to him, ne giue him meat nor drinke and thus he shall dye, for they spare no man y' hath done a trespasse, for loue, lordeship riches nor noblenes, but they do him right after y' he hath deserved.

CAP. XCIIII.

Of an yland where men wed theyr owne daughters & kinswomen.

THERE is another yle where there is great plenty of people & they eate neuer flesh of hares, nor of hens, nor geese, yet is there many of them but they eate of all other beastes, and they drink mylk, in this countrey they wed theyr owne daughters and other of theyr kyn as them liketh, and if there be x or xii men in one house, eche one of theyr wyves shal be comon to other, & at night shal one haue one of y' wives and another night another. And if she haue any chylde, she may give it to whome she would so that no man knowe if it be his or not. In this land & many other places of Inde, are many cocodrilles, that is a maner of a long serpent, and on nights they dwell on water, and on dayes they dwell on land and rocks, and they eat not in winter.

These serpents sley men and eate them weping,[1] and
they haue no tongue. In this countrey and many other,
men caste sede of cotton, and sow it eche yeare and it
groweth as it were small trees, and they bere cotton.   In
Araby is a kynde of beast that some men call Garsantes,[2]
that is a fayre beast, & he is hyer than a great courser
or a stead[3] but his neck is nere xx cubytes long, and his

crop and his taile lyke a hart and he may loke ouer a
high house and there is many Camilions,[4] that is a lytle
beaste, & he eateth nor drinketh never, and he chaungeth
his colour often, for sometime he is of one colour &
sometime of another, and he may chaunge him into all
colours that he will, saue black and red.   There are
many wilde swine of many colours and as great as Oxen,

---

[1] This curious belief gave rise to the term "Crocodile's tears,"
i.e., hypocritical tears.
[2] Giraffes.   [3] A steed or horse.   [4] Chameleon.

& they are spotted as it were smal fawnes, and there are
lions all white, and there be other beastes as great steedes
that men call Lauhorans,[1] and men call them Toutes,
and their head is blacke, and three long hornes in his
fronte, as cutting as sharp swords, and he chaseth and
wil sley Olifants. And there is many other maner of
beastes, of whom it were to long to write all.

CAP. XCV.

Of an ylande wherein dwell full good people and true.

THERE is another yland good and great, and plen-
tiouse, where are good men and true and of godly
lyfe after their faith, & all if they be not christen neverthelesse of kinde they are full of good vertues and they
fly all vices, and all sinne and malice, for they are not
envious, proud, covetous, lecherous nor glotenus, and
they do not unto another man but that they wold he did
to them, and they fulfill the x commaundementes and
they make no force of ryches nor of having, & they
Swere not, but they say ye and nay, for they say he that
swereth will deceive his neighbour, and some men call
this yle the yle of Bragamen, and some call it the land
of faith, and through it runneth a great river that men
call Thebe, and generally al men in those iles, and other
iles thereby are truer and rightwiser than in other
countreys. In this ile are no theves, murderers nor
beggers. And for as much as they are so true and so

---

[1] A rhinoceros is here evidently meant.

good, there is no tempest nor thunder, warre, hunger, nor tribulation, and thus it semeth well that God loveth them wel, and he is well payed of theyr dedes, and they beleve in God yᵗ made all thing & him they worship and they live so ordinately in meate and drinke that they live right longe, and many of them dye without sick- nesse, that kinde[1] faileth them for age.

CAP. XCVI.

How King Alexander sent his men thither for to winne that lande.

AND King Alexander sometime sent his men to win that lande, and they sent him letters that sayde thus, What behoveth a man to have all the worlde, that is not content therewithal : thou shalt fynde nothing at al in us, why that thou shouldest make warre upon us, for we haue no ryches nor treasure, and all the cattell of our countrey are common, our meates that we eate are our riches, and instede of gold and silver, we make our treasure peace & concorde of love, and we have nought but a cloth uppon our bodies, our wyves are not arrayed rychely to pleasing, for we holde it a great foly for a man to tryme up his body with costly aparel to make it seme fairer than God made it.   We haue ben evermore in peace til now yᵗ thou wilt disherite us.   We haue a king among us, not for nede of the law, nor to judge any man, for there are no trespassours among us, but all

_____
[1] They only die of old age.

onely to learne us to be obedient to him & so maist you take from us but our good peace. And when King Alexander saw this letter he thought he shold doe to much harme if he troubled them, and sent to them that they should kepe well theyr good maners, & haue no dread of him.

CAP. XCVII.

How the Emperour Prester John when he goeth to batayle, he hath three crosses borne before him of fine gold.

THIS Emperour Prester John, when he goeth to batayle, he hath no baner borne before him, but he hath borne before him three crosses of fine gold, & those are large & great, and well set with precious stones, & for to kepe eche crosse, is ordeyned a thousand[1] men of armes, in maner as men kepe a standerde in other countreys, and he hath men without number when he goeth in any batayle against any other lord. And when he hath no battayle but rydeth with privy company, then doth he beare before him a crosse of tree[2] not painted, and without gold or precious stones, and all playne in token that our lord Jesu Christ suffered death on a cross of tree. And also he hath borne before him a platter of gold ful of earth, in token y^t lordship and noblenesse shal tourne to nought, & his flesh shall turne to earth. And also he has borne before him another vessell full of Jewels, and golde and precious stones, in token of his noblenes and of his might.

[1] Others say 10,000.   [2] A wooden cross.

CAP. XCVIII.

Of the moste[1] dwelling place of Prester John in a citie called Suse.

AND he dwelleth commonly at the citie of Suse, & there is his principall palaice that is so riche that marvayle is to tell, & about the principall toure of the palaice are two pomels[2] of gold all round, and eche one of those hath two carbuncles great & large, y[t] shine ryght clere in the night, and y[e] principal gates of this palaice are of precious stones that men call Saraine[3] & the borders of the barres are of Ivory, & windowes of the hall and chambers are of Cristall, and tables that they eate of, some Emerandes, some are of Mayk,[4] some of golde and precious stones, and the pillers that beare the tables are of such stones also, and the greces on the which y[e] Emperour goeth to his sege where he sitteth at meat, one is of Mastik,[5] another of Cristal, another of green Jasphy,[6] another of Diasper,[7] another of Serdin,[8] another of Cornelin,[9] another of Seuton, & that he setteth his fote upon, is of Crisolites, and all these greces are bordered with fine gold, and well set with great

---

[1] The greatest.   [2] A ball or knot.   [3] ? Sardonyx.
[4] Another edition says Amethysts.
[5] Another edition says Onyx.   [6] Probably Jasper.
[7] Another edition says Amethyst, but as the whole is so apocryphal it does not much matter.
[8] Sardine or Sardonyx.
[9] Cornelian. What Seuton is I will not even venture to guess at.

perles and other precious stones, and ye side of the sege
are Emerauds bordred with gold and with precious
stones, the pillers in his chambre are of fine gold with
many Carbuncles and other such stones that giue great
light in the night, and all if the Carbuncles giue great
light, neuerthelesse there burneth xii[1] great vessels of
Cristall full of balme to giue good smell, and to drive
away evill ayre.   The fourme[2] of his bedde is all of
Saphire well bound with gold to make him slepe well &
for to destroy lechery, for he will not lye by his wiues
but thrise[3] a yeare, after the seasons, and all onely for
getting of children.   And he hath also a fayre palayce
in the city of Nyse where he dwelleth when he wil, but
the aier there is not so well tempered as it is in the citie
of Suse.   And he hath euery day in his courte more
than xxx thousand men, besides comers and goers, but
xxx thousand there or in the court of the great Caane
spendeth not so much as xii thousand in our countrey.
He hath euermore vii kinges in his court to serve him
and eche one of them serveth a moneth, and with these
kinges serue alway Lxxii Dukes & CCC[4] erles, and
euery day eat in his court xii archbishops and xx
byshops.   The patryarke of saint Thomas is as he were
a pope and Archbishops and byshops & abbotes, all are
kings in that countrey, and some of the lordes is master
of the hall, some of the chambre, some steward, some
marshal, and other officers, and therefore he is ful rychley
served.   And his land lasteth in breadth four moneths
journey and it is of length without measure.

---

[1] Another edition says, " a great vessel."
[2] The framework.
[3] Others say four times.   [4] Elsewhere it is 360.

CAP. XCIX.

Of the wildernesse wherein groweth the trees of the sonne
& the Moone.

AND beyond that river is a great wildernesse as men
that haue ben there say.   In this Wildernesse as
men saye are the trees of the Sonne and of the Mone
that spake to Kyng Alexander and tolde him of his
death, and men saye that folke that kepe these trees &
eate of the fruits of them, they live foure or five hundred
yeare through vertue of the fruite, and we woulde gladly
haue gone thyther, but I beleve that an hundred thousand
men of armes shold not passe that wildernesse for great
plenty of wilde beastes, as dragons and serpents that
sley men when they pass that way.   In this lande are
many Oliphantes all white and blew without number,
and unicornes & lyons of many maners.[1]   Many other
yles are in the land of Prester John that were to long to
tell, and much ryches and nobly of precious stones in
great plenty.   I beleve y[t] we haue herd say why this
Emperour is called Prester John but for those that know
it not I wil declare.   There was sometime an Emperour
that was a noble prince, & doughty, & he had many
christen Knights with him and y[e] Emperour thought hee
woulde see the service in Christen churches, and then
was churches of christendome in Turkey, Surry and
Tartary, Hierusalem, Palistine, Araby and Alappy,[2] and

---

[1] Kinds or sorts.   [2] ? Aleppo.

all the lordes[1] of Egypte.   And thys Emperour came
with a Christen Knight into a church of Egipt and it
was on a saterday after Whit sonday when the byshop
gaue orders, and he behelde the service and he asked of
the Knight what folke those should be that stode before
the Byshop, and the Knight sayd they should be prestes,
& he sayde he wold no more be called Kinge ne Emperour but preest, and he would haue the name of him that
came first out of the prestes and he was called John,
and so haue all the Emperors sythen[2] be called Prester
John.   In this lande are many Christen men of good
faith & good lawe, and they haue prestes to sing masse,
and they make the sacrements as men of Grece do, but
they say not but that ye Apostles said as saint Peter,
and saint Thomas, and other apostles when they song
masse and said *Pater noster*, and the wordes with the
which Gods body is sacred ; we haue many addicions of
Popes that haue bene ordeyned of which men in those
countreys know not.

CAP. C.

Of a great yland and kingedome called Taprobane.[3]

TOWARDE the East side of Prester John's lande is
an yle that men call Taprobane, & is right good
and fructuous,[4] and there is a great Kyng and a rych,

[1] Other editions read *land*.   [2] Since then.
[3] There seems a difference of opinion whether this island is
Ceylon or Sumatra.
[4] Fruitful.

and he is obedient unto Prester John & the King is
alway made by eleccion.   In this yle is ii wynters and
two somers, and they shere[1] corne twise in the yere, all
times in the yeare gardeins florysheth.   There dwelleth
good people and reasonable and many Christen men
among them that are full rich, and the water betwene
the syde of Prester John and this yle is not full depe for
men may see the grounde in many places.

CAP. CI.

*Of two other yles, one is called Orel, & the other Argete
where are many gold mines.*

THERE are more eastward two other yles—ye one
is called Orell and the other Argete of whom all
the land is mine of gold & silver.   In those yles many
men se no sters[2] clere shining, but one starre y^t is called
Canapos[3] and there many men se not ye Mone but in
the last quarter.   In that yle is a great hyll of golde
that pismyres[4] kepe, & they do fine golde from the other
that is not fine golde, and the pismyres are as great as
houndes, so that no man dare come there for dread of
pismyres that should assayle them so that men may not
worke in that gold nor get thereof but by subtiltie, and
therefore when it is righte hote the pismyres hide them
in the earth from undern[5] to none of the daye, and then

---

[1] Reap.   [2] Stars.
[3] Canopus, a star of the first magnitude, in the rudder of the
constellation *Argo*.
[4] Ants.   [5] See footnote, *ante*, p. 125.

P

men of the countrey take Cameles and dormedaries and
other beastes & go thither and charge them with gold
and go away fast or the pismyres come out of the earth.
And other times when it is not so hot y' the pismyres hide
them not, they take mares that haue foles, and they lay
upon these mares two long vessels as it were two small
barels and the mouth upwards and drive them thether
and holde theyr foles at home, and when the pismyres se
these vessels they spring therein, for they haue[1] of kinde
to leue no hole nor pyt open, and anone they fyl these
vessels with golde, and when men think that the vessels
be full they take the foles and bring them as nere as
they dare, and then they whine, and the mares heare
them, and anone they come to theyr foles and so they
take the gold, for these pismyres will suffer beastes for
to go among them, but no men.

CAP. CII.

*Of the darke countrey and hils and roches of stone nigh to
Paradise.*

BEYOND the yles of the lande of Prester John and
his lordeship of wildernesse to go right East, men
shall not finde but hils, great rocks and other myrke[2]
lande, where no man may see a day or night as men of
the countrey say, and this wildernesse and myrke land
lasteth to Paradise terrestre, where Adam and Eve were
sette, but they were there but a lyttle while, and that is

[1] For it is their habit.   [2] Dark, murky

toward the East at the beginning of the earth, but that
is not our East that we call where the Son ryseth in
those countreys towarde Paradise, and then it is mid-
night in our countrey for the roundnesse of the earth,
for our Lorde made the earth all rounde in the middest
of ye fyrmament.   Of Paradise can I not speake properly
for I haue not bene there, but that I haue heard I shall
tell you.   Men say that Paradise terrestre is the highest
lande in all the worlde, and it is so high that it toucheth
nere to the cyrcle of the Mone, for it is so high y^t Noes
floude might not come thereto which covered all the
earth about.

CAP. CIII.

A lyttle of Paradise terrestre.

THIS Paradise terrestre is enclosed al about with a
   wall, and that wall is all covered with mosse as it
semeth, y^t men may see no stone nor nothing else whereof
it is, and in the highest place of Paradise in the middest
of it is a well that casteth out the foure flouds that run
through divers landes.   The first floud is called Phison
or Ganges, and that runneth through Inde, in that river
are many precious stones and much *Lignum Aloes* &
gravel of golde.   Another is called Nilus or Gison, and
y^t runneth through Ethiope & Egipt.   The third is called
Tigre & that runneth through Assyry & Armony the
great.   And the fourth is called Eufrates, y^t runneth
through Armony and Percy & men say that the sweete
and fresh waters of ye world take their springing of them.

The first river is called Phison, that is to say, gathering
of many rivers together & faling into one, and some call
it Ganges, for a King y' was in Inde that men cal Gan-
geras, for it runneth through his land & this river is in
some places cleane, in some places troble,[1] in some places
hot, in some places cold.   The second river is called
Nilus or Gison, for it is ever trouble, for Gison is to say
troble.   The third river is called Tigris that is to say
fast running, for it runneth faster than any of the other,
& so is a beast that men call Tigris for he runneth fast.
The fourth ryver is called Eufrates y' is to say well
bearing, for there groweth many good things upon that
ryver.   And ye shall understande that no man living
may go unto y' Paradise, for by land he may not go for
wylde beastes which are in the wyldernesse, and for hylls
and rocks where no man may passe.   Nor by those
ryvers may no man passe, for they come with so great
course and so great waves that no ship may saile against
them.   Many great lordes haue essayed many times to
go by those rivers to Paradise, but they might not spede
in theyr way, for some dyed for werynesse of rowinge,
some waxt blynde and some defe for noise of the waters,
so no man may passe there but through speciall grace of
God—for I can tell you no more of that place.   I shall
tell you of that I haue seene.

[1] Troubled or muddy.

CAP. CIIII.

How Prester Johns land lyeth foote against[1] foote to Englande.

THESE yles of the land of Prester John, they are under the earth to us, & other yles are there whoso wold pursue them for to environ the earth whoso had grace of God to hold the waye, he mighte come right to the same countreys that he were come of and come from & so go about the earth, and for that it asketh so long tyme, & also there are so many perils to passe that fewe men assay to go so, and yet it might be done, & therefore men come from these yles to other yles costing of the lordship of Prester John, & men come in the coming to one yle y[t] men cal Cassoy, & that country is nere Lx journeys long & more than L of bredth, that is the best land that is in those countreys saue Cathay & if marchants came thither as commonly as they do to Cathay, it would be better than Cathay, for it is so thick of cities & towns y[t] when a man goeth out of a citie he seeth another on eche side. There is great plenty of spices and other goods. Ye king of this ile is rich & mighty & he holdeth his land of y[e] great Caan for y[t] is one of y[e] xii princes[2] that the great Caan hath under him beside his owne lande.

---

[1] Antipodes.   [2] Misprint for provinces.

CAP. CV.

Of the Kingedome of Ryboth.

FROM this yle men go another kyngdome that is called Riboth, and that is also under yᵉ great Caan. This is a good countrey and plentious of corne, wine & other things, men of this lande haue no houses but they dwell in tentes made of tree. And the principall citie of the countrey is all blacke made of black stones and white and all the streetes are paved with such stones and in the citie is no man so hardy to spil blood of man ne beast, for worship of a mawment[1] that is worshiped there. In that citie dwelleth the Pope of their lawe, that they call Lopasse, and he giveth all dignities & benefices that fall to yᵉ mawmet. And men of religion and men that haue churches in that countrey are obedient to him as men here to the pope. In this yle they haue a custome through all the countrey that when a mans father is dead they wil do him great worship, they send after all his friends, religious priests and many other, and they beare the body to an hill with great Joy and myrth, and whan it is there, the greatest prelate smiteth of his head, & laieth it upon a great plate of gold, or silver, and giveth it to his sonne and his son taketh it to his other friends, singing and sayinge many orysons,[2] and then the prestes and the religious men cut

---

[1] A puppet or doll, or mammet—an idol—probably so called as a contraction for Mahomet.

[2] Prayers.

the flesh of[1] the body in peces and say orysons, and the byrds of the countrey come thether, for they know well the custome, and they flye about them as they were egles and other birds that eate flesh, and the priestes cast the pieces unto them, and they beare it away a little from thence and then they eate it, and as priestes in our countrey sing for soules *subvenite sancti dei* and so forth, so those prestes ther syng with high voyce in their language in this maner wyse. Se and beholde how good and gracious a man this was, that ye aungels of God come for to fetch him & beare him into Paradise. And then thinketh y[e] son of the same man that he is greatly worshipped when birds haue eaten his father, and where are most plenty of byrds, there is most worship. And then cometh the sonne home with all his friendes, and maketh them a great feast, the sonne maketh cleane his fathers head and giveth them drynke thereof, & the fleshe of the head he cutteth of, and giveth it to his moste speciall fryends, some a lyttle, & some a lyttle, for deynty. And in remembrance of this holy man that the birds haue eaten, the sonne doth make a cuppe of the scalpe[2] & thereof drinketh he all his life, in remembrance of his father.

[1] Off.   [2] Skull.

CAP. CVI.

Of a rych man that is neyther king, prince duke nor erle.

AND from this men go ten journeys through the land of the great Caan, which is a full good yle & a great kingdom & the king is ful mighty. And in this yle is a rich man which is no king prince Duke nor Erle, but he hath eche yere cccc [1] thousand horses charged [2] with ryce and corne, and he hath a noble & a rich life after the maner of the countrey, for he hath L damosels that serve him every day at his meate & bed and do what he wil. And when he sytteth at the table they bring him meat, & at eche time fiue meates togither, and they sing in the bringing a song, and they cut his meate and put it in his mouth, and he hath righte long nayles on his hands, that is a great nobility in that countrey & therefore they let theyr nayles grow as long as they may,[3] and some let them growe so long that they come about theyr handes and y[t] is a great nobility & gentry, and the gentry of a woman is to haue small fete, and therefore anon as they are borne, they binde their feete so straight that they cannot wax halfe as they shoulde. And he hath a full faire palaice, & rich, wher he dwelleth, of which the wall is two myle about, & there is many faire gardeins, and all the pavement of the hal, & chambres, is of gold & silver, and in the midst of one of these

---

[1] Other editions say 300,000.   [2] Loaded.
[3] Similar to the Chinese custom of the upper classes.

gardeins is a lyttle hyl, whereon is a place made wyth toures and pynacles all of golde, and there he wyll syt often to take the ayer and disport, for it is made for nothing else. From this land men may go through ye land of the great Caane.

CAP. CVII.

How all these landes yles and kingdomes, and the men therof afore rehersed, haue some of the articles of our faith.

AND ye shall understand that all these men & folke that haue reason y^t I haue spoken of, haue some articles of our faith, all[1] if they be of divers lawes and divers beleves, yet they haue some good poynts of our fayth, & they beleve in God of kinde as theyr prophecie sayth, *Et metuent eum omnes fines terræ*, That is to say, And all endes of the earth shall dread him. And in another place, *Omnes gentes servient ei*, That is to say, All folk shall serve him, but they cannot speak parfitly but as theyr kyndly wit teacheth them, neither of the Son nor of the Holy Ghost can they speake, but they can speake well of the Byble, and specially of Genesis, and of the bokes of Moyses. And they say that those creatures y^t they worship are no gods, but they worship them for great vertue that is in them which may not be without special grace of God, & of simulacre and ydoles, they say that all men haue simulacres, and that, say

[1] Even.

they, for us christen men haue ymages of our Lady &
other, but they wot not that we worship not the ymages
of stone nor of wood, but the saynts of whome they are
made, for as the letter teacheth clarkes how they shal
beleve, so ymages and paynture teacheth lewde[1] men.
They say also that the aungell of God speaketh to them
in their ydoles & do miracles, they say soth,[2] but it is
the evil aungell that doth myracles to maintaine them
in their ydolatrie.

CAP. CVIII.

*How John Maundevyl leveth many mervailes unwrytten &
the cause wherefore.*

THERE are many other countreys where I haue not
yet ben nor sene & therefore I can not speke properly of them. Also in countreys where I haue bene are
many marvailes that I speke not of, for it were to long a
tale and therefore hold you payd at this time y[t] I haue
sayd, for I will say no more of mervailes that are there,
so that other men that go thither may fynde ynough for
to say that I haue not tolde.

[1] Unlearned.   [2] Truly.

CAP. CIX.

What time John Maundevil departed out of England.

AND I John Maundevil that went out of my countrey
and passed the sea, the yeare of our lord MCCCXXII
and I haue passed through many landes and yles and
countreys, and now am come to rest. I haue compyled
this boke and do wryte it the yeare of our Lord
MCCCLXVI at XXXIV yeare after my departing from my
countrey, & for as much as many men beleve not that
they 'see with theyr eyen, or y' they may conceive &
know in their mynde, therefore I made my way to Rome
in my coming homewarde, to shew my boke to the holy
father the pope,[1] and tell him of the mervayles y' I had
sene in diverse countreys; so that he with his wise
counsel wold examine it, with diverse folke y' are at
Rome, for there dwell men of all nations of the world,
and a lytle time after when he & his counsel had examined it all through, he sayde to me for a certayne
that it was true for he sayd he had a boke of latin contayning all that and much more, of y' which *Mappa
Mundi* is made, the which boke I saw, & therefore the
pope hath ratyfied & confirmed my boke in all poyntes.
And I pray to all those that rede this boke, that they
will pray for me and I shall pray for them, & all those
that say for me our Lord's prayer & that God forgive
me my sinnes, I make them parteners & graunt them

---

[1] Urban V.

part of all my good pylgrimages and other good dedes which I ever dyd or shall do to my lyves ende & I pray to God of whome all grace cometh, that he will, all the readers and hearers that are christen, fulfil with his grace, and saue them body and soule & bring them to his Joy that euer shall last.   He that is in the Trinitie, the Father, the Sonne, and the Holy Ghost, that liveth & raigneth God without ende

Amen

Imprinted at London in Breadstreat at the nether ende by Thomas East.   An 1568
. The 6 day of October

Here beginneth the journall of Frier Odoricus, one of the order of the Minorites, concerning strange things which hee sawe among the Tartars of the East.

LBEIT many and sundry things are reported by divers authors concerning the fashions and conditions of this world : notwithstanding I frier Odoricus of Friuli, de portu Vahonis being desirous to travel unto the foreign and remote nations of infidels, sawe and heard great and miraculous things, which I am truly able to avouch. First of al therefore sayling from Pera by Constantinople, I arrived at Trapesunda.[1] This place is right commodiously situate, as being an haven for the Persians and Medes, and other countries beyonde the sea. In this lande I behelde with very great delight a very strange spectacle, namely a certain man leading about with him more than foure thousande partriges. The man himselfe walked upon the grounde, and the partriges flew in the aire, which he ledde unto a certaine castle called Zavena, being three days journey distant from Trapesunda. The saide partriges were so tame, that when the man was desirous to lie downe and rest, they would all come flocking about him like chickens. And so hee led them

[1] Trebizonde.

unto Trapesunda, and unto the palace of the Emperour,
who tooke as many of them as he pleased, and the reste
the saide man carried unto the place from whence he
came.   In this citie lyeth the body of Athanasius, upon
the gate of the citie.   And then I passed on further unto
Armenia major, to a citie called Azaron,[1] which had
been very rich in olde time, but nowe the Tartars haue
almost layde it waste.   In the saide citie there was
abundance of bread and flesh, and of all other victuals
except wine and fruits.   This citie also is very colde,
and is reported to be higher situated, then any other city
in the world.   It hath most holesome and sweete waters
about it : for the veines of the saide waters seeme to
spring and flow from the mighty river of Euphrates,
which is but a dayes journey from the saide city.   Also,
the saide citie stands directly in the way to Tauris.[2]
And I passed on unto a certaine mountaine called
Sobissacalo.   In the foresaide countrey there is the very
same mountaine whereupon the Arke of Noah rested ;
unto the which I would willingly haue ascended, if my
company would haue stayed for me.   Howbeit the
people of that countrey report, that no man could euer
ascend the saide mountaine, because (say they) it
pleaseth not the highest God.   And I travailed on further
unto Tauris that great and royal city, which was in olde
time called Susis.   This city is accompted for traffique
of merchandize the chiefe citie of the world : for there
is no kinde of victuals, nor any thing else belonging unto
merchandize, which is not to be had there in great abundance.   This citie stands very commodiously : for unto
it all the nations of the whole worlde in a maner may

---

[1] Erzeroum.   [2] Tauris, a city of Persia.

resort for traffique.   Concerning the saide citie, the
Christians in those parts are of opinion, that the Persian
Emperour receives more tribute out of it, then the King
of France out of all his dominions.   *Neare unto the saide
citie there is a salt-hill yeelding salt unto the city : and of
that salt ech man may take what pleaseth him, not paying
ought to any man therefor.*   In this city many Christians
of all nations do inhabite, over whom the Saracens beare
rule in all things.   Then I traveiled on further unto a
city called Soldania,[1] wherein the Persian Emperour
lieth all Sommer time : but in Winter hee takes his progresse unto another city standing upon the sea called
Baku.[2]   Also the foresaide city is very great and colde
having good and holesome waters therein, unto the
which also store of marchandize is brought.   Moreover
I travelled with a certaine company of Caravans toward
upper India : and in the way, after many days journey,
I came unto the citie of the three wise men called
Cassan,[3] which is a noble and renowned city, saving that
the Tartars haue destroyed a great part thereof, and it
aboundeth in bread, wine, and many other commodities.
From this citie unto Jerusalem (whither the three foresaid wisemen were miraculously led) it is fifty days
journey.   There be many wonders in this citie also,
which for brevities sake, I omit.   From thence I departed unto a certain city called Geste, *whence the sea of
sand is distant one dayes journey, which is a most wonderful and dangerous thing.*   In this city there is abundance
of all kinds of victuals and especially of figs, raisins, and
grapes : more (as I suppose) then in any part of the

[1] Or Sultania.   [2] The Caspian Sea.
[3] Or Cassibin.

whole world besides.   This is one of the three principall
cities of all the Persian Empire.   Of this city the
Saracens report, that no Christian can by any means
live therein above a yeere.   Then passing many dayes
journey on forward, I came unto a certain city called
Comum [1] which was a huge and mightie citie in olde
time, conteyning well nigh fiftie miles in circuite, and
hath done in times past great damage unto the Romanes.
In it there are stately palaces altogether destitute of inhabitants, notwithstanding it aboundeth with great store
of victuals.   From hence travailing through many
countreys, at length I came unto the land of Job called
Hus, which is full of all kinde of victuals and very plea-
santly situated.   Thereabouts are certaine mountaines
having good pastures for cattell upon them.   Here also
Manna is found in great aboundance.   Four partriges
are here solde for lesse than a groat.   In this countrey
there are most comely olde men.   Here also the men
spin and card, and not the women.   This land bordereth
upon the North part of Chaldea.

Of the maners of the Chaldeans, and of India.

FROM thence I traveled into Chaldæa, which is a
great kingdome and I passed by the tower of
Babel.   This region hath a language peculiar unto
itselfe, and there are beautiful men and deformed
women.   *The men of the same countrey used to haue their
haire kempt, and trimmed like unto our women : and they*

---

[1] Como.

weare golden turbants upon their heads richly set with
pearle, and pretious stones.   The women are clad in a
course smock onely reaching to their knees and having long
sleeves hanging downe to the ground.   And they goe bare-
footed, wearing breeches which reach to the ground also.
They weare no attire upon their heads, but their haire
hangs disheaveled about their eares : and there be many
other strange things also.   From thence I came into the
lower India, which the Tartars overran & wasted.   And
in this countrey the people eat dates for the most part,
whereof 42 li are there sold for lesse than a groat.   I
passed further also many dayes journey unto the Ocean
Sea & the first lande where I arrived, is called Ormes,[1]
being well fortified, and having great store of merchandize and treasure therein.   Here also they use a kinde
of Bark or shippe called Jase, being compact together
onely with hempe.   And I went on board into one of
them, wherein I could not finde any yron at all, and in
the space of 28 days I arrived at the city of Thana,[2]
wherein foure of our friers were martyred for the faith
of Christ.   This countrey is well situate having abundance of bread and wine, and of other victuals therein.
This Kingdome in olde time was very large and under the
dominion of King Porus, who fought a great battell with
Alexander the great.   The people of this countrey are
idolaters worshipping fire, serpents and trees.   And ouer
all this land the Saracens do beare rule, who tooke it by
maine force, and they themselues are in subjection unto
King Daldilus.   There be divers kinds of beasts, as
namely blacke lyons in great abundance, and apes also,

[1] Ormus.
[2] Thana, whereof Frederick Cæsar maketh mention.

Q

and monkeis, and battes as bigge as our doves.   And
there are mise as bigge as our countrey dogs, and therefore they are hunted with dogs, because cats are not
able to encounter them.   Moreouer in the same countrey
every man hath a bundle of great boughs standing in a
water-pot before his doore, which bundle is as great as a
pillar, and it will not wither, so long as water is applied
thereunto : with many other novelties and strange things,
the relation whereof would breed great delight.

How peper is had : and where it groweth.

MOREOUER, that it may be manifest how peper
is had, it is to be understood that it groweth in a
certaine kingdome whereat I myself arrived, being called
Minibar,[1] and it is not so plentifull in any other part of
the worlde as it is there.   For the wood wherein it
growes conteineth in circuit 18 dayes journey.   And in
the said wood or forrest there are two cities one called
Flandrina,[2] and the other Cyncilim.   In Flandrina both
Jewes & Christians doe inhabite, betweene whom there
is often contention and warre : howbeit the Christians
overcome the Jewes at all times.   In the foresaid wood
pepper is had after this maner : first it groweth in leaves
like unto pot-hearbes, which they plant neere unto great
trees as we do our vines, and they bring forth pepper in
clusters, as our vines doe yeeld grapes, but being ripe,
they are of a green colour, and are gathered as we

[1] Malabar.   [2] Or Alandrina.

gather grapes, and then the graines are layd in the
Sunne to be dried, and being dried are put into earthen
vessels : and thus is pepper made and kept. Now, in
the same wood there be many rivers, wherein are great
store of Crocodiles, and of other serpents, which the inhabitants of that countrey do burne up with strawe and
with other dry fewel, and so they go to gather their
pepper without danger. At the South End of the said
forrest stands the city of Polumbrum,[1] which aboundeth
with marchandize of all kinds. All the inhabitants of
that countrey do worship a living oxe, as their god, whom
they put to labour for sixe yeres, and in the seventh yere
they cause him to rest from al his worke, placing him in
a solemne and publique place : and calling him an holy
beast. *Moreouer they use this foolish ceremonie: Every
morning they take two basons, either of silver or of gold,
and with one they receive the urine of the oxe, and with the
other his dung. With the urine they wash their face, their
eyes, and all their fiue senses. Of the dung they put into
both their eyes, then they anoint the bals of their cheeks
therewith, and thirdly their breast: and then they say that
they are sanctified for all that day : And as the people
doe, euen so doe their king and Queene.* This people wor-
shippeth also a dead idole which from the navel upward,
resembleth a man, and from the navel downward an oxe.
The very same Idol delivers oracles unto them, and
sometimes requireth the blood of fourtie virgins for his
hire. And therefore the men of that region do conse-
crate their daughters and their sonnes unto their idols,
euen as Christians do their children unto some Religion
or Saint in heaven. Likewise they sacrifice their sonnes

---

[1] *Query*, whether this is not *Kaulam* or *Ballád-ul-Falfal*, the
Pepper Country, or Malabar, latinized into Columbum or Columbus.

and their daughters, and so, much people is put to death
before the said Idol by reason of that accursed ceremony.   Also, many other hainous and abominable vil-
lainies doeth that brutish beastly people commit : and I
saw many more strange things among them which I
meane not here to insert.   Another most vile custome
the foresaide nation doeth retaine : *for when any man
dieth they burne his dead corpse to ashes : and if his wife
surviveth him, her they burne quicke, because (say they) she
shall accompany her husband in his tilthe and husbandry,
when he is come unto a new worlde.   Howbeit the said
wife having children by her husband, may if she will, remaine still alive with them, without shame or reproche :
notwithstanding, for the most part, they all of them make
choice to be burnt with their husbands.*   Now, albeit the
wife dieth before her husband, that law bindeth not the
husband to any such inconvenience but he may marry
another wife also.   *Likewise, ye said nation hath another
strange custome, in that their women drink wine, but their
men do not.   Also the women haue the lids & brows of their
eyes & beards shaven, but the men haue not :* with many
other base and filthie fashions which the said women
do use contrary to the nature of their sexe.   From that
kingdome I traveiled 10 daies journey unto another
kingdome called Mobar,[1] which containeth many cities.
Within a certaine church of the same countrey, the
body of S. Thomas the Apostle is interred, the very
same church being full of idols : and in 15 houses round
about the said Church there dwell certaine priests who
are Nestorians, that is to say, false, and bad Christians
and schismatiques.

[1] Malabar.

Of a strange and uncouth idole : & of certaine customes
and ceremonies.

IN the kingdome of Mobar there is a wonderfull
strange idole, being made after the shape and resem-
blance of a man, as big as the image of our Christopher,
& consisting all of most pure and glittering gold.   And
about the necke thereof hangeth a silke riband, ful of
most rich & precious stones, some one of which is of
more value than a whole kingdome.   The house of this
idol is all of beaten gold, namely the roofe, the pavement, and the sieling of the wall within and without.
Unto this idol the Indians go on pilgrimage, as we do
unto St. Peter.   Some go with halters about their necks,
some with their hands bound behind them, some with
knives sticking on their armes or legs : and if after their
peregrination, the flesh of their wounded arme festereth
or corrupteth, they esteeme that limme to be holy, &
thinke that their God is wel pleased with them.   *Neare*
unto the temple of that idol is a lake made by men in an
open and common place, whereinto the pilgrimes cast gold,
silver and precious stones, for the honour of the idol and the
repairing of his temple.   And therefore when anything is
to be adorned or mended. they go unto this lake taking up
the treasure which was cast in.   Moreouer at euery yerely
feast of the making or repairing of the said idol, the king
and queene, with the whole multitude of the people, & all
the pilgrimes assemble themselues, & placing the said idol
in a most stately & rich chariot, they cary him out of their

*temple with songs, & with all kinds of musical harmonie,
and a great companie of virgins go procession-wise two and
two in a rank singing before him.* Many *pilgrims also put
themselves under the chariot wheeles,* to the end that *their
false god may go ouer them, and* al they ouer *whom the
chariot runneth,* are crushed in pieces, & divided asunder
in the midst, and slaine right out. Yea, & in *doing this,
they think themselves to die most holily & securely, in the
service of their god.* And by this meanes every yere,
there die under the said filthy idol, mo then 500 persons,
whose carcases are burned, and their ashes are kept for
reliques, because they died in that sort for their god.
Moreover they haue another detestable ceremony. For
when any man offers to die in the service of his false god,
his parents & all his friends assemble themselues together
with a consort of musicians, making him a great &
solemne feast : which feast being ended, they hang 5
sharpe knifes about his neck carrying him before the idol
& so soone as he is come thither, he taketh one of his
knives crying with a loud voice, For the worship of my
god do I cut this my flesh, and then he casteth the mor-
sel which is cut, at ye face of his idol : but at the very
last wound wherewith he murthereth himselfe, he uttereth
these words : " Now do I yeeld myself to death in the
behalfe of my god " and being dead his body is burned,
& is esteemed by al men to be holy.   The king of the
said region is most rich in silver, gold, and precious
stones, & there be the fairest unions in al the world.

Traveling from thence by the Ocean sea 50 daies
journey southward, I came unto a certaine land named
Lammori,[1] where, *in regard of extreeme heat, the people*

---

[1] Perhaps he meaneth Cammori.

both men and women go stark-naked from top to toe : who seeing me apparelled, scoffed at me, saying that God made Adam and Eve naked. In this countrey al women are common, so that no man can say, this is my wife. Also when any of the said women beareth a son or a daughter, she bestowes it upon anyone that hath lien with her, whom she pleaseth. Likewise al the land of that region is possessed in common, so that there is not mine & thine, or any propriety of possession in the division of lands : howbeit euery man hath his owne house peculiar unto himselfe. Mans flesh, if it be fat, is eaten as ordinarily there as beefe in our countrey. And albeit the people are most lewd, yet the countrey is exceeding good, abounding with al commodities, as fleshe, corne, rise, silver, gold, wood of aloes, Camphir, and many other things. Marchants coming unto this region for traffique do usually bring with them fat men, selling them unto the inhabitants as we sel hogs, who immediately kil and eat them. In this island towards the south, there is another kingdome called Simoltra,[1] where both men and women marke themselves with red-hot yron in 12 sundry spots of their faces : and this nation is at continual warre with certaine naked people in another region. Then I traveled further unto another island called Java, the compasse whereof by sea is 3000 miles. The king of this Iland hath 7 other crowned kings under his jurisdiction. The said Island is throughly inhabited & is thought to be one of the principall Ilands of y⁰ whole world. In the same Iland there groweth great plenty of cloves, cubibez, and nutmegs, and in a word all kinds of spices are there to be had, and great aboundance of all victuals except wine.

---

[1] Sumatra.

The king of the said Iland of Java hath a brave and sumptuous pallace, the most loftily built, that euer I saw any, & it hath most high greeses [1] and stayers to ascend up into the roomes therein contained, one stayre being of silver, & another of gold, throughout the whole building. Also the lower roomes were paved all ouer with one square plate of silver, & another of gold. All the walls upon the inner side were seeled ouer with plates of gold, wherupon were ingraven ye pictures of knights, having about their temples, ech of them a wreath of golde, adorned with precious stones. The roofe of the palace was of pure gold. With this King of Java the great Can of Catay hath had many conflicts in war; whom notwithstanding the said king hath always overcome and vanquished.

Of certaine trees yeelding meale, honey, and poyson.

NEERE unto the said Iland is another countrey called Panten, or Tathalamasin.[2] And the king of the same countrey hath many Ilands under his dominion. In this land there are trees yeelding meale, hony, & wine & the most deadly poison in all ye whole world : for against it there is but one only remedy : & that is this : if any man hath taken of ye poyson, & would be delivered from the danger thereof, let him temper the dung of a man in water, & so drinke a good quantitie thereof, & it expels the poyson immediatly, making it to avoid at the fundament. Meale is produced out of

---

[1] Steps.   [2] *Query*, The Tathsiaulu of Marco Polo, or Thibet.

the said trees after this maner. They be mighty huge trees and when they are cut with an axe by the ground, there issueth out of the stock a certain licour like unto gumme, which they take and put into bags made of leaues, laying them for 15 days together abroad in the sunne, & at the end of those 15 dayes, when the said licour is throughly parched, it becometh meale. Then they steepe it first in sea water, washing it afterward with fresh water, and so it is made very good & savorie paste, whereof they make either meat or bread, as they thinke good. Of which bread I my selfe did eate, & it is fayrer without & somewhat browne within. By this countrey is the sea called Mare mortuum, which runneth continually Southward, into y' which whosoever falleth in (is) never seene after. In this countrey also are are found canes of an incredible length, namely of 60 paces high or more, & they are as bigge as trees. Other canes there be also called Cassan,[1] which overspread the earth like grasse, & out of euery knot of them spring foorth certaine branches, which are continued upon the ground almost for the space of a mile. In the said canes there are found certaine stones, one of which stones, whosoever carryeth about with him, cannot be wounded with any yron : & therefore the men of that countrey for the most part, carry such stones with them, whithersoever they goe. Many also cause one of the armes of their children, while they are yong, to be launced, putting one of the said stones into the wound, healing also, and closing up the said wound with the powder of a certaine fish (the name whereof I do not know) which powder doth immediatly consolidate and cure the said wounde.

[1] An exaggeration for bamboos.

And by the virtue of these stones the people aforesaid doe for the most part triumph both on sea and land. Howbeit there is one kinde of stratageme, which the enemies of this nation, knowing the vertue of the sayd stones, doe practise against them : namely, they provide themselues armour of yron or steele against their arrowes, & weapons also poisoned with the poyson of trees & they carry in their hands wooden stakes most sharpe and hard pointed, as if they were yron : likewise they shoot arrowes without yron heads, & so they confound and slay some of their unarmed foes trusting too securely unto the vertue of their stones. Also of the foresayd canes called Cassan they make sayles for their ships, and litel houses, and many other necessaries. From thence after many dayes travell, I arrived at another kingdome called Campa, a most beautiful and rich countrey, & abounding with all kind of victuals : the king whereof, at my being there, had so many wives & concubines, that he had 300 sonnes & daughters by them. This king hath 10004 tame Elephants, which are kept even as we keepe droves of oxen or flocks of sheepe in pasture.

Of the abundance of fishes, which cast themselues upon the shore.

IN this countrey there is one strange thing to be observed, y^t euery several kind of fishes in those seas come swimming towards the said countrey in such abundance, that, for a great distance into the sea, nothing can be seene but the backes of fishes : *which casting themselues upon the shore when they come neere unto it, do suffer*

men, for the space of 3 *daies to come &* **take** *as many of* *them* **as** *they please, &* **then** *they return* **again** *to the sea.* *After that kind of fishes comes another kind, offering itselfe* *after the same maner, &* *so in like sort all* **other** *kinds* *whatsoever : notwithstanding they* **do this but** *once in a* *year.* *And I demaunded of the inhabitants there* **how,** *or* *by what meanes this strange accident could* **come to passe :** *They answered, that fishes were taught, even by* **nature to** *come* **and do** *homage unto their Emperour.* There be Tor-
toises also as bigge as an oven. Many other things I
saw which are incredible, unlesse a man should see them
with his own eies.   In this countrey also dead men are
burned, & their wives are burned aliue with them, as
in the city of Polumbrum aboue mentioned : for the men
of that countrey say that she goeth to accompany him
in another world, that he should take none other wife in
mariage.   Moreouer I traveled on further by the ocean-
sea towards the South, & passed through many countries
and islands, whereof one is called Moumoran, & it containeth in compasse ii. M miles, wherein men & women
haue dogs faces, and worship an oxe for their god : and
therefore euery one of them cary the image of an oxe
of gold or silver upon their foreheads.   The men &
women of this country go all naked, saving that they
hang a linen cloth round their loins.   The men of the
said country are very tall and mighty, and by reason
that they goe naked, when they are to make battell,
they cary yron or steele-targets before them, which do
cover and defend their bodies from top to toe : and
whomsoever of their foes they take in battel not being
able to ransome himselfe for money, they presently devoure him : but if he be able to redeeme himselfe for
money, they let him go free.   Their king weareth about

his necke 300 great & most beautiful unions,[1] and saith euery day 300 prayers unto his god. He weareth upon his finger also a stone of a span long, which seemeth to be a flame of fire, and therefore when he weareth it, no man dare approach unto him : and they say that there is not any stone in the whole world of more value than it. Neither could at any time the great Tartarian Emperour of Katay either by force, money, or policie obtain it at his hands, notwithstanding that he hath done the utmost of his indeavour for this purpose.

Of the Island of Sylan: and of the mountaine where Adam mourned for his sonne Abel.

I PASSED by also another island called Sylan,[2] which conteineth in compasse aboue ii M miles, wherin are an infinit number of serpents, & great store of lions, beares, & al kinds of ravening & wild beasts, and especially of elephants. In the said countrey there is an huge mountaine, whereupon the inhabitants of that region do report that Adam mourned for his son Abel ye space of 500 yeres. In the midst of this mountaine there is a most beautiful plain, wherin is a litle lake conteining great plenty of water, which water ye inhabitants report to haue proceeded from the teares of Adam & Eve : howbeit I proved that to be false, because I saw the water flow in the lake. This water is ful of horsleeches, & blood suckers, & of precious stones also, which precious stones the king taketh not unto his owne use,

---

[1] Large and fine pearls.   [2] Ceylon.

but once or twise euery yere he permitteth certaine
poore people to diue under water for ye said stones
& al that they may get he bestoweth upon them, to the
end that they may pray for his soule.   But y⁴ they may
with less danger dive under water, they take limons [1]
which they pil, [2] anointing themselves with the juice
thereof, & so they may diue naked under yᵉ water, the
hors-leeches not being able to hurt them.   From this
lake the water runneth even unto the sea, and at a low
ebbe the inhabitants dig rubies, diamonds & perles, and
other precious stones out of the shore : wherupon it is
thought, that ye king of this island hath greater abundance of pretious stones, then any other monarch in the
whole earth besides.   In the said countrey there be all
kinds of beastes and foules : & the people told me, that
those beasts would not invade nor hurt any stranger but
only the natural inhabitants.

*I saw in this island fouls as big as our countrey geese,
having two heads, and other miraculous things, which I
will not here write off.   Traveling on further South, I
arrived at a certaine island called Bodin, [3] which signifieth
in our language unclean.   In this island there do inhabit
most wicked persons, who devour & eate rawe flesh, com-
mitting all kinds of uncleannes & abominations in such
sort, as it is incredible.   For the father eateth his son, &
the son his father, the husband his owne wife & the wife
her husband : & that after this maner.   If any mans
father be sick, the son straight goes unto the sooth-saying or
prognosticating priest, requesting him to demand of his
god, whether his father shall recover from his infirmity or
no ; Then both of them go unto an idol of gold or silver,*

---

[1] Lemons.   [2] Peel.   [3] Or Dadin.

making their prayers unto it in maner folowing: Lord,
thou art our god, & thee we do adore, beseeching thee to
resolve us, whether such a man must die, or recover of such
an infirmity or no: Then the divel answereth out of y
aforesaide idol : if he saieth (he shal liue) then returneth
his son and ministreth things necessary unto him til he
hath attained unto his former health : but if he saith (he
shall die) then goes y priest unto him, & putting a cloth
into his mouth doth strangle him therewith : which being
done, he cuts his dead body into morsels, & al his friends
and kinsfolk are invited unto the eating thereof, with
musique & all kinde of mirth: howbeit his bones are
solemnely buried. And when I found fault with that
custome demanding a reason thereof, one of them **gaue**
me this answere ; this we doe lest the wormes should eat
his flesh, for then his soule should suffer great torments,
neither could I by any meanes remoove them from that
errour. Many other novelties and strange things there
bee in this countrey, which no man would credite, unles
he saw them with his owne eyes. Howbeit, I (before
almighty God) do here make relation of nothing but of
that onely, whereof I am as sure, as a man may be sure.
Concerning the foresaid islands, I enquired of divers wel-
experienced persons, who al of them, as it were with one
consent, answered me saying, that this India contained
4400 islands under it, or within it, in which islands there
are sixty and foure crowned kings : and they say moreouer, that the greater part of those islands are wel inhabited. And here I conclude concerning that part of
India.

Of the upper India : and of the province of Mancy.[1]

FIRST of al therefore, having traveled many dayes journey upon the Ocean-sea towards the East, at length I arrived at a certaine great province called Mancy, being in Latine named India.　Concerning this India I inquired of Christians, of Saracens, & of Idolaters, and of al such as bare an office under the great Can ; who all of them with one consent answered, that this province of Mancy hath mo then 2000 great cities within the precincts thereof & that it aboundeth with all plenty of victuals, as namely with bread, wine, rise, flesh, and fish.　All the men of this province be artificers & marchants, who, though they be in never so extreme penurie, so long as they can help themselues by the labor of their handes, will neuer beg almes of any man. The men of this province are of a faire and comely personage, but somewhat pale, having their heads shaven but a little, but the women are the most beautiful under the sunne.　The first city of the said India which I came unto, is called Ceuskalon, which being a daies journey distant from the sea, stands upon a river, the water whereof, nere unto the mouth, where it exonerateth it selfe into the sea, doth overflow the land for the space of 12 daies journey.　All the inhabitants of this India are worshippers of idols.　The foresaid city of Ceuskalon hath such an huge navy belonging there-

---

[1] Or China.

unto, that no man would beleeve it unlesse he should see
it. In this city I saw 300 li of good and new ginger
sold for lesse than a groat. There are the greatest, and
the fairest geese, & most plenty of them to be sold in
al the world, as I suppose : they are as white as milke,
& haue a bone upon the crowne of their heads, as bigge
as an egge, being of the colour of blood : under the
throat they haue a skin or bag hanging down halfe a
foot. They are exceeding fat and wel sold. Also they
haue ducks and hens in that countrey, one as big as two
of ours. There be monstrous great serpents likewise,
which are taken by the inhabitants & eaten ; whereupon
a solemne feast among them without serpents is not
set by.

And to be briefe, in this city there are al kinds of
victuals in great abundance. From thence I passed by
many cities & at length I came unto a citie named
Caitan,[1] wherein ye friers Minorites haue two places of
abode, unto which I transported the bones of the dead
friers, which suffered martyrdom for the faith of Christ,
as it is aboue mentioned. In this citie there is abundance of al kind of victuals very cheap. The said city
is as big as two of Bononia,[2] & in it are many monasteries of religious persons, al which do worship idols.

I myselfe was in one of those monasteries, & it was
told me, that there were in it III M religious men, having
XI M idols ; and one of ye said idols which seemed unto
me but litle in regard of the rest, was as big as our
Christopher. These religious men euery day do feed
their idol-gods : wherupon at a certaine time I went to
behold the banquet : and indeed those things which they

---

[1] Thsiuanchau or Chiuchau, the great mediæval port of China.
[2] Bologna.

brought unto them were good to eate, & fuming hote
insomuch that the steam of the smoke thereof ascended
up unto their idols, and they said that their gods were
refreshed with the smoke: howbeit all the meat they
conveyed away, eating it up their owne selves, and so
they fed their dumb gods with the smoke only.

Of the citie of Fuco.

TRAVELING more eastward, I came unto a city
named Fuco,[1] which containeth 30 miles in circuit,
wherein be exceeding great & faire cocks, *and al their
hens are as white as the very snow, having wool in stead of
feathers, like unto sheep.* It is a most stately & beautiful
city & standeth up the sea. Then I went 18 daies
journey on further, & passed by many provinces & cities,
and in the way I went over a certain great mountaine,
upon ye one side whereof I beheld al living creatures to
be as black as a cole, & the men and women on that
side differed somewhat in maner of living from others;
howbeit, on the other side of the said hil every living
thing was snow-white & the inhabitants in their maner
of living, were altogether unlike unto others. There, al
maried women cary in token that they haue husbands, a
great trunk of horne upon their heads. From thence I
traveled 18 dayes journey further and came unto a certaine great river, and entered also into a city, whereunto
belongeth a mighty bridge to passe the said river. And

---

[1] Probably Fuchau in Fokieu.

R

mine hoste with whom I sojourned, being desirous to
show me some sport, said unto me, Sir, if you will see
any fish taken, goe with me.   Then hee led me unto the
foresaid bridge, carrying in his armes certain dive-doppers [1]
or water-foules, bound unto a company of poles, and
about every one of their necks he tied a thread, lest they
should eat the fish as fast as they took them: and he
carried three great baskets with him also; then loosed
he the dive-doppers from the poles, which presently went
into the water, & within lesse then the space of one
houre, caught as many fishes as filled the 3 baskets:
which being full, mine hoste untied the threeds from
about their neckes, and entering a second time into the
river they fed themselves with fish, and being satisfied
they returned and suffered themselves to be bound unto
the said poles as they were before.   And when I did
eate of those fishes, we thought they were exceeding
good.   Travailing thence many dayes journeys, at length
I arrived at another city called Canasia,[2] which signifieth
in our language, the city of heaven.   Never in all my
life did I see so great a city: for it containeth in circuit
an hundreth miles; neither sawe I any plot thereof,
which was not throughly inhabited: yea, I sawe many
houses of tenne or twelve stories high, one aboue the
other.   It hath mightie large suburbs containing more
people then the citie it selfe.   Also it hath twelue principall gates: and about the distance of 8 miles, in the
high way unto euery one of the saide gates standeth a
city as big by estimation as Venice, and Padua.   The
aforesaide city of Canasia is situated in waters or
marshes, which always stand still, neither ebbing nor

---

[1] Cormorants.   [2] Now Hangchau.

flowing : howbeit it hath a defence for the winde like unto Venice. In this citie there are mo than 10002 bridges, many whereof I numbered and passed over them : and upon every of those bridges stand certaine watchmen of the citie, keeping continuall ward and watch about the saide citie, the great Can the Emperour of Catay. The people of this countrey say, that they haue one duetie injoyned unto them by their lord : for euery fire payeth one Balis in regard of tribute : and a Balis is five papers or pieces of silk, which are worth one floren and an halfe of our coine. Tenne or twelue housholds are accompted for one fire, and so pay tribute but for one fire only. Al those tributary fires amount unto the number of 85 Thuman, with other foure Thuman of the Saracens, which make 89 in al : And one Thuman consisteth of 10000 fires. The residue of the people of the city are some of them Christians, some marchants, and some traueilers through the countrey. Whereupon I marveiled much how such an infinite number of persons could inhabite and liue together. There is great aboundance of victuals in this city, as namely of bread and wine, and especially of hogs-flesh with other necessaries.

Of a Monastery where many strange beastes of divers kindes doe live upon an hill.

IN the foresaide citie foure of our friers had converted a mighty and rich man unto the faith of Christ, at whose house I continually abode, for so long time as I

remained in the citie, Who upon a certain time said unto
me: Ara, that is to say, Father, will you go and beholde
the citie? And I said, yea. Then embarked we our-
selves, and directed our course unto a certaine great
Monastery: where being arrived, he called a religious
person with whom he was acquainted, saying unto him
concerning me: this Raban Francus, that is to say, this
religious Frenchman commeth from the Westerne parts
of the world and therefore you must show him some rare
things, that when he returnes into his owne countrey, he
may say, this strange sight or novelty haue I seene in
the citie of Canasia. Then the said religious man tooke
two greate baskets full of broken reliques which remained
of the table, & led me unto a little walled parke, the
doore whereof he unlocked with his key, and there appeared unto us a pleasant faire green plot, into the which
we entred. In the said greene stands a litle mount in
forme of a steeple, replenished with fragrant herbes, and
fine shady trees. And while we stood there, he tooke a
cymbal or bell, and rang therewith, as they used to ring
to dinner or bevoir in cloisters, at the sound whereof
many creatures of divers kindes came downe from the
mount, some like apes, some like cats, some like mon-
keys, and some having faces like men. And while I
stood beholding of them, they gathered themselves
together about him, to the number of 4200 of those
creatures, putting themselues in good order, before whom
he set a platter, and gaue them the saide fragments to
eate. And when they had eaten he rang upon his cymbal the second time, and they all returned unto their
former places. Then, wondring greatly at the matter, I
demanded what kind of creatures those might be? They
are (quoth he) the Soules of noble men which we do

here feed, for the love of God who governeth the world:
and as a man was honorable or noble in this life, so his
soule after death, entreth into the body of some excellent
beast or other, but the soules of simple and rusticall
people do possesse the bodies of more vile and brutish
creatures. Then I began to refute that foule error:
howbeit my speech did nothing at all to prevaile with
him, for hee could not be perswaded that any soule
might remaine without a body. From thence I departed
unto a certaine citie named Chilenso, the walls whereof
contained 40 miles in circuit. In this citie there are 360
bridges of stone, the fairest that euer I saw, and it is
wel inhabited, having a great navie belonging thereunto,
& abounding with all kinds of victuals and other commodities. And thence I went unto a certaine river called
Thalay which where it is most narrow, is 7 miles broad:
and it runneth through the midst of the land of the
Pygmœi whose chiefe city is called Cakam, and is one
of the goodliest cities in the world. These Pygmœans
are three of my spans high, and they make larger and
better cloth of cotton and silke, then any other nation
under the sunne. And coasting along by the said river,
I came unto a certaine city named Janzu, in which citie
there is one receptacle for the Friers of our order, and
there be also three Churches of the Nestorians. This
Janzu is a noble and great citie, containing 48 Thumans
of tributarie fires, and in it are all kindes of victuals, and
great plenty of such beastes, foules, and fishes, as Christians doe usually liue upon. The lord of the same citie
hath in yeerely revenues for salt onely, fiftie Thuman of
Balis, & one balis is worth a floren and a halfe of our
coyne: insomuch that one Thuman of balis amounteth
unto the value of 15000 florens. Howbeit the sayd lord,

favoureth his people in one respect, for sometimes he for-
giveth them frely 200 Thuman, lest there should be any
scarcity or dearth among them.   There is a custome in
this citie, that when any man is determined to banquet
his friends, going about unto certaine tavernes or cookes
houses appointed for the same purpose, he sayth unto
euery particular hoste, you shall haue such and such of
my friends, whom you must entertain in my name, and
so much I will bestowe upon the banquet.   And by that
means his friendes are better feasted at diverse places,
then they should haue beene at one.   Tenne miles from
the sayde citie, about the head of the foresayd river of
Thalay, there is a certaine other citie called Montu,
which hath the greatest navy that I saw in the whole
world.   All their ships are as white as snow, & they
haue banquetting houses in them, and many other rare
things also, which no man would beleeve unlesse he had
seene them with his owne eyes.

Of the citie of Cambaleth.

TRAVELING eight dayes journey further by divers
territories and cities, at length I came by fresh
water unto a certaine citie named Leucyn, standing upon
a river of Karavoran[1] which runneth through the midst
of Cataie, and doeth great harme in the countrey when
it overfloweth the bankes, or breaketh foorth of the
chanell.   From thence passing along the river Eastward,

[1] Karamoron.

after many dayes travell, and the sight of divers cities, I
arrived at a citie called Sumakoto,[1] which aboundeth
more with silke then any other citie in the worlde: for
when there is a great scarcity of silke, fortie pound is
solde for lesse then eight groates.   In this citie there is
abundance of all merchandize, and all kinds of victuals
also, as of bread, wine, flesh, fish, with all choise and
delicate spices.   Then traveiling on still towards the East
by many cities, I came unto the noble and renowned
citie of Cambaleth, which is of great antiquitie, being
situate in the province of Cataie.   This citie the Tartars
tooke, & neere unto it within the space of halfe a mile,
they built another citie called Caido.   The citie of
Caido hath twelve gates, being each of them two miles
distant from another.   Also the space lying in the midst
betweene the two foresayde cities is very well and
thoroughly inhabited, so that they make as it were but one
citie betweene them both.   The whole compasse or circuit of both cities together is 40 miles.   In this citie the
great emperour Can hath his principall seat, and his
Imperiall palace, the wals of which palace containe foure
miles in circuit : and neere unto this his palace are many
other palaces and houses of his nobility which belong
unto his court.   Within the precincts of the said palace
Imperiall, there is a most beautifull mount, set and replenished with trees, for which cause it is called the
Greene mount, having a most royall and sumptuous
palace standing thereupon, in which, for the most part,
the great Can is resident.   Upon the one side of the
sayde mount there is a great lake, whereupon a most
stately bridge is built, in which lake a great abundance

---

[1] Sumacoto.

of geese, ducks, & all kinds of water foules, and in the
wood growing upon the mount, there is a great store of
all birdes and wilde beastes.   And therefore when the
great Can will solace himselfe with hunting or hauking,
he needs not so much as once to step forth of his palace.
Moreover, the principall palace, wherein he maketh his
abode, is very large, having within it 14 pillers of golde,
and all the walles thereof are hanged with red skinnes,
which are said to be the most costly skinnes in all the
world.   In the midst of the palace stands a cisterne of
two yards high, which consisteth of a precious stone
called Merdochas, and is wreathed about with golde, &
at ech corner thereof is the golden image of a serpent, as
it were furiously shaking and casting forth his head.
This cisterne also hath a kinde of network of pearle
wrought about it.   Likewise by the sayd cisterne there
is drinke conveyed thorow certaine pipes and conducts
such as useth to be drunke in the emperours court, upon
the which also there hang many vessels of golde, wherein
whosoever will may drinke of the said licour.   In the
foresayd palace there are many peacockes of golde : &
when any Tartar maketh a banquet unto his lorde, if
the guests chance to clap their hands for joy and mirth
the said golden peacocks also will spread their wings
abroad, and lift up their traines, seeming as if they
danced, and this I suppose to be done by arte magicke
or by some secret engine under the grounde.

Of the glory and magnificence of the great Can.

MOREOVER, when the great emperour Can sitteth
on his imperiall throne of estate, on his lefte
hand sitteth his queene or empresse and upon another
inferior seate there sit two other women, which are to
accompany the emperour, when his spouse is absent, but
in the lowest place of all, there sit all the ladies of his
kinred. *All the married women weare upon their heads a*
kind of ornament in shape like unto a man's foote of a
cubite and a halfe in length, and the lower part of the said
foote is adorned with cranes feathers, and is all ouer thicke
set with great and orient pearles. Upon the right hande
of the great Can sitteth his first begotten sonne and heire
apparent unto his empire, and under him sit all the
nobles of the blood royall. There bee also foure Secre-
taries, which put all things in writing that the emperour
speaketh. In whose presence likewise stand his Barons
and divers others of his nobilitie, with great traines of
folowers after them, of whom none dare speake so much
as one worde, unlesse they haue obtained licence of the
emperour so to doe, except his jesters and stage players,
who are appointed of purpose to solace their lord.
Neither yet dare they attempt to doe ought, but onely
according to the pleasure of their emperor, and as hee
enjoineth by lawe. About the palace gate stand certaine
Barons to keepe all men from treading upon the thres-
hold of the sayd gate. When it pleaseth the great Can
to solemnize a feast, he hath about him 14000 Barons,

carying wreathes & litle crownes upon their heads, and
giving attendance upon their lord, and eueryone of them
weareth a garment of golde and precious stones, which
is worth ten thousand florens. His court is kept in very
good order, by governours of tens, governours of hundreds, and governours of thousands, insomuch that euery
one in his place performeth his dutie committed to him,
neither is there any defect to bee found. I Frier
Odoricus was there present in person for the space of
three yeares and was often at the sayd banquets: for
wee friers Minorites have a place of aboad appointed
out for us in the emperours court, and are enjoined to
goe and to bestow our blessing upon him. And I enquired of certain courtiers concerning the number of
persons pertaining to the emperors court. Moreouer,
when he will make his progresse from one countrey to
another, hee hath foure troupes of horsemen, one being
appointed to goe a dayes journey before, and another to
come a dayes journey after him, the third to march on
his right hand and the fourth on his left, in the maner
of a crosse, he himselfe being in the midst, and so euery
particular troupe haue their daily journeys limited unto
them, to the ende they may provide sufficient victuals
without defect. Nowe the great Can himselfe is caried
in maner following: hee rideth in a chariot with two
wheeles, upon which a majesticall throne is built of the
wood of Aloe, being adorned with gold and great pearles
and precious stones, and foure elephants bravely furnished doe drawe the sayd chariot, before which elephants foure greate horses richly trapped and covered
doe lead the way. Hard by the chariot on both sides
thereof, are foure Barons laying hold and attending
thereupon, to keepe all persons from approching neere

unto their emperour. Upon the chariot two milke-white
jer-falcons doe sit, and seeing any game which hee would
take, hee letteth them fly, and so they take it, and after
this maner doeth hee solace himselfe as hee rideth.
Moreover, no man dare come within a stone's cast of the
chariot, but such as are appointed. The number of his
owne followers, of his wives attendants, and of the traine
of his first begotten sonne and heire apparent, would
seem incredible to any man ; unless he had first seene it
with his owne eyes. The foresayd great Can hath
divided his Empire into twelue parts or provinces, and
one of the said provinces hath two thousand great cities
within the precincts thereof. Whereupon his empire is
of that length and breadth, that unto whatsoever part
thereof he intendeth his journey, he hath space enough
for six moneths continual progress, except his islands
which are at the least 5000.

*Of certaine Innes or hospitals appointed for traveilers
throughout the whole empire.*

THE foresayd Emperor (to the end that travailers
may haue all things necessary throughout his
whole empire) hath caused certaine Innes to be provided
in sundry places upon the highwayes, where all things
pertaining unto victuals are in a continuall readinesse.
And when any alteration or newes happen in any part
of his Empire, if he chance to be farre absent from that
part, his ambassadors upon horses or dromedaries ride
post unto him, and when themselves and their beaste are

weary, they blowe their horne, at the noise whereof, the
next Inne likewise provideth a horse and a man, who
takes the letter from him that is weary, and runneth
unto another Inne : and so by divers Innes, and divers
postes, the report, which ordinarily could skarce come
in 30 dayes, is in one naturall day brought unto the
Emperour : and therefore no matter of any moment can
be done in his empire, but straightway he hath intelli-
gence of it. Moreouer when the great Can himselfe will
go on hunting, he useth this custome. Some 20 days
journey from the citie of Kambaleth there is a forrest
containing six dayes journey in circuit, in which forrest
there are so many kinds of beasts and birds as it is incredible to report. Unto this forrest, at the ende of
euery thirde or fourthe yeere, himself with his whole
traine resorteth, and they all of them together environ
the said forrest, sending dogs into the same, which by
hunting doe bring foorth the beasts : namely lions and
stags, and other creatures, unto a most beautifull plaine
in the midst of the forrest, because all the beasts of the
forrest doe tremble, especially at the cry of hounds.
Then cometh the great Can himselfe, being caried upon
three elephants, and shooteth fiue arrowes into the whole
herd of beasts, and after him all his Barons, and after
them the rest of his courtiers and family doe all in like
maner discharge their arrowes also, and euery mans
arrow hath a sundry marke. Then they all goe unto the
beasts which are slaine (suffering the living beasts to
returne into the wood that they may haue more sport
with them another time) and euery man enjoyeth that
beast as his owne, wherein he findeth his arrow sticking.

*Of the foure feasts which the great Can solemnizeth euery
yeere in his court.*

FOURE great feasts in a yeere doeth the emperor
Can celebrate: namely the feast of his birth, the
feast of his circumcision, the feast of his coronation, and
the feast of his mariage. And unto these feasts he in-
viteth all his Barons, his stage players, and all such as
are of his kinred. Then the great Can sitting in his
throne, all his Barons present themselves before him,
with wreaths and crowns upon their heads, being diversely
attired, for some of them are in greene, namely the principall: the seconde are in red, and the third in yellow:
and they hold each man in his hand a little Ivorie table
of elephants tooth, and they are girt with golden girdles
of halfe a foote broad, and they stand upon their feete
keeping silence. About them stand the stage-players
or musicians with their instruments. And in one of the
corners of a certaine great pallace, all the Philosophers
or Magicians remaine for certaine howers, and do attend
upon points or characters; and when the point and
hower which the sayd Philosophers expected for, is
come, a certain crier crieth out with a loud voice, saying,
Incline or bowe your selves before your Emperour; with
that all the Barons fall flat upon the earth. Then hee
crieth oute againe: Arise all, and immediately they all
arise. Likewise the Philosophers attend upon a point
or character the second time, and when it is fulfilled the
crier crieth out amaine: Put your fingers in your eares;
and foorthwith againe he saieth: Plucke them out.

Againe, at the third point he crieth, Boult this meale.
Many other circumstances also doe they performe, all
which they say haue some certaine signification, howbeit
neither would I write them, nor giue any heed unto
them, because they are vaine and ridiculouse. And
when the musicians houre is come, then the Philosophers
say, Solemnize a feast unto your Lord : with that all of
them sound their instruments, making a great and
melodious noise. And immediately another crieth,
Peace, Peace, and they are all whist. Then come the
women-musicians, and sing sweetly before the Emperour,
which musike was more delightfull unto me. After them
come in the lions and doe their obeisance unto the great
Can. Then the juglers cause golden cups full of wine
to flie up and downe in the ayre & to apply themselves
unto mens mouths that they may drinke of them. These
any many other strange things I sawe in the court of
the great Can, which no man would beleeve unlesse he
had seen them with his owne eies, and therefore I omit
to speake of them. I was informed also by certaine credible persons of another miraculous thing, namely, that
in a certaine Kingdome of the sayd Can, wherein stand
the mountains called Kapsei (the Kingdomes name is
Kalor) there *groweth great Gourds or Pompions,*[1] *which
being ripe, doe open at the tops, and within them is found
a little beast like unto a yong lambe, even as I my selfe
have heard reported, that there stand certain trees upon the
shore of the Irish Sea, bearing fruit like unto a gourd,
which at a certaine time of the yeere doe fall into the water,
and become birds called Bernacles, and this is most true.*

[1] Pumpkins.

Of *divers provinces & cities.*

AND after three yeeres I departed out of the empire of Cataie, traveiling fiftie dayes journey towards the West.   And at length I came unto the empire of Prete-goani,[1] whose principall citie is Kasan, which hath many cities under it.   From thence passing many dayes travel I came unto a province called Casan, which is for good commodities, one of the onely provinces under the Sunne, & is very well inhabited, insomuch that when we depart out of the gates of one city we may beholde the gates of another city, as I myselfe sawe in divers of them.   The breadth of the said province is 50 dayes journey and the length aboue sixtie.   In it there is great plenty of all victuals, and especially of chesnuts, and it is one of the twelve provinces of the great Can.   Going on further, I came unto a certaine Kingdome called Tebek,[2] which is in subjection unto the great Can also, wherein I thinke there is more plenty of bread and wine then in any other part of the worlde besides.   The people of the sayd countrey do, for the most part, inhabit in tents made of blacke felt.   Their principall city is invironed with faire and beautifull walls, being built of most white and blacke stones, which are disposed checkerwise one by another, and curiously compiled together : likewise all the high wayes in this countrey are exceedingly well paved.   In the said countrey none dare shed the bloud of a man, or of any beast, for the reverence of a certaine idol.   In the

---

[1] Prester John.   [2] Or Thibet.

aforesayd citie their Abassi, that is to say, their Pope is
resident, being the head and prince of all idolaters (upon
whom he bestoweth and distributeth gifts after his maner)
euen as our Pope of Rome accounts himselfe to be the
head of all Christians. The Women of this countrey
weare aboue an hundreth tricks & trifles about them,
and they haue two teeth in their mouthes as long as the
tuskes of a boare. *When any mans father deceaseth
among them, his sonne assembleth together all the priests
and musicians that he can get, saying that he is determined
to honour his father : then causeth he him to be caried into
the field (all his kinsfolks, friends, and neighbours, accom-
panying him in the sayd action) where the priests with
great solemnity cut off the fathers head, giving it unto his
sonne, which being done, they divide the whole body into
morsels, and so leaue it behinde them, returning home with
prayers in the company of the said sonne. So soone as
they are departed, certain vultures, which are accustomed
to such bankets, come flying from the mountains, and cary
away all the sayd morsels of flesh : and from thenceforth
a fame is spread abroad, that the sayd party deceased was
holy, because the angels of God carried him into paradise.
And this is the greatest and highest honour, that the sonne
can devise to performe unto his father. Then the sayd
sonne taketh his fathers head, seething it and eating the
flesh thereof, but of the skull he maketh a drinking cup,
wherein himselfe with all his family and kinred do drinke
with great solemnitie and mirth, in the remembrance of his
dead and devoured father.* Many other vile and abominable things doth the sayd nation commit, which I
meane not to write because men neither can nor will
beleeue, except they should haue a sight of them.

Of a certaine riche man, who is fed and nourished by 50
virgins.

WHILE I was in the province of Mancy, I passed
by the palace of a certaine famous man, which
hath fifty virgin damosels continually attending upon
him, feeding him euery meale as a bird feeds her yoong
ones.   Also he hath sundry kinds of meat served in at
his table and three dishes of ech kinde : and when the
said virgins feed him, they singe most sweetly.   This
man hath in yeerely revenues thirty thuman of tagars of
rise, euery of which thuman yeeldeth tenne thousand
tagars, and one tagar is the burthen of an asse.   **His**
palace is two miles in circuit, the pavement thereof is
one plate of golde and another of silver.   Neere unto the
wall of the sayd palace there is a mount artificially
wrought with golde and silver, whereupon stand turrets
and steeples, and other delectable things for the solace
and recreation of the foresayd great man.   And it was
tolde me that there were foure such men in the sayd
kingdome.   It is accounted a great grace for the men of
that countrey to haue long nailes upon their fingers, and
especially upon their thumbes which nailes they may
folde about their handes : but the grace and beauty of
their women is to haue small and slender feet : and
therefore the mothers when their daughters are yoong,
do binde up their feete that they may not grow great.
Travelling on further towards the South, I arrived at a
certain countrey called Melistorte, which is a pleasant

S

and fertile place.   In this countrey was a certain aged
man called Senex de monte, who round about two
mountaines had built a wall to inclose the said mountaines.   Within this wall there were the fairest and most
chrystall fountaines in the whole world : and about the
sayd fountaines there were the most beautifull virgins in
great number, and goodly horses also, and in a word,
euery thing that could be devised for bodily solace and
delight, and therefore the inhabitants of the countrey
call the same place by the name of Paradise.   The olde
Senex, when he saw any proper and valiant yoong man,
he would admit him into his paradise.   Moreover by
certain conducts he makes wine and milke to flow abun-
dantly.   This Senex when he hath a minde to revenge
himselfe or to slay any king or baron, commandeth him
who is governor of the sayd paradise, to bring thereunto
some of the acquaintance of the sayd king or baron,
permitting him a while to take his pleasure therein, and
then to give him a certaine potion being of force, to cast
him into such a slumber as should make him quite voide
of all sense, and so being in a profound sleepe to convey
him out of his paradise : who being awakened and seeing
himselfe thrust out of the paradise, would become so
sorrowfull, that he could not in the world devise what to
do, or whither to turne him.   Then would he goe unto
the foresaid old man, beseeching him that he might be
admitted again into his paradise, who saith unto him,
You cannot be admitted thither, unlesse you will slay
such or such a man for my sake, & if you will giue the
attempt onely, whether you kill him or no, I will place
you againe in paradise, that there you may remain
always : then would the party without faile put the same
in execution, indevouring to murther all those against

whom the old man had conceived any hatred. And therefore all the kings of the east stood in awe of the sayd olde man, and gaue unto him great tribute.

Of the death of Senex de monte.

AND when the Tartars had subdued a great part of the world, they came unto the sayd olde man, and tooke from him the custody of his paradise: who being incensed thereat, sent abroad divers desperate and reso-lute persons out of his forenamed paradise, and caused many of the Tartarian nobles to be slaine. The Tartars seeing this, went and beseiged the citie wherein the sayd olde man was, tooke him, and put him to a most cruell and ignominious death. The friers in that place haue this special gift and prerogative, namely, that by the vertue of the name of Christ Jesu, & in the vertue of his precious blood, which he shedde upon the crosse for the salvation of mankinde, they doe cast foorth devils out of them that are possessed. And because there are many possessed men in those parts, they are bound and brought ten dayes journey unto the sayd friers, who being dis-possessed of the uncleane spirits, do presently beleeve in Christ, who delivered them, accounting him for their God, and being baptised in his name, and also delivering immediately unto the friers all their idols and the idols of their cattell, which are commonly made of felt or of womens haire: then the sayd friers kindle a fire in a publicke place (whereunto the people resort, that they may see the false gods of their neighbors burnt), and

cast the sayd idols thereinto : howbeit at first those idols
came out of the fire againe. Then the friers sprinkled
the sayd fire with holy water, casting in the idols the
second time, and with that the devils fled in the likenesse of black smoake, and the idols still remained till
they were consumed unto ashes.   Afterward, this noise
and outcry was heard in the ayre : Beholde and see how
I am expelled out of my habitation. And by these
means the friers doe baptise great multitudes, who presently revolt againe unto their idols ; insomuch that the
sayd friers must eftsoones, as it were, underprop them,
and informe them anew. *There was another terrible
thing which I saw there : for passing by a certaine valley,
which is situate beside a pleasant river, I saw many dead
bodies, and in the said valley also I heard divers sweet
sounds and harmonies of musike, especially the noise of
citherns, whereat I was greatly amazed. This valley conteineth in length seven or eight miles at the least, into the
which whosoeuer entreth, dieth presently, and can by no
means passe aliue thorow the middest thereof; for which
cause all the inhabitants thereabout decline unto the one
side. Moreover, I was tempted to go in & to see what it
was. At length, making my prayers and recommending
my selfe to God in the name of Jesu, I entred, and saw
such swarmes of dead bodies there, as no man would
beleeve unless he were an eyewitnesse thereof. At the one
side of the foresayde valley upon a certaine stone, I saw
the visage of a man, which behelde me with such a terrible
aspect that I thought verily I should haue died in the same
place. But alwayes this sentence, the word became flesh,
and dwelt amongst us, I ceased not to pronounce, signing
my selfe with the signe of the crosse, and neerer than seven
to eight pases I durst not approach unto the sayd head :*

but I departed & fled unto another place in the sayd valley,
ascending up into a little sande mountaine, where look-
ing about, I saw nothing but the sayd citherns, which
methought I heard miraculously sounding and playing
by themselves without the helpe of musicians. And
being upon the toppe of the mountaine, I found silver
there like the scales of fishes in great abundance, and I
gathered some part thereof into my bosome to shew for
a wonder, but my conscience rebuking me, I cast it upon
the earth, reserving no whit at all unto my selfe, and so,
by God's grace I departed without danger. And when
the men of the countrey knew that I was returned out
of the valley alive, they reverenced me much, saying
that I was baptised and holy, and that the foresayd
bodies were men subject unto the devils infernall who
used to play upon citherns, to the end they might allure
people to enter, and so murther them. Thus much concerning these things which I beheld most certainly with
mine eyes, I frier Odoricus haue heere written : many
strange things also I haue of purpose omitted, because
men will not beleeue them unlesse they should see them.

Of the honour and reverence done unto the great Can.

I WILL report one thing more, which I saw, concerning
the great Can. It is an usuall custome in those
parts, that when the foresayd Can traveileth thorow any
countrey, his subjects kindle fires before their doores,
casting spices thereinto to make a perfume, that their
lord passing by may smell the sweet and delectable

odours thereof, and much people come forth to meet him. And upon a certaine time when he was comming towardes Cambaleth, the fame of his approch being published, a bishop of ours with certaine of our minorite friers and myselfe went two dayes journey to meet him : and being come nigh unto him, we put a crosse upon wood. I my selfe having a censer in my hand, and began to sing with a loud voice : Veni creator spiritus. And as we were singing on this wise he caused us to be called, commanding us to come unto him : notwithstanding (as it is above mentioned) that no man dare approche within a stones cast of his chariot, unlesse he be called, but such onely as keep his chariot. And when we came neare unto him, he vailed his hat or bonet being of an inestimable price, doing reverence unto the crosse. And immediately I put incense into the censour, and our bishop taking the censer perfumed him, and gaue him his benediction. Moreouer, they that come before the said Can, do alwayes bring some oblation to present unto him, observing the ancient law : Thou shalt not appear in my presence with an empty hand. And for that cause we carried apples with us, and offered them in a platter with reverence unto him : and taking out two of them he did eate some part of one. And then he signified unto us, that we should go apart, lest the horses comming on might in ought offend us. With that we departed from him, and turned aside, going unto certaine of his barons, which had been converted to the faith by certaine friers of our order, being at the same time in his army : and we offered unto them of the foresayd apples, who received them at our hands with great joy, seeming unto us to be as glad, as if we had giuen them some great gift. All the premisses

above written frier William de Solanga hath put downe
in writing euen as the foresayd frier Odoricus uttered
them by word of mouth, in the yeere of our Lord 1330
in the moneth of May, and in the place of S. Anthony
of Padua. *Neither did he regard to write them in difficult
Latine, or in an eloquent style, but even as Odoricus himselfe rehearsed them, to the end that men might the more
easily understand the things reported.* I Odoricus frier,
of Friuli, of a certaine territory called Portus Vahonis,
and of the order of the minorites, do testifie and beare
witnesse unto the reverend father Guidotus minister of
the province of S. Anthony, in the marquisate of Tre-
viso (being by him required upon mine obedience so to
doe) that all the premisses above written, either I saw
with mine owne eyes, or heard the same reported by
credible and substantiall persons. The common report
also of the countreys where I was, testifieth those things,
which I saw, to be true. Many other things I haue
omitted because I behelde them not with my owne eyes.
Howbeit from day to day I purpose with my selfe to
travell countreys or lands, in which action I dispose myselfe to die or to live, as it shall please my God.

Of the death of frier Odoricus.

IN the yeere therefore of our Lord 1331 the foresayd
frier Odoricus preparing himselfe for the perform-
ance of his intended journey, that his travel and labour
might be to greater purpose, he determined to present
himselfe unto Pope John the two and twentieth, whose

benediction and obedience being received, he with a
certaine number of friers willing to beare him company
might convey himselfe unto all the countreys of infidels.
And as he was travelling toward the pope, and not farre
distant from the city of Pisa, there meets him by the
waye a certaine olde man, in the habit and attire of a
pilgrime, saluting him by name and saying: All haile
frier Odoricus. And when the frier demaunded how he
had knowledge of him: he answered: Whilest you were
in India I knew you full well, yea, and I knew your holy
purpose also: but see that you returne immediately unto
the coven [1] from where you came, for tenne dayes hence
you shall depart out of this present world. Wherefore
being astonished and amazed at these words, (especially
the olde man vanishing out of his sight, presently after
he had spoken them) he determined to returne. And so
he returned in perfect health feeling no crazednesse nor
infirmity of body. And being in his coven at Udene
in the province of Padua, the tenth daye after the foresayd vision, having received the Communion, and preparing himselfe unto God, yea, being strong and sound
of body, hee happily rested in the Lord: who sacred
departure was signified unto the Pope aforesaid, under
the hand of the publique notary in these words following.

In the yeere of our Lord 1331, the 14 day of Januarie,
Beatus Odoricus a Frier minorite deceased in Christ, at
whose prayers God shewed many and sundry miracles,
which I Guetelus publique notarie of Utina, sonne of M.
Damianus de Porto Gruaro at the commandment and
direction of the honorable Conradus of the Borough of

---

[1] Convent.

Gastaldion, and one of the Councell of Utina, haue written as faithfully as I could, and haue delivered a copie thereof unto the friers minorites, howbeit not of all, because they are innumerable, and too difficult for me to write.

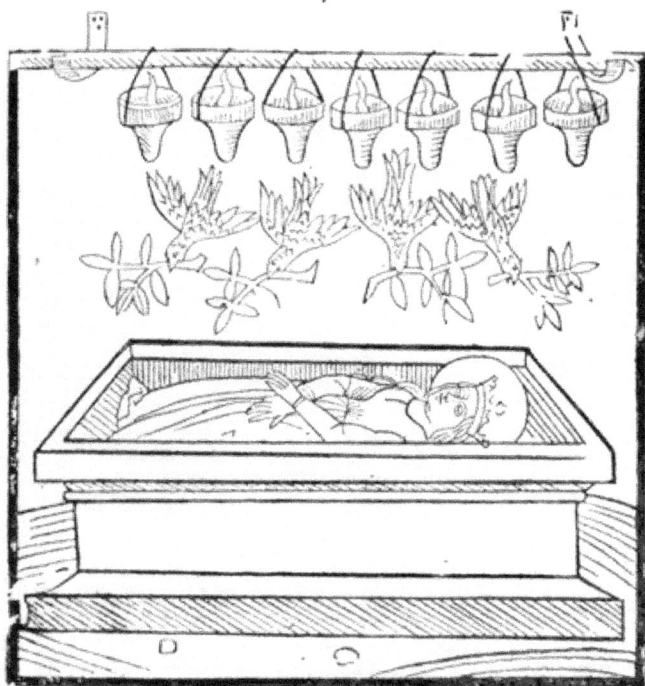

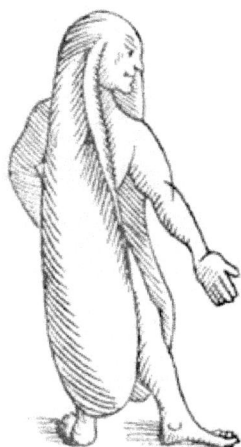

LIST OF THE EDITIONS

OF THE VOYAGES AND TRAVELS OF SIR JOHN MANDEVILLE
NOW (1884) IN THE BRITISH MUSEUM.

CHRONOLOGICALLY ARRANGED.

MSS.

EGERTON MSS. 672. Johannis de Maundevilla Itinerarium ad partes Ierusolumitanas, &c. Vellum, 14 Cent., small 4°.

Grenville XXXIX. A 14 Cent. MS. fol. on vellum in double columns, which evidently has belonged to one of the French Royal Libraries, as the binding testifies. It commences "Ci comence le liure qui parle des diuersités des pais qui sunt par universe monde : le quel liure fut compile par mesire Jehan Mandeuille chlr ne dangleterre de la uille con dit Saint Albain."

Harl. 3954. A MS. on vellum, end of 14th Cent., with unfinished illuminations ; fine copy.

Sloane, 1464. Voyage in 1356. Vellum, in French. Early 15 Cent.

Harl. 212 (1). Le Geste de Sr John Maundeville de Mervailles de Monde. Small 4°. French. Vellum. Early 15 Cent. MS. note at end seems to place it as having been written previous to 1425.

Harl. 212 (2).   La Copie de la Lettre maunde ovesque cest
Escrit a tres noble Prince Monsire E. de Wyndesore Roy
d'Engleterre, et de Fraunce, par Monsire Johan de Maundeville, autour susdit.

Cotton, Tit. C. 16. English MS. 4°. Vellum. Early 15 Cent.

Sloane, 560.   De la Terre Seinte, que houme l'appelle Terre
de Promissionis de Ierusalem.   Vellum.   French.   15 Cent.

Add. MSS. 17,335.   Travels of Sir John de Mandeville
translated into German by Otto von Diemeringen, Canon of
Metz.   Vellum and paper, 15 Cent., with coloured drawings.
Fol.

Add. MSS. 10,129.   The Voyages and Travels of Sir John
Mandeville ; in German.   On paper.   15 Cent.   Fol.

Egerton MSS. 1982.   " Ye buke of (*the voiage and travaile*
of Sir) John Maundeville."   The text differs considerably from
that of the printed editions, and the prologue does not include
the apocryphal passage found in Cotton MS. Titus C. xvi., in
which the author states that he translated the work from Latin
into French, and from French into English. *Vellum.*   15
Cent.   On the fly-leaf, f, 2, is a note by E. Hill, M.D., 22
Mar. 1803, stating that on a leaf of paper pasted on the inside
of the old cover, was written, " Thys fayre Boke I have fro
the Abbey of Saint Albons in thys yeare of our Lord
M.CCCCLXXXX the sixte daye of Apryll.   Willyam Caxton,"
together with the name of Richard Tottyl, 1579, by whose
descendant, the Rev. Hugh Tuthill, the book was given to E.
Hill.   Small quarto.

Harl. 82 (4).   Itinerarium D. Joannis de Maundevyle
Militis, ἀχέφαλοι, et in fine Truncatum.   Vellum, fol. 15 Cent.
In Latin.

Harl. 175.   Itinerarium Dñi Johannis de Maundeville Militis,
de Mirabilibus Mundi.   In Latin, 15 Cent. 12°.   Vellum.

Harl. 204.   In French. On vellum. 4°. 15 Cent. On the
last page is a copy of the letter to Edward III.

Harl. 3589 (2). A Latin MS. commencing " Incipit Itinerarius magistri Johannis de Mandevelt ad partes Hierosoly-mitanas, et ulteriores partes transmarinas; qui obiit Leodii A.D. 1382." Paper. 15 Cent.

Harl. 3940. Le Livre de Jeh. de Mandeville, chevalier, le queil fut ney du pais d'engleterre, le queil parle de l'estat de la terre, et de marveilles que il y a veues. 15 Cent. Vellum. French. 4°.

Harl. 4383. Voiage de D. Jean Maundeville. 15 Cent. Vellum. French. Fol.

Harl. 1739. A French 4° MS. of 15 Cent. on vellum and paper, with letter to Edward III., in Latin, at the end.

Arundel, 140 (2). English MS. Fol. Paper, 15 Cent., ending "Her endys the boke of Johne Maundevile, Knyghte, of wayes to Ierusalem and of merveyles of Ynde and othere contrees."

Add. MSS. 18,026. The Voyages and Travels of Sir John Mandeville Knight; translated into German, and written by Johann Segnitz de Castel. 1449. Paper. 4°.

Egerton MSS. 1781, f. 129. Translation into Irish of the Travels of Sir John Mandeville made by Fineen Mac Mahon in 1475.

Cotton, App. 4, art. 2. Iter. Johannis Mandevill. Vellum. Small fol., in Latin. Late 15 Cent.

Grenville XII. An English MS. on paper, fol., end of 15 Cent., commencing "Here begynñth the boke of Moundevyle Knyzt that techyth the weyes to Jeslm and of the Meruelis of ynde and of the londe of Pst John, and of the grete Cham. and of Constantinople and of many oder Contreys."

PRINTED EDITIONS.

GRENVILLE, 6775. This is, probably, the oldest printed "Mandeville" extant, certainly the oldest dated copy, except a folio copy printed at Lyons on the 8th day of February of the same year, and there was also an Italian 4° edition previously printed at Milan. As far as is known this copy is unique, and it is in B. L. double columns, fol. It has, unfortunately, no name of printer, nor place of publication. "Ce liure est eppelle mandeuille et fut fait et compose par monsieur jehan de mandeuille cheualier natif dangleterre de la uille de sainct alein.[1] Et parle de la terre de promission cest assauoir de ierusalem et de pluseurs autres isles de mer et les diuerses et estranges choses qui sont es dites isles. Cy finist ce tres plaisant liure nome Mande ville parlant moult autentiquement du pays et terre doultre mer Et fut fait lan Mil. ccccLxxx le iiii iour dauril." Folio. B. L.

Grenville, 6702. Itinerario. Explicit Johannes de Mandeuilla impressus Mediolani ductu et auspiciis *Magistri Petri de corneno* pridie calendas augusti MCCCCLXXX. 4°. B. L. This is said to be the first Italian edition.

Grenville, 6700. Itinerarius Domini Johannis de Mandeville militis. This is a curious edition, printed in semi-Gothic Letter, and is the first known of the Latin editions. Its date is unknown, as is also the place where it was printed, but its date is fixed *circa* 1480.

C. 32, m. 5. Mandeville (*Sir* John) *the Traveller*. The travels of Sir J. M. translated into Dutch. G. L. (no place). 1470? Fol.

566, f. 6/1. Mandeville (*Sir* John) *the Traveller*. Begin-

---

[1] St. Albans.

ning (fol. 4, verso) Liber prĩs cui auctor feřt johãñes de mãdeville militari ordĩs, agit de divers patrijs, etc. G. L. Alosta? 1478? 4°. Imperfect.

Grenville, 6774. Hie hebt sich an das püch (*sic*) des Ritters herz Hannsen von Monte Villa. Gedrucht zü Augspurg *von hannsen schönsperger* am freitag nach Galli. Anno domini (MCCCCLXXXII). Fol.

Grenville, 6773. Johannes von Mondeuilla, Ritter. Getruckt zii Strassburg Johannes Prüssz. 1484. Fol. B. L. This is a very rare German edition, and is attributed to Michelfeld or Michelfelser.

Grenville, 6728/3. Explicit Itinerarius a terra Anglie in partes Ierosolymitanas et in vlteriores transmarinas editus primo in lingua gallicana a domino Johanne de Mandeville milite suo auctore. Anno incarnacionis domini MCCCLV in civitate leodiensi et paulo post in Eadem civitate translatus in dictam forinam latinam. Quod opus ubi inceptum simul et completum sit ipã elementa seu singularum seorsum caracteres literarum quibus impressum vides venatica, monstrant manifeste. 4°.[1]

789, a. 19. Mandeville (*Sir* John) *the Traveller.* Tractato de le piu maravegliose cose e piu notabile che si trovino ĩ le parte del mondo reducte e colte sotto brevita in lo p̃sente compẽdio dal strenuissimo cavalier a speron doro J. de Mandavilla anglico, &c.

G. L. p. U. Rugeriũ boñ (*oniæ*). 1488. 4°.

Grenville, 6703. Another copy of Sir John Mandeville's travels printed at Bologna, "*per mi Ugo di Rugerii.*" 1488. 4°. B. L.

Grenville, 6704. Another copy of Sir John Mandeville's travels, printed at Venice, "*per mi Nicolo de li ferari de pralormo.*" 1491. 4°. B. L.

---

[1] This edition has no date, but *Brunet* says (vol. iii. p. 1359) that it is printed from the same type used by *Gerard Leeu* at Antwerp in 1484 or 1485. As *Graesse* also confirms this, I attribute that date to it.

C. 4, h. 11.   Mandeville (*Sir* John) *the Traveller*.   Joanne de Mandavilla.   G. L.   Nicolo de li ferari de pralormo. Venetia, 1491.   4°.

Grenville, 6705.   Tractato belissimo, delle piu marivigliose cose, &c. scripte dallo cavaliere asperondoro Giov. Mandavilla Frazese ridocto in lingua thoscana.   Impresso ne la cipta di Firenze, *per Lorenzo de* Morgiani et Giovanni da Maganza. Adi VII. di Giugno MDCCCCLXXXXII.   4°.   This edition is very rare.

Grenville, 6706.   Johanne de Mandauilla.   Bologna, *per mi Joanne jacobo et Joanne antonio di benedetti da Bologna.* 1492.   4°.   B. L.

Grenville, 6709.   Another copy of Sir John Mandeville's travels, printed at Milan, *per Ulderico Scinzenzeler.*   1497. 4°.   B. L.

Grenville, 6707.   A Dutch copy of Sir John Mandeville's travels, printed at Antwerp bii nuy Govaerdt Back.   1494. 4°.   B. L.

Grenville, 6699.   Itinerarius in partes Iherosolimitanas.   Et in ultiores transmarinas.   B. L.   4°.   There is no certainty when or where this was printed, but it contains a MS. note attributing its production to P. Friedberg, of Maintz, *circa* 1495.

Grenville, 6713.   The boke of John Maunduyle Knyght of wayes to Ierusalem and of maruelys of ynde and of other countrees, Emprented *by Richard Pynson.*   4°.   B. L.   This is considered the oldest English printed version extant, older even than that of Wynkyn de Worde's of 1499.   It is unfortunately undated.   Pynson began to print 1493.

Grenville, 6708.   Tractato, etc.   Venexia, *per Maestro Manfredo da Monferato da Streuo da Bonello.*   1496.   4°.

789, a. 20.   Mandeville (*Sir* John) *the Traveller*.   Johanne de mandauilla.   Tractato de le piu maruegliose cose e piu notabili che si trouino in le parte del mondo, etc. per Maestro Manfredo da Mōferato da streno de Bonello.   Venice, 1496.   4°.

100 77, b. Mandeville (*Sir* John) *the Traveller*. Johanne de mandavilla. Tractato de le piu maravegliose cose e piu notabile che se trouino in le parte del mõdo, etc.

G. L. Stãpado p Ulfrycho scienzēzeler, Milaõ. 149(7). 4°.

Grenville, 6710. Che tracta de le piu marauegliose cose e piu notabile che si trouyns in le parte del Mondo. Bologna, *per mi Piero et Jacobo fratelli da Campii*, 1497. 4°. B.L.

C. 32, e. 2/2. Mandeville (*Sir* John) *the Traveller*. Johannis de montevilla Itinerari in partes Iherosolimitanas. Et in ulteriores transmarinas. G.L. 1500 ? 4°.

Grenville, 6711. Another copy of Sir John Mandeville's travels. Impressa in Venetia, per *Zuan Baptista Sessa*. Anno 1504. Adi 29, Luio. 4°. B.L.

280, f. 32. Mandeville (*Sir* John) *the Traveller*. I. de Mandavilla. Tractato de la piu maraviliose cose e piu notabili che si trovino in le parte del monde redutte . . . . sotto brevita in lo presente compendio, etc.

Manfredo da sustrevo dacã Bonis. Venezia, 1505. 8°.

148, c. 3. Mandeville (*Sir* John) *the Traveller*. Von . der. erfarung . des. streugen . Ritters. johannes . võ. montaville.

G. L. J. Knoblouch. Strassburg, 1507. 4°.

Grenville, 6701. Tractato bellissimo delle piu marauigliose cose, et piu notabile che si trouino nelle parte del mondo. Impresso nella excelsa cipta di Firenze appetitione *di Ser Piero da Pescia*, etc. Circa, 1512. 4°.

Grenville, 6712. Another copy of Sir John Mandeville's travels printed at Milan, *per Rocho et fratelli da Valle*. 1517. 4°. B. L.

Grenville, 6656. Another copy of Sir John Mandevilles travels, printed at Venice, *per Marchio Sessa e Piero de rauani*. 1521. 8°.

1051, c. 1/1. Mandeville (*Sir* John) *the Traveller*. I. de Mandavilla, qual tratta della piu maravegliose cose e piu notabile che si trovino, etc. Venetia, 1537. 8°.

567, i. 5. Mandeville (*Sir* John) *the Traveller*. Juan de

T

Mandavila. Libro de las Marauillas del mundo y del viage
d' la tierra santa di Hierusalē & de todas las provincias &
hombres monstrussos que hayen las Indias.   G. L. Valencia,
1540, fol.

149, e. 6.   Libro de las maravillas del mondo que trata
del viage de la Tierra Santa de Hierusalem y de todas
las provincias y Ciudades de las Indias y de los hombres
mostruosos que ay en el mundo.   Alcala de Heuares.   1547,
fol.

1074, k. 4/1.   Mandeville (*Sir* John) *the Traveller*.   Maistre
Iehan Mandeville Chevalier natif du pays Dangleterre, lequel
parle des grandes Adventures des pays estrange, tant par mer,
que par terre . . . . Ensemble la terre de promission & du
sainct voyage de Hierusalem.   G. L. *Jehan Bonfons*.   Paris,
1560? 4°.

Grenville, 6657.   Another copy of Sir John Mandeville's
travels.   Nel quale si contengono di molte cose maravigliose.
Venetia, 1567.   8°.

1046, a. 26/4.   Mandeville (*Sir* John) *the Traveller*.   I. de
Mandavilla, nel quale si contengono di molte cose maravigliose,
etc.   Venetia, 1567.   8°.

1045, h. 2.   Mandeville (*Sir* John) *the Traveller*.   The
Voiage and travayle of Syr I. M. which treateth of the way
toward Hierusalem, and of marvayles of Inde, with other Ilands
and Countryes.   B. L. Lond. 1568.   8°.

10,076, a.   Mandeville (*Sir* John) *the Traveller*.   Reysen
und Wander schafften, durch das Gelobte Land, Indien und
Persien, dess . . . . Ritters J. de Montevilla . . . . von ihm
in Frantzösischer unnd Lateinischer Sprach . . . . beschrieben.
Nachmals durch O. von Dameringer . . verteutscht . . . . auffs
neuw corrigieret und mit . . . . Figuren gezieret.

Franckfurt am Mayn, 1580.   8°.

790, m. 16.   Mandeville (*Sir* John) *the Traveller*.   Reysen
ins gelobte Land . . . . Persien, Indien, Tartary, etc.   1584,
fol.

Grenville, 6714. Another copy of Sir John Mandeville's travels in English, unfortunately mutilated, said to be probably printed by Thomas East or Este[1]—but it is unlike his type—and the engravings are totally different.

791, l. 12. Mandeville (*Sir* John) *the Traveller*. Reysen . . . . durch das gelobte Landt, Indien, und Persien, etc. 1609, fol.

Grenville, 6715. Another copy of Sir John Mandeville's travels. "Wherein is set downe the way to the Holy Land, and to Hierusalem: as also to the land of the great Caane, and of Prester John; to Inde, and diuers other countries: together with the many and strange Meruailes therein. London, *by Thomas Stansby*. 1618. 4°. B. L.

10,056, bbb/2. Mandeville (*Sir* John) *the Traveller*. De wonderlijcke Reyse van I. Mandevijl, be schrijvende eerst de Reyse ende gheschiedenisse van den H. Lande . . . . Daer na de ghestaltenisse ende zeden van den Lande van Egipten, Syrien, Persen . . . Indien, ende Ethiopien, &c.—t'Amsterdam. 1650. 4°.

Grenville, 6716. Voyages and travels, wherein is set down the way to the Holy Land, &c. London, 1657. 4°. B. L.

791, l. 25. Mandeville (*Sir* John) *the Traveller*. Reysen unnd Wanderschafften durch das gelobte Landt, Indien und Persien . . . durch Otto von Demeringen . . . . verteutscht. 1659, fol.

10,055, a. Mandeville (*Sir* John) *the Traveller*. The voyages and travels of Sir J. Mandevile, Knight. Wherein is set down the way to the Holy Land, and to Hierusalem; as also to the lands of the Great Caane, and of Prester John, &c. (Woodcuts). B. L. Lond. 1670. 4°.

12,410, f. 10. Mandeville (*Sir* John) *the Traveller*. De Wonderlycke Reyse van I. Mandevyl. Naer het H. Landt, ghedan in 't Jaer 1322 &c. Antwerpen, 1677. 4°.

---

[1] The dated works of Est, Este, East, or Easte range from 1565 to over 1600.

Grenville, **6717**. Another copy of Sir John Mandeville's travels. London, for R. Scot, 1684. 4°.

1045, h. 30. Mandeville (*Sir* John) *the Traveller*. The voyages of Sir I. M., &c. B. L. Lond. 1684. 4°.

Grenville, **6718**. Another copy of Sir John Mandeville's travels. London, for R. Chiswell, &c. 1696. 4°. The woodcuts in this edition are the same as in Grenville 6717.

12,315, c. 5/4. Mandeville (*Sir* John) *the Traveller*. Des vortrefflich Welt-Erfahrnen . . . Ritters Johannis de Montevilla, curieuse Reiss-Beschreibung wie derselbe in das gelobte Land, Palästinum, Jerusalem, Egypten, Türkey, Judäam, Indien, Chinam, Persien, angekommen, und fast den ganzen Erd-und Welt. Kriebs durchzogen seye ; . . . . Nunmehrins Teutsche übersetzt . . . . Jetzt von neuem auferlegt, vermehrt und verbessert, &c. (no place named) 1700 ? 8°.

1077, g. 35/2. Mandeville (*Sir* John) *the Traveller*. The voyages and travels of Sir J. M., &c. Lond. 1705. 4°.

10,056, c. Mandeville (*Sir* John) *the Traveller*. The voyages and travels of Sir J. Mandevile . . . where in is set down the way to the Holy Land. . . . As also to the lands of the Great Caan, and of Prester John ; to India, and divers other countries, &c. Lond. 1710. 4°.

10,055, a. Mandeville (*Sir* John) *the Traveller*. The Travels and voyages of Sir J. M., &c. Lond. 1720? 12°.

Grenville, **2247**. Another copy of Sir John Mandeville's travels. London, for J. Osborne. (A chap book.) No date ? 1720-30. 12°.

683, f. 18. Mandeville (*Sir* John) *the Traveller*. The voiage and travaile of Sir I Maundevile, which treateth of the way to Hierusalem, and of marvayles of Inde, with other ilands, and countreyes. Now publish'd entire from an original MS. in the Cotton Library. Lond. 1725. 8°.

Note. There is another title page, with the date 1727.

149, b. 8. Another edition of the same in the King's Library—without the 1727 title page.

The Grenville Library also has copies of the 1727 edition of the Cotton M.S. and Halliwell's reprint of same, edition 1839.

212, e. 6. Mandeville (*Sir* John) *the Traveller.* Receuil ou abrègè des voiages et observations de, &c. (Receuil de divers Voyages Curieux, &c.) Vol. 2. 1729. 4°.

435, a. 1. Mandeville (*Sir* John) *the Traveller.* The Travels and Voyages of Sir I. M. Lond. 1730? 8°.

454, f. 6. Mandeville (*Sir* John) *the Traveller.* See Bergeron (P.) *Parisien* Voyages faits principalement en Asie dans les XII. XIII. XIV. et XV siecles, &c. 1735. 4°.

100,56, cc. Mandeville (*Sir* John) *the Traveller.* De Wonderlÿke Reyse van Ian Mandevyl, &c. Amsterdam, 1742? 4°.

790, b. 34. Mandeville (*Sir* John) *the Traveller.* De wonderlyke Reize van Jan Mandevyl, &c. Amsterdam 1750? 4°.

1077, i. 14/23. Mandeville (*Sir* John) *the Traveller.* The foreign travels of Sir I. M., &c. (A chap book.) Aldermary Church Yard, Lond. 1750? 12°.

10,056, aa. Mandeville (*Sir* John) *the Traveller.* De wonderlyke Reize van Ian Mandevyl, &c. Amsterdam, 1760. 4°.

10,055, b. Mandeville (*Sir* John) *the Traveller.* De wonderlyke Reize von I. Mandevyl, &c. Amsterdam, 1779. 4°.

12,315, aaa. 6/3. Mandeville (*Sir* John) *the Traveller.* The foreign travels of Sir I. M., &c. London, 1780? 12°. (A chap book.)

1295, c. Mandeville (*Sir* John) *the Traveller.* De wonderlyke Reyse van Ian Mandevyl, naer het H. Land, gedden in 't jaer 1622 (1322) . . . Menheeft desen nieuwen Gendsehen Druk van alle Touten gesuyverd, &c. Gend. 1780? 4°.

1076, l. 3/12. Mandeville (*Sir* John) *the Traveller.* The foreign travels and dangerous voyages of Sir I. M. (A chap book). London, 1785? 12°.

209, h. 11. Mandeville (*Sir* John) *the Traveller.* Liber Præsens . . . agit de diversis patriis . . . & insulis, Turcia,

Armenia, &c.   Hakluyt's Collection of the early Voyages, &c.
Vol. 2.   1809, &c.   4°.

790, g. 17.   Mandeville (*Sir* John) *the Traveller*.   The
Voiage and Travaile of Sir I. Maundeville . . . which treateth
of the way to Hierusalem ; and of Marvayles of Inde, with
other Islands and Countryes.   Reprinted from the Edition of
A.D. 1725, with an Introduction, Additional Notes, and Glossary, by J. O. Halliwell.   Lond. 1839.   8°.

836, i. 23(1).   Mandeville (*Sir* John) *the Traveller*.   Biblio-
graphische Untersuchungen über die Reise.   Beschreibung
des Sir I. M., &c.   1840.   4°.

2101, a.   Mandeville (*Sir* John) *the Traveller*.   Early Travels
in Palestine, comprising the narratives of Arculf, Willibald . . .
Sir I. Mandeville (the latter entitled The Book of Sir I. M.
A.D. 1322-1356), &c.—Bohn's Antiquarian Library, 1847, &c.
8°.

1007, 6, aa.   Mandeville (*Sir* John) *the Traveller*.   Des
edlen engelländischen Ritters . . . J. v. Montevilla . . . Reis
Beschreibung . . . von Neueman's Licht gestellt durch O. F. H.
Schönhuth.

Reutlingen, 1865.   8°.

10,075, g.   Mandeville (*Sir* John) *the Traveller*.   The Voiage
and Travaile of Sir J. Maundevile . . . Reprinted from the
edition of 1725.   With an introduction, additional notes, and
glossary, by J. O. Halliwell, &c.   Lond. 1866.   8°.

11,900, bb.   Mandeville (*Sir* John) the *Traveller*.   A Translation of a portion of Sir J. M.'s travels.   (Irish.)   See *Todd*
(J. H.), *D.D.*   Some account of the Irish manuscript, &c.
1867.   8°.

12,226, bbbb.   Mandeville (*Sir* John) *the Traveller*.   I.
Viaggi di G da Mandavilla.   Volgarizzamento antico Toscano,
ora ridotto a buona lezione coll' ainto di due testi a penna per
cura di F. Zambrini.   2 vols.   Bologna, Imola (printed) 1870.
8°.

10,027, aaa.   Mandeville (*Sir* John) *the Traveller.*   The English Explorers, &c.

Note. Forming part of "Nimmo's National Library," Lond. Edinburgh (printed), 1875.   8°.

Ac. 9057.   Mandeville (*Sir* John) *The Traveller.*   Mandevilles Rejse, på danok fra 15de århundrede, . . . udgiven af M. Lorenzen.   1881, &c.   8°.

CHISWICK PRESS:—C. WHITTINGHAM AND CO., TOOKS COURT,
CHANCERY LANE.

www.ingramcontent.com/pod-product-compliance
Lightning Source LLC
Chambersburg PA
CBHW021214270326
41929CB00010B/1126